# THE PRISONER'S RELEASE

# THE PRISONER'S RELEASE

## A Study of the Employment of Ex-Prisoners

by

KEITH SOOTHILL

Foreword by Lord Donaldson

LONDON SCHOOL OF ECONOMICS
AND POLITICAL SCIENCE

GEORGE ALLEN & UNWIN LTD
RUSKIN HOUSE   MUSEUM STREET   LONDON

First published in 1974

ISBN 0 04 364008 7 Hardback
0 04 364009 5 Paperback

Printed in Great Britain
in 10 *point Times Roman type*
by Clarke, Doble & Brendon Ltd
Plymouth

# FOREWORD

BY LORD DONALDSON
*Chairman*, NACRO

The Apex experiment is one which everyone concerned in the field of prison after-care has been watching with interest. Its main objective, to find suitable work for men discharged from prison, with a distinct bias in favour of 'difficult' cases, is being carried out with some success. But it is of interest, above the normal run of such ventures, because it has incorporated in its work a system of records which makes possible an objective assessment of the effectiveness of the methods used. Dr Soothill was appointed as a research worker to undertake this assessment and the present volume presents his findings.

As in all attempts to help deviant groups, there is a fair share of failure to report. Dr Soothill says, 'We have shown that this particular service . . . is not a panacea. . . . We have probably moved a little way towards . . . [identifying] more closely the men who *may* be helped by such a placing service'. He peers into a future where prediction techniques might be able to classify men as likely to respond to different forms of assistance and treatment, so that they could be sentenced accordingly by a computer-assisted judge.

The book is valuable for its survey of the past as well as its guesses at the future. The history of after-care has not before been described in detail (the late Frank Dawtry had in mind such a task but unfortunately died before it could be accomplished). The first two chapters of this book fill this gap accurately, and fully enough to make any further history unnecessary.

There can be little doubt that men coming out of prison need help, and little doubt that a great deal of this help is wasted. Any analysis which will help the helpers to be less ineffective is welcome – Dr Soothill's report will be used by Apex to improve their methods and will be an example to others to do the same.

# ACKNOWLEDGEMENTS

Rarely can the originator of any enterprise be traced so definitively as in the case of the Apex Charitable Trust. Mr Neville Vincent conceived the idea of setting up a specialist employment agency for discharged prisoners and took on all the work of the gestation period of setting up the organization. It was agreed to carry out this research project as the main work of Apex during the first three years and I am grateful for the way in which Mr Neville Vincent and the other Trustees, the late Mr Douglas Gibson and Mrs Marna Glyn, directed their efforts towards ensuring that the project was completed.

The work of Apex was financed mainly by grants from the City Parochial Foundation, Goldsmiths' Company, the Hilden Charitable Fund and the Leverhulme Trust Fund and given financial support from other trusts, foundations, trades unions, firms and individuals. However, the present research was possible as a result of a grant from the Noel Buxton Trust during the planning stage and a generous three-year grant from the Nuffield Foundation during the operation of the project.

For this study, which was submitted as a doctoral thesis, I was particularly fortunate that Professor Terence Morris agreed to supervise the research, for he had the rare ability of allowing the research to progress when everything was going well and of giving appropriate suggestions when advice was needed. His direction led me to the range of computer and statistical facilities offered at the London School of Economics and other institutions within the University of London. Professor John Martin and Mr Douglas Webster were helpful in giving me some idea of what a project of this kind would involve and subsequently helped me in overcoming some of the problems of coding this type of material.

One must emphasize that this study could not have been started or completed without the full support and co-operation of the Home Office. My thanks are due to the Administrators of the Head Office of the Prison Department and the Probation and After-Care Department, and the Governor and the staff at Wormwood Scrubs and Pentonville prisons. The Home Office Research Unit made an enormous contribution by arranging for the co-operation of the Criminal Record Office. One could not fail to be impressed by the interest and helpful attitude of the Department of Employment towards this study and, in particular, by the way in which the London and South Eastern Regional Office was willing to provide information which must have taken some time to collate.

A*

The key figure in a project concerned with placing ex-prisoners after release is the person who makes the contacts with employers. Mr Edwin Horlington did this for the first part of the Wormwood Scrubs study and then the work was shared for a short time by Mrs Eliane Gibson and Mrs Marna Glyn. The present Director of Apex, Mr Freddie Pentney, completed the Wormwood Scrubs study and did all the placing work for the Pentonville study. As a research worker there is the danger that I will remember the meticulous way he kept a record of his placing activities but fail to emphasize his determination to ensure that every man had a suitable interview to attend on release. However, all those who have been actively engaged in the placing work at Apex are the first to emphasize that it is the many employers who have in fact made this project possible. Apex continues to appreciate the interest employers show in the work of the Trust.

My thanks are also due to Mrs Nancy Hodgkin and Mrs Nancy Tapsfield for their help in the follow-up study, and to Mrs Mary Fleuty, Mrs Sally Marston, Miss Daphne Wagstaff, Miss Jean Lewis, Mrs Jean Elliott and Mrs Anita Leech for their secretarial assistance.

The Apex project stresses employment in isolation from other factors impinging on a man's life. I am well aware of the dangers of this approach, but a more comprehensive programme to meet the prisoner's needs was outside the scope of this project.

I myself was perhaps more fortunate. At Apex I worked with a sympathetic employer; at home I returned to a sympathetic wife.

## AUTHOR'S PREFACE

In the same week as this report was completed, I received a letter from the first person I interviewed in prison with a view to the Apex Trust trying to find him suitable employment on release. There were five years separating that prison interview and the receipt of the letter. His life during those five years was a most suitable reminder of the difficulties of integrating into the community after many years in prison, and a reminder that helping a man to settle down after release is much more complex than simply providing him with a job. If the present report fails to indicate this truth, I think that this letter from the first Apex client written a few days after he had suffered the effects of a stroke may help.

> At the moment I am taking it easy at home. The left side of my face has fallen and is paralysed – I cannot speak at all – not intelligibly anyhow – only thickly.
>
> Just my luck, isn't it. All the year I work hard and then I have an accident – then what, an act of God!
>
> At least it gives me time to review my present life and I must say that I don't find it satisfactory. It is just an existence, I am achieving nothing. I have been leaving home at 6.45 a.m. and returning at 6.45–7.0 p.m., then the day has – apart from watching TV – been over. I am somehow going to change this – my job pays well, but it doesn't help me, for I am on my own there, and don't talk – or have the chance to talk to anyone. The [Circle] Club has been an eventful evening for me – I believe it has helped me to realize what life is all about.
>
> It could well be that I am feeling rather depressed at the moment – but I don't think so. . . .

KEITH SOOTHILL

*London School of Economics,*
*September 1971*

*Come, sleep! O Sleep, the certain knot of peace,*
*The baiting-place of wit, the balm of woe,*
*The poor man's wealth, the prisoner's release,*
*Th' indifferent judge between the high and low*

SHAKESPEARE, *Sonnet* XXXIX

# CONTENTS

# TABLES

# INTRODUCTION

## The Prisoner's Release

We always hear much more about the people who go into our prisons than about the people who come out. The newspaper headlines constantly remind us that more and more people are being literally imprisoned from society – '1,000-a-month rise in gaol population',[1] '40,000 in prison by the early 1970s',[2] 'Gaol population graph rising',[3] 'Gaol to open early to ease "bulge" '.[4] If our information were restricted to newspaper banner headlines we would assume that our prisons are crammed full of murderers, rapists, and train robbers. With the prominence given by the mass media to escapes from prison, one could perhaps be excused for believing that no one is legitimately released from prison through the front gate. On the few occasions when a legitimate release becomes prominent, there is almost invariably the hint of disaster – 'Murderer returns to prison'[5] or 'Strangler sentenced again'.[6] It is easy to forget that the vast majority of men and women in prison and being released from prison are people who have been incarcerated away from the community for comparatively trivial offences. It is the persistence rather than the enormity of the criminal behaviour which characterizes most occupants of our prison cells. The persistence of criminal activity after release results for a fair proportion of offenders in a phenomenon known as the 'revolving door' or 'life sentence by instalments'. Occasionally a case history of one of the men who has 'graduated' through the entire prison system is featured in a national newspaper almost as though he were as unique as the murderer who murders again. A front-page feature on 'What 30 years' jail has done to Bill Fletcher' occupied a total of thirty-six column inches. It began:

Bill Fletcher has spent only seven months out of prison in the last 30 years. All his sentences have been for petty thieving. The sum of his unlawful gains has been less than £40 in that period, during which it has cost the State around £31,000 to keep him locked up. . . . He is now so accustomed to prison life that he feels deeply insecure away from it. Frightened to enter a cafe alone, he prefers to take his meals at railway station trollies. Repelled by the shared and sometimes squalid facilities of a hostel, he sleeps in the open when he hasn't enough money for a private room. . . . He has recently begun committing petty crimes with the conscious aim of getting sent back to prison. Ironically, the police and the courts, appalled by his life story, have at the same time become increasingly reluctant to charge or convict him, so that he is failing even in this enterprise.[7]

It is not until the last paragraph that we are reminded that this man – to use Professor Morris's term,[8] a failure 'across the board', a failure in society and a failure even in crime – is not unique but that 'there are between 1,000 and 2,000 men and women in Britain with similar case-histories'.

To allow men like Bill Fletcher to flounder briefly in society and then return to a prison routine which has failed again and again to help them adapt to a non-institutional life is clearly a wasteful and expensive procedure. Such a history indicates that there is a strong case on both humanitarian and economic grounds for considering ways of modifying this tragic pattern. From a humane point of view the community has an obligation to assist these men since it has, at times, contributed in making them as they are. Economically, the case is equally strong. Apart from the direct cost to the country of £1,203[9] per annum to keep a person in prison, there is the fact that his family may well be receiving social security benefits whilst the potential breadwinner is in prison. Clearly it is only common sense to try to get men and women being released from prison on to a sound economic and social footing.

Bill Fletcher is, of course, not a typical prisoner, but, without pressing the analogy too far, he is as typical of prisoners as terminal cancer cases are typical of cancer sufferers. All the problems of the ex-prisoner can be highlighted by a study of his case-history. On release he is jobless, homeless, friendless in society, in fact a visitor from prison whose only sense of belonging is to prison. Although Bill Fletcher is fairly characteristic of the stage army of prisoners who have completed thirty years' goal, the majority of men and women in prison are simply not old enough to exhibit the same long, pathetic career pattern. Some in fact reach the stage of utter despair and loss of hope very much earlier in life, perhaps even before arriving in prison. Generally, though, men arrive in prison for their first sentence at an age when it would make economic sense to ensure that they had no necessity to return, for the failures will often continue to fail for at least another forty years or so.

It is easier to argue the sense of the policy than to make a convincing demonstration of how to set about effecting it. Even at the most superficial level, one can soon recognize the numerous obstacles to achieving a sensible rehabilitation programme which will break at least for some the tragic pattern of repeated prison sentences.

Professor Terence Morris has recently reminded us that it is not a truism that 'after-care has to be seen in the context of the treatment of offenders as a whole'.[10] Even if one disregards all the social effort in bringing the offender to trial and the effect of this effort on the offender, the sentencing court is only tangentially considering how a prison sentence could effectively modify a person's future behaviour. Where the court does consider it, the decision is sometimes potentially more disastrous than if the reformation of the offender had not been considered. The newspaper report outlining the appeal judgement of a man reconvicted while part of the Apex project indicates the type of obstacle erected by an apparently well-meaning judge:

'Long prison sentences do not cure drug addiction', Lord Parker, the Lord Chief Justice, said in the Court of Appeal yesterday. An Inner London Sessions judge had imposed a three-year sentence on a drug addict because he thought that a substantial term might cure him. That was a misconception, Lord Parker said. No long period of imprisonment effected a drug addiction cure. . . . The three judges substituted three years' probation, conditional on his undergoing non-residential hospital treatment, and living where directed by the probation officer.[11]

There are other types of offenders, such as the habitual drunk, where there is a great need to consider alternative methods of treatment than the simple dichotomy of fine or prison. The recent Home Office working party report on 'habitual drunken offenders'[12] accepts, though, that prisons will always have men whose basic problem is drink, emphasizing that the prison service needs an increased awareness of the problems of alcoholism and must make efforts to identify and deal with drink problems.

The particular problem of the alcoholic highlights the second major obstacle in the development of after-care. The facilities available and the training of the personnel involved in the prison system are often inadequate or inappropriate to begin to prepare men and women for life on the outside. Seventy-five years ago the Chairman of the Commissioners of Prisons regarded the after-care of prisoners as 'outside work, it is not our work'.[13] Almost from the moment he uttered those words, there has been a steady trend away from that belief, but the fact remains that there is still comparatively little activity in prison that is consciously geared to preparing a man for the outside. Inevitably the Prison Department has been sidetracked in considering how to house the projected number of inmates and there has been little opportunity to evaluate some of the schemes which have been put into operation. Security is the other issue which has dominated the desks of the prison administrators and presumably the postbags of the newspapers. The result has been over-kill. Resources which were desperately needed for pursuing some tentative moves to make the prison an instrument of effective change have been directed to producing a security level in closed prisons which is often higher than is necessary to deal with most of the inmates. Expectations of prison reform have been disappointed and replaced by a fairly obsessional concern with security. The young lag who promised the long-termers to say his piece on his release after his first prison sentence indicates the disappointment when expectations are raised: 'Mr X has a particular animus against the Labour Government which promised prison reform and, in his view, left prisoners to stew in their own juice in the age-old manner'.[14]

Whatever is happening or failing to happen in prison to prepare a man for his release, the age-old gap between him and society widens rather than narrows while he is in prison. He needs more help than that of other socially handicapped people because of the stigma involved in serving a prison sentence. It may be, as Professor Morris suggests,[15] that by separating the prisoner from other groups at each move we may reinforce his stigmatization; but if there is any attempt at an alternative development, say, placing after-care within the responsibility of the local authority department, there must be a more ready appreciation of the number of fronts on which the social casualty from prison is often battling. Ideally, to re-establish himself he usually needs help not only in material terms but also in the more subtle aspects of normal social functioning.

In the past there has perhaps been a lack of appreciation of the number of difficulties a person leaving prison has often to overcome, and if there was any realization of the deleterious effects of continued stigmatization, this was thought to be after all what he deserved, for he had brought it all on himself. Alternatively, a more generous explanation of the traditional approach is that it was felt that an ex-prisoner cannot be helped on all the various problem fronts and that by concentrating on one particular aspect, traditionally by finding the ex-prisoner work, all the other problems would somehow disappear. In other words, if the man has a job on release, this will act as a catalyst and lead to a solution of all other material problems, as well, presumably, as any psychological ones. The possession of a job will enable suitable accommodation to be secured and any problems within the family will be solved by his assuming his traditional role of breadwinner.

It is fascinating that the single-salvo approach in after-care has almost invariably concentrated on the finding of work. It reflects how work is regarded as perhaps the central value in our society. Men who are unemployed and seeking work claim they have a right to work, while men who are unemployed but not seeking work are told they have a duty to work. Within the context of a work culture, the most obvious way of helping a man to return to society is to offer him a job. The after-care worker who states that 'there is no substitute for steady work when it comes to getting an ex-prisoner settled into normal life again',[16] is not only repeating a recipe concocted well over a hundred years ago but is also indicating how work remains the central value in our society. We have never waxed as enthusiastic over a belief that, say, 'there is no substitute for a happy marriage when it comes to settling an ex-prisoner into normal life again'. Somehow we have come to believe that steady work is the integrating feature of normal life, whereas a steady relationship is not.

The present work ethic of our society can easily be traced back to the Victorian era when virtually by a historical accident our present prison system also originated. The familiar thesis of Max Weber that Puritan ideas largely influenced the development of capitalism can easily be extended to suggest that Puritan ideas dominated the development of prison after-care. With the religious reverence for work, it was easy for a Victorian to recognize the attributes of a good citizen; to make a bad citizen good, work was the obvious solution. The fact that the remedy of available work was such a rare commodity simply reinforced the belief in its possible efficacy.

The enthusiasm with which finding employment for the discharged prisoner as the overall solution to his problems was proclaimed in official government reports up to the Second World War and their disappointment that the placing efforts of the after-care workers should be so limited is described in Chapter 1. Since the Second World War there has been a slow transition towards a more professional casework approach culminating in the Probation Service taking over the statutory responsibility for the whole of after-care. After the war there was a somewhat speedier transference of much of the task of finding work for ex-prisoners to the Ministry of Labour, and its success in this activity is discussed in Chapter 2.

While recognizing all the efforts that after-care organizations and the Department of Employment have put into the placing of ex-prisoners over the years, there is no escaping the fact that a careful assessment of the effectiveness of an active placing policy for ex-prisoners has never been carried out. In the mid-1960s the formerly held view of the supreme value of finding work for the ex-prisoner was at an all-time low. The present writer was one among several keenly interested in Neville Vincent's initiative in establishing a central agency designed solely to assist ex-prisoners to find work, for the time seemed ripe to demonstrate that one could justify this type of activity on both humane and economic grounds. The present writer's belief was that it would be the exception rather than the rule for anyone to fail to benefit significantly from such a service. For this reason it seemed appropriate to set forth the hypothesis that such a placing service would reduce the reconviction rate of a group we tried to help compared with a control group who were not helped in this way. In fact, in reconviction terms there is virtually nothing to suggest that the placing service had any overall beneficial effect at all. A personal belief has changed in five years to the present belief that it is the exception rather than the rule for the finding of employment in isolation to modify an ex-prisoner's subsequent criminal pattern. It should be emphasized that this should not be interpreted to mean that employment is irrelevant, but that concentrating on the particular activity of finding employment for ex-prisoners without considering any other factors is likely to have limited economic returns. Instead of abandoning Apex-type activities, though, the more appropriate move is to try to identify more closely the particular group whom one has enabled to have a more humane post-release experience in terms of settling into work satisfactorily. The main lesson of the Apex project is the very small proportion of men for whom this placing service could have made an impact. The disappointing outcome from the majority who accepted the offer does not mean that one should jettison the small minority for whom this may have been the after-care action that was needed. It should help us to recognize that there is not a simple panacea for prisoners after release. There are few who would now postulate a single cause for crime, and similarly we must try to avoid assuming that there is a single method of assisting men and women discharged from prison.

It should be emphasized, though, that the effectiveness of any particular after-care enterprise will not remain constant throughout time. A relevant variable for any placing activity is likely to be the market conditions. While no one would support a straightforward relationship between unemployment and crime, Glaser and Rice[17] have produced evidence to indicate that variations in economic opportunity have a significant influence upon the rate at which adult males commit crime. They suggest that previous investigations failed to indicate consistent relationships between crime and unemployment because opposite types of relationship existed for persons in different age ranges. They found some evidence that crimes by juveniles increase somewhat during periods of full employment for adults, perhaps because there is less supervision of children at those times, whereas juvenile crimes tend to decrease somewhat with unemployment, perhaps because unemployment fosters more cohesive relationships at home between parents and children. In contrast, crime by adults old enough to be economically independent of their parents increased with unemployment and decreased with full employment. This study certainly indicates that the market situation may well be relevant to the amount or even the type of crime committed. Even though the general market conditions may be important in planning appropriate after-care, it may not make much difference to the outcome of the efforts of a placing agency operating in isolation unless there is a variation in the value-system of the men discharged from prison. For example, if market conditions somehow forced a high proportion of reasonable-calibre but redundant white-collar workers to resort to crime and they were imprisoned 'pour encourager les autres', these men would be likely to share the middle-class Protestant ethic in which work plays such a central role. With the small proportion of white-collar workers in the present project, it is still evident that these men tend to respond more favourably to an employment-providing service.

It is perhaps too glib to suggest that one of the most significant developments in British industrial sociology is the realization that few of us actually enjoy our work. Most people in fact regard work as a dreary obligation and expect to find their pleasure and fulfilment in their leisure and private life. The 'orientation to work' approach to the analysis of industrial behaviour emphasizes the needs and expectations that the worker brings with him to the work situation as a result of previous social experience in the home, school, and community and in his jobs. Goldthorpe and his colleagues studying a comparatively affluent group of workers at the Vauxhall motor works in Luton have usefully developed the debate by indicating that these car workers had a strongly instrumental orientation to work, seeing it as purely a means to an end and not expecting any reward apart from relatively high earnings. Goldthorpe in fact predicts that 'in the conditions of modern British society, the tendency will increase for industrial workers, *particularly unskilled or semi-skilled men*, to define their work in a largely instrumental manner'.[18] He could almost have in his mind the skilled mail-bag workers who have been discharged from the prisons over the years when he goes on to suggest that 'in the case of those men at least who do not possess skills which are in high demand there will be mounting inducements to relegate work to the level of merely instrumental activity and to seek employment which offers a high economic return if only as compensation for its inherent "disutility"'.[19] This tendency will considerably heighten an already existing problem, for, as Glaser has shown, 'prisoners have expectations of extremely rapid occupational advancement during the years immediately following their release, expectations which are unrealistic in the light of their limited work experience and lack of vocational skills'.[20]

This introduces us to the whole area of what a placing agency operating in isolation fails to do even in the field of employment. There is no opportunity of changing or improving a person's market chances, for one is operating with the legacy of a man's previous work experience. Dr Pauline Morris clearly indicated how 'family relationships following upon conviction and imprisonment will follow a pattern set by family relationships existing before imprisonment'.[21] This could be generalized to other spheres of a prisoner's existence, including his work experience.

Dr Morris's work in fact is highly relevant when one begins to consider the effects if one accepts Goldthorpe's thesis that the worker's occupational life is likely to be narrowed down more and more to one of a largely economic kind. As Goldthorpe points out: 'One major outcome of this is to bring the conjugal family into a more central position than previous in the life of the manual worker, and thus to widen and strengthen the expectations which are held of him as husband, father and family provider'.[22]

When the pursuit of satisfactions is restricted to workers' out-of-work lives, it is clearly necessary for the out-of-work life to be reasonably satisfactory. With the evidence from Dr Pauline Morris's work on the problems of the married prisoner and the knowledge that a high proportion of unmarried prisoners are mobile, hostel dwellers, we realize that even if they were able to obtain employment which maximized economic returns, they have so much to learn on the pursuit of extrinsic ends. This in effect is the after-care chicken-and-egg conundrum and the attempt to procure a result by the simple provision of finding employment on release begins to seem rather inadequate, if not pathetic. Providing a job is only one aspect of the work situation, even without considering the ex-prisoner's other areas of need. After interviewing well over four hundred men and examining the records of a further three hundred or so men, the present writer is almost reluctant to admit that he genuinely believed at the outset that this simple solution would have a profound effect on the subsequent careers of a fairly signifi-cant proportion of men. There is in fact much more to be learned from the Apex project than simply the recognition of the naïveté of the author!

If one builds research into the framework of a rehabilitation programme, then clearly one should be prepared for a series of shocks when one begins to evaluate the results. In most cases, what could be called providing services simply sit back and wait for their clients to present themselves at the front door. The Apex technique of calling up and interviewing a random sample of prisoners means that we know much more about the type of characters who are not interested in the Apex service instead of simply being restricted to those who actually present themselves for help. So often social work organizations who attract a certain clientele assume that if only they had the resources everyone could be helped by their particular approach. A bitter pill to swallow, perhaps, but there are clearly ex-prisoners who do not need and others who cannot use a placing service on release.

An even more startling possibility is that those who reject the Apex service actually seem to have a lower reconviction rate after release compared with those who accept the service. It is certainly a heretical view if one suggests that a helping service actually harms, but it is a possibility which must always be faced. In the present case, the higher reconviction risks (in other words, the poorer calibre men) tend to accept the Apex service. If one then begins to take these factors into account, those who accept the service seem to perform more satisfactorily in reconviction terms than those who reject the service. Taking, for example, those who have spent a considerable proportion of their working life in custody, those who have accepted the Apex service seem to have fewer re-convictions after release than those who have rejected the Apex service. Within a paragraph one has swung from results which would depress anyone in the Apex Trust and perhaps in the after-care field, to results which seem to provide a clear indication of successful help if one takes into account – as one must – that men with different criminal records have a somewhat different likelihood of reconviction.

In fact neither of these interpretations of the results is accurate, for one must stress the importance of a control group who did not have the advantage (or perhaps disadvantage!) of this extra influence on their post-release chances. The Apex project had a control group which had also been randomly selected, and the surprising result was that there was virtually nothing to suggest any difference in the subsequent reconviction rate of this group compared with the reconviction rate of all those interviewed and offered the Apex service. There are some who reject the service who seem to do perfectly well after release without the intervention of Apex, while others who accepted the Apex service would probably have done just as well if Apex had never arrived on the scene.

Does this mean that any beliefs on the part of the Apex staff that they are helping a proportion of the men to settle down are totally unjustified? Does this mean that the letters of appreciation from clients saying how grateful they are for the help and support they received from Apex are totally inappropriate? It is impossible at this juncture to make a judgement on this, but what is clearly established is that a placing service in isolation does not have the significant impact on the majority of men leaving prison that one had originally believed.

By tracing carefully the outcome for all the men who accepted the Apex service, one begins to appreciate that it is only a small proportion of these men on whom Apex could have made much of an impact at all. There is considerable evidence to indicate the difficulty of helping those who probably needed the help the most. In the final analysis, though, there are a small group of men who settled satisfactorily at the jobs arranged by Apex, but the numbers are too small (which is another way of saying that the measures used in the study are too crude) to indicate whether the efforts of Apex had any beneficial effects over and above what would have happened to them without the help of Apex.

The message is clear. One needs a procedure by which one can identify the men who may be significantly helped by the Apex service. This study at least attempts to lay the foundations for producing a screening device by which it should be possible to predict men who are most unlikely to be helped by the Apex service, leaving a residual group among whom there will be those men who may significantly benefit from this particular after-care activity.

What this study means in a wider framework is that one should abandon a belief in a single or simple solution for the after-care of prisoners. Placing men into employment is admittedly only one type of 'single solution' but it may serve as a 'demonstration' to indicate the poverty of this type of approach. Already, in fact, there is probably a tacit recognition of the need for the individualization of treatment, and this study briefly pushes the point a stage further by suggesting the use of computer techniques in attaining this goal.

It is perhaps worthwhile to appreciate the extent to which the primary object of after-care was once regarded as the reinstatement of the ex-prisoner in employment. Part I describes this era and then indicates how the specific task of finding jobs for ex-prisoners gradually became a peripheral activity considered as the responsibility of the Department of Employment.

Part II describes the research design of the Apex project. From two London prisons 439 men were randomly selected and offered the services of a specialist employment agency. These men are compared with a control group of 324 men randomly selected from the same prisons.

Part III considers the outcome of those who fully accepted the Apex service, and the necessity for the individualization of treatment clearly becomes evident.

Part IV considers critically some of the assumptions upon which the Apex project was based, and the possible use of computer techniques in the individualization of treatment is briefly discussed.

## REFERENCES

1 The *Guardian*, 14.10.70.
2 The *Guardian*, 27.11.69.
3 The *Guardian*, 12.6.69.
4 The *Guardian*, 31.12.70.
5 The *Guardian*, 29.5.71.
6 The *Guardian*, 13.11.70.
7 The *Observer*, 29.8.71.
8 Morris, T., *After-Care in the Seventies*, NACRO (1971), p. 2.
9 *Report on the Work of the Prison Department*, London, HMSO, Cmd. 4724 (1970), p. 69.
10 Morris, op. cit., p. 1.
11 The *Guardian*, 19.12.70.
12 *Habitual Drunken Offenders, Report of Working Party*, London HMSO (1971).
13 *Report from the Departmental Committee on Prisons* (c. 7702, 1895), Minutes of Evidence, p. 367, para, 10,879.

14 The *Guardian*, 11.5.71.
15 Morris, op. cit., p. 9.
16 The *Birmingham Post*, 15.4.67.
17 Glaser, D., and Rice, K., 'Crime, Age and Employment', *Am. Sociological Rev.*, 24, No. 5 (1959), pp. 679–86.
18 Goldthorpe, J. H., *et al.*, *The Affluent Worker: Industrial Attitudes and Behaviour*, Cambridge University Press (1968), p. 174. (Goldthorpe's italics.)
19 Ibid., p. 175.
20 Glaser, D., *The Effectiveness of a Prison and Parole System*, Indianapolis, The Bobbs–Merrill Co. Inc. (1964), p. 358.
21 Morris, P., *Prisoners and their Families*, London, Allen and Unwin (1965), p. 280.
22 Goldthorpe, *et al.*, op. cit., p. 175.

# PART I

# Past and Present Provision for Discharged Prisoners with Particular Reference to Employment

## CHAPTER 1

### Historical Development of After-Care

In trying to trace early examples of prisoners adjusting to the outside world after their release from prison, one cannot but be impressed by the case of Joseph which is recorded in the first book of the Bible.[1] From the outset this is an unusual case, for he is imprisoned in effect as a result of refusing to perform the sexual act. While in prison he correctly interprets the two dreams of the chief butler and the chief baker. This ability of being able to interpret dreams – an ability which he seems to have developed in prison – eventually secures his release when he interprets Pharaoh's dreams of famine. His immediate appointment as Prime Minister of Egypt completes the remarkable rehabilitation of this ex-prisoner.

There were probably at least three unusual features in the case outlined above compared with what has tended to happen in this country over the last hundred and fifty years. In the first place, one suspects, or at least hopes, that the majority of men and women imprisoned have not been falsely accused. Secondly, it is most exceptional that any activity which has been developed or carried out in a prison setting has been of much use in helping a person to settle down to a non-criminal career after release. Finally, most prisoners are fortunate if after their release they manage to retain the same level of occupation as that prior to their imprisonment. From servant of the captain of the guard to Prime Minister is a remarkable achievement by any standard.

The important question of the number of innocent persons who serve a prison sentence can reasonably be regarded as beyond the present terms of reference, but the other two points are very relevant to any discussion of the employment of prisoners. There is a ready distinction between the employment of prisoners serving their sentence and the employment of prisoners after their release. Logically there would appear to be a close connection between these two periods of an employment career, but it is perhaps some sort of epitaph to the fight for penal reform that these have remained, and can still be examined as, largely separate subjects. However, it could be argued that there has been some progress inasmuch as before the Report from the Departmental Committee on Prisons in 1895, neither subject was recognized as worthy of much discussion. In their introduction to the section on prison labour the authors of the 1895 report hasten to point out that 'it has been necessary to go at length into this branch of the subject, both because of its great intrinsic importance and because in previous inquiries it has been passed over with but little notice'.[2] The result of their deliberations on prison labour was to produce as one of their principal recommendations that 'unproductive labour should be abolished wherever possible'.[3] Important though this is in its own right, it is the change in the underlying philosophy that this recommendation represents which makes this report an outstanding document. This change can be summarized in their belief that 'the main fault of our prison system is that it treats prisoners too much as irreclaimable criminals, instead of as reclaimable men and women'.[4] Hence, the report recognized that the prison system should try to play a positive part in the rehabilitation of offenders and even went so far as to suggest – a suggestion which did not, however, appear in the list of principal recommendations – that 'as Prisoners' Aid Societies are charged to a considerable extent with the responsibility of seeing to a prisoner's position after discharge, it is advisable that they should be consulted upon the kind of work likely to be most useful to the class of prisoners to be found in the particular prison'.[5]

It is reasonable to argue that this is the high point of considering the possible relationship between the activity of prisoners during a prison sentence and their employment plans after release. It had never been considered in such terms previously and, except for a small minority of prisoners, it has never been put into action on any meaningful scale subsequently.

Before 1895 it is fair to say that the prison authorities regarded prison labour, in so far as they regarded it at all, as a tool of deterrent theory on the theoretical level and as a tool of containment on the practical level. The First Report of the Prison Inspectors in 1836 in which they describe their inspection of Newgate mentions their concern at 'the want of employment':

Another feature in the Newgate system . . . is the utter absence of all employment for the prisoners: an evil which imparts to indiscriminate association nearly all its force and malignity; since even the mischief of association would, in a measure, be mitigated, by keeping them in constant employment.[6]

While the Prison Inspectors were extremely honest in their recognition of the atrocious conditions at Newgate, there is no doubt that the use of employment in the prison setting was seen as a way of avoiding trouble. Indeed, there were already indications of how the State at this juncture regarded the activities of such persons as Mrs Fry who had formed the Ladies' Association for the Improvement of the Female Prisoners at Newgate. There was the veiled hint that perhaps such organizations would not be needed in, or would even be a hindrance in, well-regulated gaols:

No one can for a moment doubt that in a miserable prison like Newgate the visits of the Ladies' Committee have greatly contributed to lessen the depravity of the place, and cannot fail to be highly beneficial *so long as the present state of the prison shall continue.*[7]

Even more remarkable in some way than the fairly well-known efforts of Mrs Fry were the 'charitable labours' which took place at Great Yarmouth Borough Gaol. The Inspectors describe how a dressmaker who 'has to earn her own livelihood by her own business' has visited the prison for seventeen years.

[The prisoners] are supplied with work according to their several abilities, and their earnings are paid to them on their discharge; in several instances they have earned sufficient to put themselves in decent apparel, and be fit for service. After their discharge, they are, by the same means, frequently provided with work, until enabled to procure it for themselves.[8]

While for both Elizabeth Fry and Sarah Martin the mainspring of their zeal and the inspiration of their work was religion, it is clear that both exerted vigorous and practical common sense in terms of the apparent needs of the prisoner. However, it is important

B

to consider why their immediate influence was largely limited to being an exemplar for the growing number of discharged prisoners' aid societies rather than having a more fundamental impact on the prison system. While the prisons were ill-organized and generally chaotic, these 'charitable labours' within prison catering to the needs of the prisoner were acceptable to the prison authorities, for they reasonably coincided with the needs of the prison system in attempting to create well-regulated gaols. However, as the prison system itself became more organized and was able to discharge its responsibility of carrying out a policy bounded by the philosophy of retribution and deterrence, any hint of a reformative element which might help the prisoner after release was left to the community.

It is at this juncture worthwhile to consider schemes which had in fact been developing to help the ex-prisoner after release. As early as the Gaol Act of 1823 there was some kind of state acceptance of a responsibility for providing aid to certain prisoners on release. The Visiting Justices were empowered to levy a county rate to provide up to £1 per head for 'deserving' prisoners and to make other types of bequest in kind, such as food, clothing and implements of labour. Although there need not have been any shortage of funds, especially for 'deserving' cases, as Young and Ashton point out, 'it is doubtful, however, whether much use was made of these powers'.[9]

Although there had probably always been some kind of private initiative by philanthropists founding charities for aiding discharged prisoners, there was already at the end of the eighteenth century the more specific development of aid societies for ex-prisoners beginning to spring up here and there throughout the country. Elizabeth Fry's Ladies' Association was one of the more famous, but perhaps more typical was the type of enterprise where the individual or the aid society was involved more specifically with persons after their release but had little or no contact with the inmate during his sentence. Sometimes there is a mention of quite specific activities such as the fact that in Manchester about the middle of the century a Mr Wright was active in finding employment for ex-prisoners.[10] These types of effort were undoubtedly spreading but they must have been rather sporadic in character.

Although justices' aid and aid by these societies often amounted to the distribution of small amounts of money by the same set of administrators, these two types of aid were in fact parallel developments. They were brought together by the Discharged Prisoners Aid Act of 1862 which was the first statutory recognition of discharged prisoners' aid societies. The Act empowered justices to exercise their powers of aid on discharge through such a society and, after due examination, to issue a certificate to the effect that the society was approved for the purpose of the Act. The justices were also empowered to suspend or revoke such a certificate. While in effect this Act placed the aid societies in the key position for administering voluntary after-care for prisoners, a position which the aid societies held for exactly one hundred years, Young and Ashton emphasize[11] that the Act brought no change to the work being done among ex-prisoners, as aid was confined to small grants of money or gifts of clothing. One suspects, however, that this Act had the fundamental effect of ensuring that after-care became an extra-mural activity rather than an integrated feature of the prison system.

When the local prisons were transferred to the Prison Commissioners by the Prison Act of 1877 the powers and duties of the justices in regard to aid on discharge were also transferred to the commissioners. Any hope that there would be any basic change in the theoretical approach towards after-care was entirely marred by the appointment of Du Cane as Chairman of the Commissioners of Prisons. Nearly twenty years later in his evidence to the Gladstone Committee he indicated how he regarded after-care: 'I think that our position is to stand outside of these agencies and to say, "You take the business in hand, it is outside work, it is not our work" '.[12]

Although one would tend to agree with Young and Ashton's generalization about the nature of the aid societies' work being confined to small grants of money or gifts of clothing, it is important to emphasize that each aid society grew up as a result of local initiative rather than as the result of initiative and planning from a central body, which is probably the more characteristic development of voluntary work. While undoubtedly it was this peculiar feature of the movement which dogged any attempt in this century to enable a successful transition to be made to an effective national system of after-care within the voluntary movement, equally this characteristic of the movement makes one consider the likelihood of an enormous variation in the effectiveness of the various local societies. In 1895 the Gladstone Committee, commenting on the aid societies, noted that 'there seems to be a great and unnecessary variation in the methods of working'.[13] Certainly the aspirations of most societies were much higher than simply doling out small amounts of money, and in this context it is fascinating to read the preamble to the Bill leading to the 1862

Act which, as we have mentioned, gave statutory recognition to the discharged prisoners' aid societies. It is noted there that these societies 'have been formed in divers Parts of England, by Persons subscribing voluntarily, for the Purpose of finding Employment for discharged Prisoners, and enabling them by Loans and Grants of Money to live by honest labour. . .' .[14] While in many cases there remained a vast discrepancy between these high ideals and the actual action taken, no one can argue that there were persons involved with these societies, particularly when they were founded, who wished 'to express the community's forgiveness and re-acceptance of the offender'.[15]

In contrast to the discharged prisoners' aid societies, which seem to have been founded from the best of humanitarian motives in trying to help the discharged prisoner in a voluntary manner after release, it is relevant to consider the development of compulsory after-care which remained as a separate and parallel system until the changes recommended in the 1963 Report of the Advisory Council of the Treatment of Offenders (referred to subsequently as the ACTO Report (1963)) were implemented. As Holborn has indicated,[16] compulsory after-care stemmed from a very different motivation from voluntary after-care. Its roots lacked any positive rehabilitative element even as an aspiration, for the original aim of compulsory after-care was to impose restrictions on the movements of habitual criminals, in the hope that society would be protected from them. It started as 'ticket-of-leave' with the 1853 and 1857 Penal Servitude Acts, whereby ex-convicts were required to report their addresses to the police. Compulsory after-care was extended to those released from a sentence of preventive detention (imposed by the 1908 Prevention of Crimes Act), when this category of prisoners was required to report to the Central Association for the Aid of Discharged Convicts which had been organized in 1910. Holborn also regards this extension of compulsory after-care as lacking any 'positive rehabilitative content'[17] but there was a distinction in theory which was noted as early as 1918–19 in the Report of the Prison Commissioners. Discussing the comparative merits of the systems of licensing on discharge from penal servitude and preventive detention, the report goes on to suggest that:

The Police licence may be described as negative in character, viz., it only prescribes that a man shall abstain from crime. The licence to the Central Association is positive, as prescribing that, under careful and kindly shepherding and supervision, a man shall actually work where work is found for him, and shall remain at work under the penalty of report for failing to observe the conditions of licence.[18]

When one considers borstal after-care, where there was a much clearer attempt from the outset to provide constructive supervision, it is impossible to make a generalization regarding the fundamental character of compulsory after-care. In fact, it is possible to argue that despite its less appealing origins compulsory after-care has had a greater and more positive influence than is perhaps generally recognized in moulding the present pattern of after-care. Although the nature of its attempts to help the discharged prisoner in the first half of the twentieth century paralleled those of the voluntary movement with local prisoners, the compulsory element ensured in general a longer period of contact with the ex-prisoner, and it was this experience which helped to highlight some of the shortcomings of a straightforward practical approach.

While it is essential not to forget the complementary system of compulsory after-care which came into existence for certain categories of prisoners, the vast majority of persons discharged from prison were in the domain of the discharged prisoners' aid societies as far as provision of after-care was concerned. Between the 1862 Act and the 1895 Report of the Gladstone Committee, there was a certain amount of activity on the part of the aid societies, but one suspects that the debate mainly concerned the two overlapping issues of the financial arrangements of the societies and the question of a central organization to co-ordinate and to develop the scope of their activities. While these problems were hydra-headed and never solved satisfactorily during the next hundred years, present space is too limited to trace this aspect of the aid society movement. Suffice it to say that the members of the Gladstone Committee, while making some pertinent comments on the work of the aid societies in their 1895 report, recognized that 'the subject is of very wide scope, and requires a special study by itself'.[19] While Young and Ashton suggest that the commissioned study by the Reverend G. P. Merrick on the discharged prisoners' aid societies 'makes depressing reading',[20] the most depressing aspect is to realize with the benefit of hindsight that as well as being a useful description of the early years of the movement it is a reasonable projection of the next forty years.

By the time of the Merrick Report in 1897, there were about forty societies employing agents to meet prisoners on their discharge and there is already a more specific emphasis, at least in theory, on finding employment: 'it is to be noted that Societies do make it the chief item in the agent's duties that he should try to procure employment for the cases committed to his care'.[21]

It is mentioned in the report that a few years previously, by the authority of the Home Office, the following note of the existence of the local discharged prisoners' aid society was ordered to be put up in the cells or corridors of the prison.

### ASSISTANCE TO PRISONERS ON DISCHARGE

As prisoners have sometimes a difficulty in obtaining employment on their discharge, certain benevolent societies have been established for the purpose of giving aid in that respect to those who desire, and are likely to profit by it, and for affording to deserving prisoners such other assistance as they may be able to give.[22]

Although this extract gives only the first paragraph of the notice, it is enough to indicate that finding employment had become the proclaimed function of the societies. In fact, though, six societies objected to the particular notice, because they felt that it promised, with reference to employment, more than they were competent to perform. Other societies objected to the notice on other grounds – for example, maintaining that it encouraged prisoners to ask for aid, whether they really wanted it or not, or, alternatively, because it might give prisoners an idea that they had a 'right to assistance'.[23] Later in his report, Merrick develops the theme that 'a very large number of the Aid Societies say that it is almost impossible to find employment for men who have undergone imprisonment'.[24] Just over a quarter of the societies felt that the reason for this difficulty was that 'trade in the locality is bad, and the prejudice of both masters and workmen against ex-prisoners is great',[25] and one society expressed the position more tersely that 'as honest men cannot get employment, an ex-prisoner has no chance',[26] so perhaps summarizing the greatest problem of the aid societies until the advent of a world war. However, one must emphasize once again the disparity between the various societies, and indeed one society proudly reported to Merrick that it had 'found employment for no less than 166 men during the course of the year'.[27] This example, however, is rather an oasis in the report, and, more important for the development of after-care, there was generally a complete lack of sympathetic response from the societies to any of Merrick's proposals for closer and more skilled supervision. This resulted in his summary of suggestions concluding the first major report on the aid societies being somewhat trite and negative. One feature, though, is that his definite emphasis that 'the special duty of the agent should be to find employment for ex-prisoners'[28] placed on record which function was to be regarded as the prime purpose of the aid societies.

The next general inquiry into English prisons was conducted by the departmental committee appointed in 1932 under the chairmanship of Major (later Sir) Isidore Salmon. Its terms of reference were 'to review the methods of employing prisoners and of assisting them to find employment on discharge'.[29] The final report was issued in two parts, so in effect ensuring that the two matters could not be regarded too closely as two sides of the same coin. The committee published its deliberations on the work of the prisoners' aid societies in 1935 and the following sentence printed in bold type probably summarizes the sentiments of the Committee: 'We are bound to say that on the whole we have not found much evidence of concentrated effort on the important task of finding work'.[30] In view of the fact that since the Gladstone Report this had been gradually acknowledged as the principal duty of the paid agent of the society, this was indeed a serious indictment. Perusal of the annual reports of the Commissioners of Prisons in which the Chaplain-Inspector makes some comments on the work of the discharged prisoners' aid societies on the basis of the annual returns to his office indicates the great disparity between their stated aim of finding work and their success in carrying it out. According to the Chaplain-Inspector, the standard variable deciding whether a society attempted to find work for ex-prisoners was the effectiveness of the particular committee in raising money ('Reports of all Societies show that the "percentage of employment found" – the real test of effective work – varies according to the sum expended on agency'),[31] while the standard excuse if the Society failed to find work was that 'the difficulty owing to local circumstances is almost insurmountable'.[32]

The totals from these annual returns of the discharged prisoners' aid societies fail to indicate the tremendous range of the quantity and quality of assistance given by individual societies, but they do give some idea of the numbers involved. Merrick in his 1897 report showed that the societies assisted in some way about 15 per cent of men and women released from the gaols of England and Wales (just under 26,000 out of a total of 169,137).[33] As the prison population increased, the numbers and proportion helped by the societies seemed to increase, so that soon they were dealing with approximately 25 per cent of the men discharged. However, the quality of the work was perhaps suspect. In the report for 1907–8, the Rev. C. B. Simpson recorded that out of 44,561 men and women helped in some way, 'it is much to be regretted that it was only found possible to procure actual work for about 3,000 exclusive of those who returned to former employers and of the lads who were sent to sea',[34] regarding this as a comparative failure to attain the aim for which the aid societies existed. The importance of defining terms is illustrated in 1909 when there was a dramatic fall of 16,553 in the number of cases helped in the course of the year. This is because Simpson wanted to restrict it to those prisoners who were 'helped *in some useful fashion*'[35] (my italics) and so he disregarded those assisted simply with the provision of 'free breakfasts' or 'packets of cocoa' as he felt that these 'can hardly be said to advance materially any prisoner's prospects'.[36] The advent of the First World War considerably eased the difficulty in finding work, and in the first year of the war it is recorded that work was found by the societies for 12,537 prisoners. To sum up the period from the turn of the century to the beginning of the First World War, it appears that the discharged prisoners' aid societies dealt in some way with between one-quarter and one-fifth of persons discharged from local prisons and in a good year work of some kind was found for between 10 and 15 per cent of these prisoners.

After the First World War the discharges from local prisons settled down to approximately a quarter of the numbers there had been before the war. The discharged prisoners' aid societies were able to deal with a higher proportion of discharges (approximately 40 per cent) but smaller gross numbers than before the war. By 1929 (just before the Salmon Committee began to deliberate) the discharged prisoners' aid societies were assisting in some way as many as three-quarters of the local prisoners. In this period the numbers who were said to be suitably placed by the societies stabilized at around 40 per cent of the prisoners whom they assisted. Remembering the very real difficulties confronting any individual or organization trying to place ex-prisoners, particularly in view of the general market situation at that time, it seems perhaps surprising that the Salmon Committee, some of whose members were very sympathetic to the discharged prisoners' aid society movement, should suggest that there was not much evidence of concentrated effort in finding work. This perhaps gives some clue to the quality of effort which was included in the category on the returns of 'found employment'. Certainly it would include those for whom the society arranged a return to their former employers. In the report for the year 1900, one aid society mentioned that '50 per cent of the prisoners have been received back into their old employment',[38] and while there is no reason to regard this as a typical proportion it does indicate that there was no reluctance to use this method of boosting the placing figures. One does suspect that specialized placing effort to help an individual case was fairly limited, and probably the general policy was simply to refer the man to employers known to be sympathetic. The Chaplain-Inspector in one annual report quotes as an example of the extreme difficulty of finding work that 'one society stated that it had to make 21 applications for temporary work for a discharged prisoner before employment was obtained'.[39] If societies were engaged in finding employment in a concentrated manner, this would not have been quoted as an unusual example.

The Salmon Committee emphasized 'the tendency [of aid societies] to concentrate on relief payments to prisoners on the day of discharge',[40] but felt (in fact almost reiterating the 1895 report) that 'the primary object of after-care should be the re-instatement of the ex-prisoner in employment and the efforts of all Societies should be concentrated on this aspect of their work'.[41]

However, while still maintaining that finding employment on discharge was the most important task, there was some consideration by this committee of other types of help, even considering the assistance of families of prisoners during their sentence. The committee felt that a reorganization of the framework of after-care was essential, but only within certain strict limits. It is revealing as to how much controversy this report stirred up within the movement when one appreciates that the committee went to great lengths to emphasize that they regarded the voluntary principle as sacrosanct: 'from every point of view – that of the public, the prisoner, and the Prison Authorities – it is, we are satisfied, of great importance to preserve the voluntary principle to the fullest extent possible'.[42]

Soon after the Salmon Committee presented the second part of its report, the Report of the Departmental Committee on the Social Services in Courts of Summary Jurisdiction was published in 1936. This report is of interest in so far as it discusses the duties of the probation officer. The probation service was only peripherally concerned with after-care in that officers sometimes acted as agents for the prisoners' aid societies or for the Central Association of Discharged Convicts, the statutory body concerned with compulsory after-care. Although the committee reporting in 1936 discussed probation officers' duties in relation to persons placed on probation, it is interesting to note that there were already hints of what we have subsequently come to regard as a casework approach and there was also some emphasis on the view that the probation

B*

officers should liaise with the local employment exchange on the specific matter of finding work for their cases.

The probationer should be steadily encouraged to find work for himself, but often he will need help. For this purpose the probation officer should be in close touch with the local employment exchange. . . . But employment exchanges cannot give preferential treatment to probationers and the probation officer will often have to rely on the probationer's efforts or his own. Many probation officers are in touch with sympathetic employers who are willing to give a chance to someone in trouble. . . . Where there is a principal probation officer it should be one of his functions to explore all the possibilities of finding employment.[43]

There was a conflict between the 1935 committee and the 1936 committee in that the former was in favour of extending the help given to the aid societies by probation officers while the latter wanted to limit the dependence on the probation service. Bearing in mind that thirty years later the probation service was in fact given the statutory responsibility for after-care as well as discharging its traditional duties, it is interesting that the Home Office had as early as 1932 noted the similarity between after-care and probation work. 'After-care in its general technique bears a close resemblance to the functions which a probation officer discharges in supervising a person placed on probation'.[44] This is a view which once more comes to the fore when it is seriously suggested that the probation service should have the statutory responsibility for all forms of after-care.

Within the discharged prisoners' aid societies' movement, there were indications that a reconstituted central body was thinking more constructively about how to help the discharged prisoner. The local aid societies had reacted strongly to the recommendations of the Salmon Committee and under the chairman of their own central society (Mr F. P. Whitbread), set up a committee from within their membership to recommend any reforms they considered necessary. The Whitbread Report opposed any change in the areas of responsibility of local discharged prisoners' aid societies but recommended the strengthening of the central body. The recommendations of the Whitbread Committee were accepted by the Government and the Central Discharged Prisoners' Aid Society was reconstituted in 1936 as the National Association of Discharged Prisoners' Aid Societies (referred to subsequently as NADPAS). The fact that NADPAS agreed to accept responsibility for appointing welfare officers to the regional (and subsequently special local) prisons is very relevant to the history of the development of after-care, for it was this move which probably extended the reign of the discharged prisoners' aid societies for a further ten years after 1953. One suspects that it was largely the work in this sphere which made the next major report in 1953, the Maxwell Report, feel that it could shift the emphasis of the societies from 'aid on discharge' to personal 'after-care'.

Meanwhile, the Wakefield Sub-Committee, with its resident secretary, Frank Dawtry (who eventually became secretary to the National Association of Probation Officers), blazed a trail which few of the local discharged prisoners' aid societies could or would follow. Even its first report, published in the 1938 NADPAS annual report, suggests that its interest was expanding to include an on-going relationship with men serving their sentence.

> Whilst the obtaining of work comes first in importance, and financial provision in its various forms is essential, a very important feature of our work is that of 'stand-by', adviser and friend, in daily contact with the men during the period of sentence.[45]

As we will show in the next chapter, the Wakefield Sub-Committee pioneered the scheme which involved the Ministry of Labour more closely in performing the placing work. Although the Maxwell Report, published in 1953, still emphasized that 'the arrangements which have been made with the Ministry of Labour should not cause the Aid Societies themselves to lose the active interest which they have shown in the past in the finding of employment',[46] this committee will mainly be remembered for its attempt to shift the emphasis away from this aspect. The theme in the Maxwell Report which is quoted with favour ten years later in the next major report is that 'the central object of after-care is to provide such guidance and moral support as will help the ex-prisoner to cope with his personal and peculiar difficulties'.[47]

The major change recommended was the appointment of prison welfare officers. The prison welfare officers were to build up relationships with selected prisoners during their sentence and 'to prepare case-histories . . . and constructive plans for their assistance after discharge and for submission to the Society to whose care they will be released'.[48]

The next ten years proved to be an interregnum period before the structure of after-care was altered in a fundamental manner by the ACTO Report 1963, when the central role for after-care was moved from the discharged prisoners' aid societies to the probation service. Most of the discussion in the 1950s was directed not towards the correctness of the Maxwell proposals but rather to the speed with which the proposals were put into practice. NADPAS, which with the Prison Commissioners had the responsibility of working out the details of the Maxwell Report, acknowledged in its memorandum submitted to the ACTO After-Care Sub-Committee that 'there has been criticism that their implementation had been incomplete or lackadaisical'.[49] NADPAS made a spirited attempt in its evidence to answer this criticism, but the real fact of the matter was that NADPAS had not had the full support of the local aid societies in its attempt to implement the Maxwell Report. As Holborn has argued, 'although some societies did attempt to make the switch, most failed – either through weight of tradition, poor quality staff, or great inefficiency'.[50] NADPAS had in fact not been given the power to alter a hundred years' history of local autonomy in somewhat less than ten years.

During what proved to be an interregnum period between the Maxwell Report and the ACTO Report 1963, another sub-committee of the Advisory Council for the Treatment of Offenders reported in 1958 on the question of whether there should be compulsory after-care for prisoners and, if so, which categories. It is only now that one can appreciate how much this report heralded the thoughts of the subsequent ACTO sub-committee. In a sense it tidied up official thinking on a few matters. The emphasis that 'voluntary after-care is no different from compulsory after-care in its aim'[51] officially brought the two strands of after-care together. To endorse this belief, the 1958 report recommended the repeal of the statutory requirement whereby certain prisoners discharged on licence were obliged to report their addresses for the information of the police. This had again been placed on the Statute Book as recently as 1952 as one clause of the Prison Act, but the recommendation of the 1958 sub-committee was put into effect by the 1961 Criminal Justice Act.

Although the 1958 report is concerned with compulsory after-care, it does begin to marshall the arguments which were to influence the views of the subsequent ACTO sub-committee in coming to its choice of the service to carry out after-care. The 1958 report states that 'the probation service combines, like no other organised body, the two essentials for effective after-care. It is composed of trained social workers. . . . Secondly, it is so spread over the whole country that a discharged prisoner will seldom live more than a few miles from his supervisor'.[52] Although this committee's recommendation for extending compulsory after-care to further categories of prisoners was incorporated in the Criminal Justice Act of 1961, these provisions have never in fact been put into effect. In reality the main effect of the deliberations of the 1958 ACTO report was almost certainly the way it began to spotlight the probation service as the most suitable candidate in any major reorganization of after-care. It is this early groundwork which makes it almost appear to be a foregone conclusion, reading the ACTO Report 1963, that the probation service would get the job.

The 1958 report is of further interest because it contains as Appendix A the results of a survey in which prisoners were questioned about after-care arrangements. This was not by any means a totally novel procedure to examine consumer reaction, for the Salmon Committee, for example, had interviewed some prisoners in taking their evidence. It is probably novel inasmuch as the prisoners interviewed were selected on the basis of a research design. The relevant feature is that the subjects name employment as a problem far more than anything else, amounting to nearly 50 per cent of the total, yet in the main report discussing resettlement difficulties it suggests that 'accommodation and employment are generally recognized as the most pressing, with accommodation probably the more serious of the two'.[53] Although this need be only an apparent discrepancy, it does perhaps illustrate how the question of employment difficulties no longer hold the centre of the stage in the minds of the policy makers. In its annual reports, NADPAS, while continuing to recognize the need for employment as a priority, similarly indicated that 'during the present period of full employment, it is one of the less difficult aspects of rehabilitation – except for the difficult minority of ex-prisoners from the professional classes'.[54] It is fascinating that in Pauline Morris's study, *Prisoners and their Families*, prisoners' wives regard the problem of their husband's work as far and away the largest single problem (over 29 per cent), although the problem seemed perhaps to be one of perseverance in work rather than one of finding work – 'wives feel that if only their husbands worked regularly, most of their problems would be solved'.[55]

Although it is perhaps difficult to assess its eventual influence, an impressive non-statutory committee was set up in February 1960 at the instigation of Mr Peter Thompson and under the chairmanship of Lord Pakenham 'to examine the present methods of assisting discharged prisoners to find and keep employment with particular reference to the reasons for the difficulties experienced'.[56] The report was criticized in several quarters for laying too much emphasis on the difficulties men encounter in getting and keeping jobs.

These difficulties, though real enough, are inseparable from the wider task of helping an ex-prisoner to resume his place in society, and sometimes in family life. He thus needs not only practical aid but less tangible forms of advice and support, and how to combine these two forms of after-care is the essential problem.[57]

Many felt that this approach was succinctly stated by Pauline Morris, who was herself a member of the Pakenham-Thompson Committee, in a Fabian pamphlet where she emphasized that assistance must be geared to the degree and kind of material aid required 'in the light of the emotional needs of the individual'.[58] Nevertheless, the importance of the Pakenham-Thompson Report must be measured in terms of the questions it raises rather than the answers it tries to provide, and it reveals that an influential section of the after-care world – many of whom could perhaps be regarded as professional observers of the penal scene – would expect any statutory committee to go beyond automatically building upon the existing superstructure.

The Report of the Departmental Committee on the Probation Service published in March 1962 was a further curtain-raiser for the far-reaching proposals of the ACTO report in the following year. The Morison Committee (1962) had a somewhat less restrictionist view than the 1936 committee which had recommended that prison after-care should cease to be undertaken by probation officers, for it felt strongly that 'we do not recommend any narrowing of the range of functions which probation officers undertake. Indeed, we shall show reasons for thinking that the demands on the service must increase'.[59] This committee endorsed with favour the possibility of the continuity of care of the offender at different stages in his criminal career, and it must have been of interest to the members of the ACTO committee carrying out a broader review of the organization of after-care to read that 'the carrying out of prison and borstal after-care by probation officers in England and Wales was almost universally endorsed by our witnesses'.[60]

It is useful to consider the type of care which the Morison Committee felt that the probation officer should be undertaking, for this provides the theoretical base for the subsequent official endorsement of the nature of after-care. The Morison Committee felt it was significant that the 1936 committee could describe the supervisory functions of the probation officer without using the terms 'social casework'. This is not so surprising when one considers that the framework of social casework theory had begun to be drawn in any coherent manner only since the Second World War. However, the Morison Committee usefully uses the term 'casework' to indicate how the emphasis is now placed on planning with the probationer rather than for him. The following extract can be taken as the theoretical model for after-care work in the late 1960s and as the background to the ACTO Report 1963 which transferred the responsibility for after-care to the probation service.

Casework, as we understand it, is the creation and utilization, for the benefit of an individual who needs help with personal problems, of a relationship between himself and a trained social worker. . . . It is a basic assumption of all casework that each person is a unique individual whose difficulties are the product of complex and interacting factors. . . . There may, in the first place, be scope for altering external influences by helping the individual to change his home or economic circumstances, his habits or companions. Here, although the need may sometimes be for direct material assistance, the caseworker's aim will be to encourage people to help themselves rather than be helped; to co-operate rather than obey. The caseworker will plan constantly for the time when his support, advice and assistance are no longer available.[61]

The recommendations of the ACTO Report, *The Organization of After-Care*, published in 1963, followed strongly on these lines by emphasizing from the outset that the committee considered that 'after-care is essentially a form of social casework'.[62] The 1963 committee considered the general principles by which after-care should be organized and within these limits it was quickly apparent that the only service geared to operate on the lines envisaged was the probation service. The committee's two main recommendations were first, the amalgamation of compulsory and voluntary after-care into a common service (the probation service), emphasizing that 'the only distinction between the two forms of after-care should lie in the legal consequences of failure to respond'[63] and second, the employment of professional social workers on after-care work both in penal institutions and in the community. It endorsed the view, which was familiar reading in reports of this kind but had never been put into practice, that

after-care, to be fully effective, must be integrated with the work of the penal institutions in which the offender serves his sentence, and must be conceived as a process which starts on the offender's reception into custody, is developed during his sentence, and is available for as long as necessary after his release.[64]

The members of the Advisory Council were not completely unanimous in presenting their report. There is a Memorandum of Dissent[65] by Professor Leon Radzinowicz, Lady Inskip and the Rev. E. Shirwell Price which is couched in fairly strong terms. They felt that the committee was 'so preoccupied with casework problems that it ignores the broader questions of community provision'. They emphasized that planning was needed on a national scale in some instances of which one of the most obvious areas concerned the provision of hostels. One person or body with greater executive powers and devoting exclusive attention to after-care was what was required, in their view, and this approach would be more likely to ensure that sufficient resources would be forthcoming for the development of after-care.

In December 1963 the government announced its acceptance in principle of the ACTO recommendations of the majority report. The following two years showed a fairly remarkable flurry of activity in implementing the proposals. This is summarized in the Report on the Work of the Probation and After-Care Department 1962-5.[67] It is not the purpose of the present chapter to discuss developments since 1963, but the evidence of Holborn's field study suggests that the ACTO proposals have not produced a panacea. At one point she suggests that 'either most discharged prisoners do not need the kind of help the 1963 Report assumed they would; or, they do need this help, but are not getting it',[68] while as a conclusion she maintains that 'the general problem of voluntary after-care was that the Service was often trying to sell something which its potential clients did not want, did not expect, or perhaps could not use'.[69] While these comments should be examined within the context of her evidence, they do provide a further justification for looking once again at the area which the majority of offenders consider as their primary need – the finding of a job on release. As we have tried to show, job-finding was considered the most important facet of after-care for nearly a hundred years, but when it was jettisoned for another viewpoint, we still did not know the value or effect of this type of after-care provision.

The ACTO Report (1963) radically altered the structure of after-care and completed the transition to the view of after-care as a form of social casework. It is perhaps a relevant epitaph on after-care in this country that even in 1963 the committee reported that 'we are not able to point to any research directed to determining the extent to which after-care of offenders discharged from prisons or borstals assists in preventing relapse into crime'.[70] The Committee goes on to say 'research in this field is, indeed, particularly difficult'.[71] It is gratifying to know that some people at least are aware of the obstacles we have to overcome in order to complete our work.

## NOTES

It is impossible to do justice to the intricacies of the development of after-care in one chapter. Two unpublished theses give a much fuller account, while the contribution of Professor John Martin concisely states some of the issues involved in planning after-care.

Holborn, J. M., 'The After-Care of Offenders: An Analysis of Recent Developments', M.A. (Econ.) thesis, University of Manchester (1968), unpublished.

Lacey, A. W., 'The Role of Voluntary Effort in the After-Care of Offenders', Ph.D. thesis, University of London (1963), unpublished.

Martin, J. P., 'After-Care in Transition' in Grygier, T., Jones, H., and Spencer, J. C. (eds), *Criminology in Transition*, London, Tavistock (1965).

It is perhaps useful to give in chronological order the reports which provide the background to the debate on after-care between the years 1935 and 1963:

*Report of the Departmental Committee*. Part II. Employment on Discharge (Cmd. 4897, 1935) – The Salmon Committee (1935).

*Report of the Committee on Discharged Prisoners' Aid Societies* (Cmd. 8879, 1953) – The Maxwell Report (1953).

*Report of the Advisory Council on the Treatment of Offenders*. The After-Care and Supervision of Discharged Prisoners. London, HMSO (1958) – The ACTO Report (1958).

Morris, P., *Prison After-Care: Charity or Public Responsibility?* London, Fabian Society Research Series, No. 218 (1960).

Pakenham-Thompson Committee, *Problems of the Ex-Prisoner: A Report*, London, National Council of Social Service (1961).

*Report of the Advisory Council on the Treatment of Offenders*. The Organization of After-Care. London, HMSO (1963) – The ACTO Report (1963).

In addition, although they may appear somewhat tangential to the main debate on after-care, it is instructive to consider the two reports on the probation service to appreciate the reluctance to involve the probation service further in after-care at the beginning of this period and the willingness to consider the possibility of its closer involvement towards the end of the period:

*Report of the Departmental Committee on the Social Services in Courts of Summary Jurisdiction* (Cmd. 5122, 1936).

*Report of the Departmental Committee on the Probation Service* (Cmd. 1650, 1962) – The Morison Committee (1962).

REFERENCES

1 Genesis, chapters 39–41.
2 *Report from the Departmental Committee on Prisons* (c. 7702, 1895), p. 18. Referred to hereafter as the Gladstone Committee (1895).
3 Ibid., p. 45.
4 Ibid., p. 16.
5 Ibid., p. 15.
6 *Reports of the Inspectors of Prisons of Great Britain*, I. Home District (1836), pp. 70–1.
7 Ibid., pp. 18–19. (My italics.)
8 Ibid., Northern District (1836), p. 69.
9 Young, A. F., and Ashton, E. T., *British Social Work in the Nineteenth Century*, London, Routledge and Kegan Paul (1956), p. 160.
10 Ibid., p. 159.
11 Ibid., p. 160.
12 The Gladstone Committee (1895), Minutes of Evidence, p. 367, para. 10,879.
13 Ibid., p. 14.
14 *Bills, Public* (Session 6 February–7 August 1862), 1862, Vol. I, p. 648.
15 Holborn, J. M., 'The After-Care of Offenders: An Analysis of Recent Developments', M.A. (Econ.) thesis, University of Manchester (1968), unpublished.
16 Ibid.
17 Ibid.
18 *Report of the Commissioners of Prisons*, London, HMSO, Cmd. 374 (1918–19), p. 13.
19 The Gladstone Committee (1895), p. 14.
20 Young and Ashton, op. cit., p. 162.
21 *Report to the Commissioners of Prisons on the Operations of Discharged Prisoners' Aid Societies*, by the Rev. G. P. Merrick (c. 8299, 1897), p. 23. Referred to hereafter as the Merrick Report (1897).
22 Ibid., p. 37.
23 Ibid., p. 37.
24 Ibid., p. 61.
25 Ibid., p. 61.
26 Ibid., p. 62.
27 Ibid., p. 62.
28 Ibid., p. 100.
29 *Report of the Departmental Committee. Part II. Employment on Discharge*, London, HMSO, Cmd. 4897 (1935), xi, p. 3. Referred to hereafter as the Salmon Committee (1935).
30 Ibid., p. 17.
31 *Report of the Commissioners of Prisons* (Cd. 8342, 1915–16), p. 18.
32 *Report of the Commissioners of Prisons* (Cd. 2723, 1904–5), p. 59.
33 The Merrick Report (1897), p. 5.
34 *Report of the Commissioners of Prisons* (Cd. 4300, 1907–8), p. 46.
35 *Report of the Commissioners of Prisons* (Cd. 5360, 1909–10), p. 35.
36 Loc. cit.
37 *Report of the Commissioners of Prisons* (Cd. 380, 1899–1900), p. 57.
38 *Report of the Commissioners of Prisons* (Cd. 380, 1899–1900), p. 57.
39 *Report of the Commissioners of Prisons* (Cd. 3169, 1905–6), p. 59.

40 The Salmon Committee (1935), pp. 15–16.
41 Ibid., p. 17.
42 Ibid., p. 20.
43 *Report of the Departmental Committee on the Social Services in Courts of Summary Jurisdiction*, London, HMSO, Cmd. 5122 (1936), p. 61.
44 Ibid., p. 86. The Report quotes from a Home Office circular to Justices of 21 October 1932.
45 *Annual Report of the National Association of Discharged Prisoners' Aid Societies* (Wakefield Sub-Committee, Report for the Year 1937), 1938, p. 22.
46 *Report of the Committee on Discharged Prisoners' Aid Societies*, London, HMSO, Cmd. 8879 (1953), p. 13. Referred to hereafter as the Maxwell Report (1953).
47 Ibid., p. 16.
48 Ibid., p. 21.
49 *Annual Report of the National Association of Discharged Prisoners' Aid Societies*, 1961–2, Appendix 2, p. 26.
50 Holborn, op. cit.
51 *Report of the Advisory Council on the Treatment of Offenders. The After-Care and Supervision of Discharged Prisoners*, London, HMSO (1958).
52 Ibid., p. 12.
53 Ibid., p. 27.
54 *Annual Report of the National Association of Discharged Prisoners' Aid Societies* (1961), p. 20.
55 Morris, P., *Prisoners and their Families*, London, Allen and Unwin (1965), p. 120.
56 Pakenham-Thompson Committee, *Problems of the Ex-Prisoners: A Report*, London, National Council of Social Service (1961), p. 9.
57 The *Observer*, 27.11.60.
58 Morris, P., *Prison After-Care: Charity or Public Responsibility?* London, Fabian Society Research Series, No. 218 (1960).
59 *Report of the Departmental Committee on the Probation Service*, London, HMSO, Cmd. 1650 (1962), p. 10. Referred to hereafter as the Morison Committee (1962).
60 Ibid., p. 44.
61 Ibid., pp. 24–5.
62 *Report of the Advisory Council on the Treatment of Offenders. The Organization of After-Care*. London, HMSO (1963), p. ii (the ACTO Report (1963)).
63 Ibid., p. 29.
64 Ibid., p. 4.
65 Ibid., p. 83.
66 Ibid., p. 86.
67 *Report on the Work of the Probation and After-Care Department*, London, HMSO, Cmd. 3107 (1962–5).
68 Holborn, op. cit.
69 Holborn, op. cit.
70 The ACTO Report (1963), p. 6.
71 Loc. cit.

## CHAPTER 2

# Development of an Employment-Placing Service for Discharged Prisoners (the Work of the Department of Employment)

We have emphasized in the last chapter how voluntary societies involved in the rehabilitation of discharged prisoners tended to regard job-finding as their primary function. Clearly there were tremendous differences throughout the country in the success of carrying out this approach relating both to the state of the market in the various regions and more directly to the resources and expertise of a particular discharged prisoners' aid society. Now that the responsibility for after-care has been transferred from the voluntary societies to the Probation and After-Care Service, there is probably no longer the same problem of a disparity of service according to which part of the country a prisoner returns to after a prison sentence. However, the Probation and After-Care Service does not regard job-finding as its main function in handling the after-care of ex-prisoners. This is partly because the probation officer operates within a framework which is aiming in the long term to encourage people to help themselves rather than to rely on being helped. Although in the short term the probation officer will sometimes recognize the need for direct material aid or assistance, he will perhaps tend to use a specialized service which is designed to answer a particular need. While most probation officers in practice have access to a few sympathetic employers who might help with a particular case, the cornerstone of the present system of job-finding for ex-prisoners rests with the Department of Employment. The aim of this chapter is primarily to describe the origins and procedure of the special arrangement that the Department of Employment has set up for dealing with men and women discharged from H.M. Prisons throughout the country.

The one great asset that the direct involvement of the Department of Employment should in theory have is that it should put the placing of ex-prisoners within the mainstream of placing activity. The Department has a national network of offices, and because it is designed for the general population it should also have a wide range of jobs to offer. The success of the Department's general placing activity has from time to time been considered critically. As an example, in the late 1950s and early 1960s, earlier workers, such as Kahn,[1] found that employment exchanges played a relatively small part in finding new jobs for redundant workers. In more recent times the Department of Employment has made definite attempts to improve its placement service, but research findings have still tended to confirm the earlier results. Reid[2] investigated the experience of 658 male workers made redundant from 23 plants in the East Midlands in the two years following the 'July measures' of 1966. Of those using the service of the employment exchange, only a third of the workers expressed satisfaction and nearly two-thirds dissatisfaction. Despite a high contact rate, the service achieved a low placement rate, and those it placed found no better jobs no more quickly than those finding them by other means. More perniciously, there was still a largely unfavourable image among its users – nearly half of whom described it as primarily a 'place where you collect dole' or a 'place for layabouts'. On the other hand, there were more favourable reports regarding the on-site offices to register and counsel redundant workers, with nearly half the users expressing satisfaction, so there is some indication that the more specific attempts of the Department to improve its service may be working. Major redundancies place a tremendous strain on the resources of the Department, but it has tried to respond positively to the challenge of this problem.

The arrangement of on-site offices for redundant workers is in fact not too dissimilar from the special arrangement in prisons by which placing officers interview prisoners before their release. However, it is essential if this particular aspect of the Department's work is to be meaningful to place it within the context of the overall development of the employment exchanges since their inception on a national basis sixty years ago. In this way one can begin to distinguish the general problem of the Department's placing service – of which the ex-prisoner is just one of many consumers – and the particular difficulties of the special arrangement for ex-prisoners. The co-operation of the Department of Employment (D.E.) has enabled a small-scale study to be made of the effectiveness of the latter procedure. The Department agreed to supply the numbers in the various groups of the Apex project who saw the D.E. official before release and of these the numbers placed by the D.E. within three months after release.

Although the Labour Exchange Act of 1909, by which the recommendation urged in both the Majority and Minority Reports of the Royal Commission on the Poor Laws in 1909 to establish labour exchanges on a permanent and co-ordinated basis was put into effect, is obviously a key date in the history of employment exchanges, it is perhaps important to emphasize that it is their proposed national distribution in this legislation which is the vital factor in their subsequent development. Similar systems had already been set up in some other European countries, particularly Germany, but even in this country some municipal authorities kept employment registers in the recession of 1891-5.[3] This kind of provision was the forerunner of a more positive attitude to the problem of unemployment, so that unemployment was no longer to be regarded as simply 'destitution' of the type with which the Poor Law had traditionally dealt. This distinction was implicit in the provisions of the Unemployed Workmen Act of 1905 that local distress committees should be set up to collect information, to discriminate between applicants for relief, to establish labour exchanges and to assist emigration.[4] Certainly the 1909 Act took a step forward, emphasizing that the only criterion for the selection of workers was industrial suitability, no regard being paid to such factors as length of unemployment. The President of the Board of Trade, Winston Churchill, who was the responsible minister, encouraged this new and positive role by saying:

> The Exchanges are primarily agencies for dealing with employment rather than unemployment and when Unemployment Insurance comes into operation . . . it will throw into labour exchanges all the business of finding employment in some of the greatest trades of the country . . . the difficulties of the system will diminish as its work increases.[5]

Unfortunately, Churchill's last sentiment has not proved accurate, for the fact of a national distribution of agencies has resulted in the employment exchanges being an attractive repository of a number of extraneous functions which have hindered the fulfilment of their original purpose as job-finding agencies. In spite of the assurances of the then responsible minister, Winston Churchill, it has been the administrative problem of unemployment which has done more than anything else to overburden the work of the Department and has caused the image of its placing work to suffer, sometimes fairly and sometimes unfairly.

The Unemployment Insurances Act of 1920 meant that the Labour Exchanges were charged with the duty of issuing unemployment insurance cards and paying unemployment benefit when claims were made for the whole of the industrial population with the exception of work-people employed in agriculture and private domestic service. Since then the Department of Employment has been struggling to cope with the very real volume of work that these Acts imposed. The first complete Annual Report of the Ministry of Labour (published 1924–5) recognized this:

> The primary function of the Exchanges is to place the unemployed worker in touch with the employer requiring labour. During the last few years this essential function has been somewhat overshadowed by the duties which the Exchanges have had to perform in relation to the payment of unemployment benefit to large numbers of unemployed workpeople.[6]

The Second World War accelerated the trend towards giving the Ministry of Labour a large number of responsibilities extraneous to its placing activity. The decision to add National Services to the duties of the Ministry of Labour was reached in August 1939. In June 1940 the administration of the Factory Acts was transferred from the Health Service to the Ministry of Labour and National Service to link the promotion of good working conditions inside the factories more closely with the arrangements for regulating labour in wartime. This is all in addition to much other work which the ministry's local offices continued to perform on an agency basis for other government departments.

On the other hand, the war brought to the fore again the importance of the ministry's placing work in manning the vital war industries quickly. The placing work of the employment exchanges was given a privileged position to the extent that the ministry was given comprehensive powers of labour control, including control over the engagement of labour. In March 1950 when these powers were finally revoked the ministry's employment exchange service had to demonstrate its value as a placing agency in a free labour market. There had been some useful preparation in the sense that the Employment and Training Act of 1948 extended the functions of employment exchanges to include the provision of employment advice and vocational guidance to workers whether they were in employment or not. Further, the Appointments Department of the Ministry of Labour which was designed to fulfil the function of a nationwide employment agency to deal with vacancies of a professional, administrative, managerial, technical or scientific nature, had been established as early as April 1918. The ministry would appear to have been reasonably prepared to improve its image, particularly with respect to the belief that the exchanges were useful only in supplying unskilled labour. However, the opportunity of cornering a large portion of the potentially lucrative parts of the market, such as the white-collar field and vocational guidance and advice, was largely lost by short-sighted economy cuts. This was disastrous for in the 1950s and early 1960s the employment exchanges were competing not only in a free labour market but also in a market where there was a general shortage of labour. J. P. Martin in his study of 97 firms in the Reading area, *Offenders as Employees*, distinguishing between recruitment for 'works' employees and 'staff' employees, showed that for 'works' employees the Ministry of Labour was the most frequently used source for the larger firms, but 'the position was quite different among the smaller firms; for only seven out of forty was it a major source'.[7] An interpretation of this is that the larger firms with more vacancies and a wider range were able to have a mutually satisfactory relationship with the local exchange. This would clearly explain the belief, particularly prevalent among prisoners, that the exchanges offer only unattractive work at low rates, for no doubt the large firms, among many other vacancies they may notify, submit such unacceptable vacancies which remain on the exchange's books for many years and are ritually offered by the counter clerk to any possible candidate who in turn rejects the offer but repeats the story elsewhere of what he was offered.

In the last few years the Department of Employment has begun to appreciate the need for a much more active employment placing service. This has resulted in some tentative but enterprising attempts such as an occupational guidance scheme for adults which was introduced early in 1966. Local exchanges have been allowed somewhat more opportunity to experiment on their own initiative. Perhaps more fundamental is the development of such practices as benefits being paid by postal draft, for not only is this likely to be a more efficient system, releasing resources for more placing activity, but it is more likely to fulfil the main objective of the employment service, 'to swing it from being an institution which is largely about unemployment benefit to being an economic agency which is predominantly about employment'.[8] While one can accept that the stage is gradually being set for a more aggressive and dynamic placing policy, one suspects that the resources, particularly in terms of personnel, are somewhat stretched to carry out such a policy effectively. This is a tentative prophecy about the future, and innovations take time to filtrate through to produce the desired effect. One must obviously stress that none of any recent improvements in the last couple of years in the placing service of the Department could have had any impact on the Apex samples at the prisons of Wormwood Scrubs and Pentonville.

We have given this short historical background to the more specialized work of the Department of Employment in prisons, for it is always worthwhile to remember that almost any specialized placing activity of the Department operates within a wider context and usually attempts to dovetail into the general organization of the Department.

## THE WORK OF THE DEPARTMENT OF EMPLOYMENT IN PRISONS

In many ways it is surprising that it was not until the Second World War that the beginnings of a special arrangement with the Ministry of Labour for a pre-discharge interview began to be forged. Sir Alexander Paterson, a prison commissioner for twenty-five years and noted for using his experience in other spheres of activity to encourage new ideas in the prison service, had after the First World War first found work with the Ministry of Labour in the rehabilitation and placing in employment of young people. Similarly, Dame Lilian Barker, CBE, who was appointed the first Director of 'The Aylesbury Association' set up for the after-care of women and girls, had worked for the Ministry of Labour until 1923 when she was persuaded 'under some pressure from the Commissioners, to take on the Governorship of the girls' Borstal at Aylesbury at a critical time in the history of that institution'.[9]

As she continued to supervise the work of the Aylesbury After-Care Association even after her appointment as the first woman Assistant Commissioner in 1935, one suspects that it was on the initiative of Dame Lilian Barker that a more direct link was contemplated. During the early part of the war, when all work had to be obtained through the Ministry of Labour, it was noted that difficulties arose for borstal girls, for when the fact that they were borstal girls was disclosed, placing became difficult. There is no reason to believe in retrospect that such difficulty was restricted to borstal girls in distinction to borstal boys or even ex-prisoners in general. However, it was for the borstal girls that a direct personal appeal was made to the Ministry of Labour by whose help it was arranged that, before leaving, a girl would be interviewed by a Ministry of Labour official who would fix her up with work to go to immediately on discharge.[10] It was then only necessary to arrange lodgings and supervision. Clearly the Ministry of Labour performed this job intelligently and conscientiously, for the Reports of the Commissioner of Prisons were full of enthusiasm for the scheme.

This is perhaps not such a surprising innovation in the penal field when one considers the parallel developments in the relationship of hospitals and the Ministry of Labour. The Inter-Departmental Committee on the Rehabilitation and Resettlement of Disabled Persons (the Tomlinson Committee) had reported and Disablement Resettlement Officers had been appointed in 1943.

The close co-operation established with hospitals and other establishments concerned from July, 1941, onwards provided for the first time a link between the hospital and the Employment Exchange service, thus enabling the process of rehabilitation to be continued through the period of medical treatment to the stage of industrial settlement.[11]

The figures indicate that this was not only an ambitious programme but also effective. The total number of persons interviewed at hospitals and Local Offices from the start of the Interview Scheme until September 1945, that is, prior to the introduction of registration under the Disabled Persons (Employment) Act of 1944, was 426,336. Of these, 310,806 (or 73 per cent) were placed in work while a further 67,001 (or 16 per cent) required no assistance in settlement. This scheme was able to get on a very satisfactory basis when there was a great shortage of labour. On the other hand, within the sector of prison and borstal after-care, there was the somewhat anomalous situation of the discharged prisoners' aid societies and to a lesser extent the statutory after-care organizations, both of which largely regarded the finding of employment for discharged prisoners as their main task. It is interesting that the Aylesbury Association enlisted the co-operation of the Ministry of Labour during the war years when many of the aid societies reported that finding employment for discharged prisoners did not constitute a serious problem. Immediately after the war, though, when there was still a shortage of labour, the aid societies indicated that there was evidence that their former difficulties were beginning to show themselves again.

Two important developments took place in 1948 which brought the Ministry of Labour and National Service into even closer involvement with the after-care of prisoners. The Prison Commissioners had consulted the Ministry of Labour in connection with the placing in industry of men and youths who had been given some training in skilled trades in prisons and borstal institutions.

In January 1948, the ministry issued a letter to its Assistant Regional Controllers giving details of the training courses then in existence, but the ministry insisted, for various reasons, that it was not possible for the men to be placed in industry under the arrangements made for those trained under the ministry's own schemes. In reality this brings up the whole question of the value of prison training in helping to place men in the open market if the qualification obtained is not a recognized trade qualification. For this reason alone, the effectiveness of this letter in trying to encourage the regions to assist men and youths to find suitable work on release is likely to have been extremely limited.

The other development is of more fundamental importance for it illustrates the willingness of the Ministry of Labour to recognize that the ex-prisoner has particular problems by the very fact of being an ex-prisoner and should perhaps be given special consideration. The aim was that discharged prisoners, when visiting an employment exchange, should not have to divulge in the hearing of other applicants the fact that they had been serving a prison sentence and, further, there was an attempt to reduce delay in the payment of grants to a minimum. A revised scheme, for co-operation between local discharged prisoners' aid societies, the Ministry of Labour and the Assistance Board, came into operation on 1 January 1948, when a simplified procedure was adopted.

The Wakefield Sub-Committee which, from its inception, had always been to the forefront in pioneer after-care work, was already co-operating closely with the Ministry of Labour in the placing in employment of trainees from the prison vocational training schemes. In the NADPAS annual report for the year ended 31 March 1949, a much grander scheme was outlined.

> We hope in the near future to formulate a scheme whereby every man due for discharge will have an early opportunity of being brought by this Committee before the Ministry of Labour for new employment, should he so desire, and thus have a job waiting for him on discharge . . . what greater aid on discharge could be supplied than the offer of immediate employment?[12]

The Sub-Committee had responsibility for the after-care of all prisoners at Wakefield serving less than four years, with the exception of those sentenced to corrective training. The calibre and potential of the men at Wakefield was higher than at any other prison in the country, although in the previous year the advent of men in the prison with more than one conviction had been noted. In their report for the year 1949 the Prison Commissioners maintained that the results of the experiment at Wakefield Prison were sufficiently encouraging to warrant its extension elsewhere.[13] The Wakefield Sub-Committee reports that the employment scheme inaugurated with the Ministry of Labour 'shows 78% of successful placing'.[14]*

There is no exact definition of successful placing, but one suspects that the ideal of a job waiting for a man on discharge had probably been compromised to some extent. Describing the extension of the scheme, the Prison Commissioners indicate[15] that arrangements were shortly to come into force whereby every prisoner serving a sentence of more than six months might, if he so wished, be interviewed before discharge by an officer of the Ministry of Labour in the hope that *suitable employment might be found for him within a few days of his release.* If he were serving a sentence at a distance from his home his case would, after interview, be brought without delay to the notice of the employment office of the Ministry in his own locality. The arrangements were for prisoners released unconditionally after a sentence of more than six months, but the extension of these arrangements to cover prisoners serving sentences of corrective training and preventive detention was also under consideration. However, for the present they were covered by the same arrangement provided for prisoners serving shorter sentences who formed the majority of the prison discharges in the course of a year. These men were to be advised by the discharged prisoners' aid societies of the help that the employment exchange service could give them in obtaining employment, and if they wished to take advantage of this offer they were to be given a suitable introduction to the employment exchange in the area in which they proposed to live.

Everyone seemed thrilled by this closer involvement of the Ministry of Labour. The Ministry of Labour emphasized that 'not only have these arrangements resulted in employment being found for discharged prisoners more rapidly, but they are reported to

* Appendix D of the Maxwell Report, which is a Memorandum submitted in evidence by the Ministry of Labour and National Service, noted the success of the Wakefield experiment. 'In the period 1st July, 1949 to 26th November, 1949, of the 63 interviewed and released, 46 had been placed in work through local Employment Exchanges; 6 had not reported to an Employment Exchange and 11, mainly those just released, were still unemployed.' (This would produce a figure of 73 per cent successfully placed. If three more of the unemployed were subsequently placed, this would produce a figure of 78 per cent.)

have improved the morale of prisoners by demonstrating to them that increased interest was being taken in their future welfare'.[16] The Prison Commissioners indicated that the Ministry of Labour had taken up its new responsibility within the prisons with enthusiasm and 'in one town, at least, the manager of the Employment Exchange goes further than the scheme requires by visiting the prison each month to give to the prisoners who are due for discharge a talk on the state of the labour market and industrial trends'.[17] The Central After-Care Association (CACA), dealing with prisoners on compulsory after-care and those serving sentences of four years or more, also developed a close liaison with the Ministry of Labour, so that the placing officers could now see those prisoners who had indicated a willingness to be interviewed prior to discharge.

The first hint that there was still some way to go before the arrangement could be called completely satisfactory came in the annual reports of the Wakefield Sub-Committee which had so much to do with the first experimental scheme.

> The co-operation between the Ministry of Labour and National Service, the Central After-Care Association, the National Assistance Board and the National Association of Discharged Prisoners' Aid Societies still requires tightening up before one can say that it has reached top gear standard.[18]

The next year there is a more definite indication that the situation had not been perfected, suggesting a surprising reversal in the development of the sub-committee's thinking about the role of the discharged prisoners' aid societies.

> It has been more difficult to place men in employment. We feel that Discharged Prisoners' Aid Societies' assistance will be welcomed by the Ministry of Labour as unemployment increases.[19]

It was at this juncture that the Report of the Committee on Discharged Prisoners' Aid Societies (the Maxwell Committee) was published. The involvement of the Ministry of Labour was very much in its scheme of recommendations that 'in future the Aid Societies should shift the emphasis of their interest from "aid-on-discharge" to personal "after-care"'.[20] It noted with favour the present arrangement in operation and suggested in addition that the interviewing of prisoners by placing officers of the ministry should be extended to prisoners with sentences of less than six months and also that 'an interview with the Placing Officer should be arranged as a matter of normal routine unless the prisoner objected'.[21] In fact it was able to note later in the report that its recommendations had been accepted by the ministry, which planned in the future to interview all prisoners with sentences of three months or over, and that these interviews would take place in every case unless the prisoner objected or there were special reasons to the contrary.

Although the Maxwell Committee was very enthusiastic about the pre-release work of the Ministry of Labour, the committee was equally anxious that the aid societies should still be involved in the field of employment.

> We consider it to be of great importance that the arrangements which have been made with the Ministry of Labour should not cause the Aid Societies themselves to lose the active interest which they have shown in the past in the finding of employment.[22]

One of the ways in which the committee suggested that the aid societies might be particularly effective in the field of employment was in the placing of professional men, for the committee maintained:

> It is . . . sometimes possible for an Aid Society to make a special appeal to individual employers with the result that a fresh chance may be offered to such a prisoner in spite of his lapse; and in this way the personal and unofficial approach of the Aid Society can be of inestimable value.[23]

This was an area that some aid societies did recognize as important, and the annual reports of NADPAS further indicate that the organization was aware of this particular problem, emphasizing that during a period of 'full' employment finding employment is one of the less difficult aspects of rehabilitation, except for the difficult minority of ex-prisoners from the professional classes.[24]

Another reason why the Maxwell Committee felt that it was a wise precaution for the aid societies to continue to be involved in employment placing was in case the economic situation changed.[25] It recognized that the Ministry of Labour could not be expected to give priority to the needs of discharged prisoners and equally recognized that in times of difficulty the ex-prisoner should not be given preference over others who might be seeking employment. It is perhaps ironical that when this situation did occur in the mid–1960s the role of the aid societies had been encouraged to change by the ACTO report 1963, and few of the aid societies were actively involved in placing ex-prisoners.

The Maxwell Committee recognized that an employer is not usually willing to engage an applicant without a personal interview and maintained that it is seldom possible actually to place a prisoner in a job *before* discharge, so that there is inevitably some interval of time after discharge before he can begin work.[26] This is undoubtedly true, but the committee failed to make the distinction between arranging an interview before release and arranging a job before release. The former is usually possible, but the latter is usually not. Failure to make this distinction has meant that in practice the Ministry of Labour simply takes the basic details of the man during a pre-release interview and notifies the relevant exchange that it has arranged for the man to come to that office after release. While it is possible that some offices may keep a vacancy on one side, knowing that a particular ex-prisoner would be suitable, one suspects that this is not the usual practice, for experience has perhaps suggested that only a proportion of the men contact the office after release as arranged. Certainly in present practice it would tend to be the exception for a vacancy to be notified to the man before release unless perhaps he were settling in the area covered by the ministry official conducting the pre-release interview.

Clearly, however, the Maxwell Committee wanted an extension of the scheme initiated in Wakefield Prison. As a result, arrangements were subsequently made by which every prisoner serving a sentence of more than three months was to be interviewed during the course of his sentence by a placing officer of the ministry unless he declined such an interview (incidentally, it is not clear when the policy of 'contracting-out' of an interview changed to the present one of 'contracting-in'). In addition, arrangements were made to ensure that the results of the efforts made by the employment exchange on his behalf were in each case known to the after-care authorities and to the governor of the prison from which he was discharged.[27] This latter procedure was very conscientiously carried out during the 1950s, but it seems to have been curtailed somewhat over recent years.

Apart from the initial experiment at Wakefield Prison, there seems to have been little or no subsequent investigation of the effectiveness of the scheme. There are, however, some passing references in other work. In the preparation of its report on 'The After-Care and Supervision of Discharged Prisoners' (1958), the Advisory Council on the Treatment of Offenders submitted questionnaires to prisoners covering various aspects of after-care. The main group was 248 prisoners serving a sentence of imprisonment who had had one, but not more than three, previous sentences of imprisonment and whose last previous sentence was more than three months and less than four years.

Within prison over half of the men did not see the Placing Officer of the Ministry of Labour or the Discharged Prisoners' Aid Societies' case committee, although over 80 per cent saw the Discharged Prisoners' Aid Society representative.[28]

A possible inconsistency in the information is that:

almost 90 per cent claimed that they had found work themselves, although when the first job or the longest job held was considered specifically, 27 per cent reported help from the employment exchange or the after-care societies.[29]

There is a failure here to distinguish placing action by the Ministry of Labour as a result of the pre-release interview and subsequent action by the Ministry of Labour when an ex-prisoner attends the employment exchange on his own initiative after release (as anyone is entitled to do).

The annual reports of the Ministry of Labour give no real indication of the progress of the scheme, for, after explaining the procedure, they simply state that 'Local Officers were able in many cases to place discharged prisoners in employment with little or no delay'.[30] The main comment of the Ministry of Labour regarding its prison commitments was its increasing involvement with the extension of the prison hostel scheme by which prisoners were available for ordinary employment outside the prison on the same terms and conditions as other workers.

To some extent the impact of the Ministry of Labour in the after-care field can be estimated by examining the reports of the sub-committees of the Regional Prisons in the NADPAS annual reports. One suspects that the committees of these special prisons were considerably more active than almost any local society in the country dealing with the local prison population. The fact that they were enthusiastic in trying to ascertain the outcome of the efforts of the various agencies to which they sent their charges almost certainly encouraged these other agencies to do their best to produce a favourable outcome.

Wakefield and Maidstone prisons were known as special prisons and were training centres for selected prisoners from prisons in the northern and southern halves of England and Wales respectively.

C

TABLE 1  Employment arrangements of men discharged from Wakefield Prison to care of NADPAS (1946–57)

| Year | | 1946 | 1947 | 1948 | 1949 | 1950 | 1951 | 1952 | 1953 | 1954 | 1955 | 1956 | 1957 |
|---|---|---|---|---|---|---|---|---|---|---|---|---|---|
| Total No. of men discharged from H.M. Prison (to care of NADPAS) | No. | 664 | 497 | 541 | 428 | 197* | 192 | 268 | 289 | 260 | 213 | 188 | 193 |
| | % | 100·0 | 100·0 | 100·0 | 100·0 | 100·0 | 100·0 | 100·0 | 100·0 | 100·0 | 100·0 | 100·0 | 100·0 |
| New employment found by Wakefield Sub-Committee | No. | 18 | 14 | 7 | 6 | 13 | 10 | 7 | 8 | 15 | 4 | 4 | 7 |
| | % of total | 2·7 | 2·8 | 1·3 | 1·4 | 6·6 | 5·2 | 2·6 | 2·8 | 5·8 | 1·9 | 2·1 | 3·6 |
| Returned to old employment arranged by Wakefield Sub-Committee | No. | 32 | 17 | 19 | 14 | 16 | 5 | 6 | 15 | 8 | 17 | 6 | 9 |
| | % of total | 4·8 | 3·4 | 3·5 | 3·3 | 8·1 | 2·6 | 2·2 | 5·2 | 3·1 | 8·0 | 3·2 | 4·7 |
| New employment found by local discharged prisoners' aid society | No. | 23 | 1 | 1 | — | 24 | 14 | 10 | 19 | 17 | 13 | 7 | 9 |
| | % of total | 3·5 | 0·2 | 0·2 | — | 12·2 | 7·3 | 3·7 | 6·6 | 6·5 | 6·1 | 3·7 | 4·7 |
| Placed in work by Ministry of Labour | No. | 24 | 32 | 21 | 69 | 36 | 40 | 27 | 59 | 43 | 36 | 37 | 40 |
| | % of total | 3·6 | 6·4 | 3·9 | 16·1 | 18·3 | 20·8 | 10·1 | 20·4 | 16·5 | 16·9 | 19·7 | 20·7 |
| Found own employment or returned to former employment | No. | 303 | 377 | 450 | 330 | 27 | 30 | 110 | 76 | 88 | 76 | 62 | 66 |
| | % of total | 45·6 | 75·9 | 83·2 | 77·1 | 13·7 | 15·6 | 41·0 | 26·3 | 33·8 | 35·7 | 33·0 | 34·2 |
| Returned to H.M. Forces or known to have enlisted | No. | 137 | 26 | 13 | 4 | 1 | 1 | — | — | 1 | 1 | 1 | — |
| | % of total | 20·6 | 5·2 | 2·4 | 0·9 | 0·5 | 0·5 | — | — | 0·4 | 0·5 | 0·5 | — |
| Total reported to be in employment | No. | 537 | 467 | 511 | 423 | 117 | 100 | 160 | 177 | 172 | 147 | 117 | 131 |
| | % of total | 80·9 | 94·0 | 94·5 | 98·8 | 59·4 | 52·1 | 59·7 | 61·2 | 66·2 | 69·0 | 62·2 | 67·9 |

* Decrease because of influx of corrective trainees who are seen by CACA.
Source: NADPAS Annual reports 1946–58.

As we have mentioned, the sub-committee of Wakefield Prison was largely instrumental in getting the special arrangement with the Ministry of Labour on a working basis. Hence, it is interesting to trace the impact on this prison of the Ministry of Labour over the twelve-year period (1946–57 inclusive); this period covers the introduction of the scheme and also the publication of the Maxwell Report which encouraged the extension of the arrangement. In examining Wakefield, there is the advantage (to counter the major disadvantage of its being a very special case!) that one variable at least remains stable over the period, for there was the same Resident Secretary of the Sub-Committee from 1948 to 1957 inclusive, so any apparent fluctuations in the figures cannot be the result of a 'new broom' in the form of a new Resident Secretary.

Table 1 shows the employment arrangements of men discharged from Wakefield Prison from 1946 to 1957. It indicates how the Ministry of Labour placed approximately 5 per cent of the men discharged in the period 1946–8 before the pre-discharge scheme was fully operational. These were men primarily placed in work after training in the engineering course at Wakefield. After the introduction of the scheme at Wakefield Prison in 1949, the number of men placed in work by the Ministry of Labour stabilized at between 16 and 20 per cent of those discharged. In 1952, there is an unexplained fall in the percentage helped by the Ministry of Labour, for, from the 20·8 per cent of the previous year, only 10·1 per cent were placed in work by the Ministry of Labour in 1952. A higher proportion of men in that year found their own employment or at least returned to their former employment than did so in the previous years, and so the apparent fall in the Ministry activity cannot be explained by any increased activity of the Wakefield Sub-Committee or local discharged prisoners' aid societies in an attempt to impress the Maxwell Committee, which was then active in investigating this area of after-care. Whatever the explanation, it does suggest how quickly the proportion helped by the Ministry can drop in a short time, but apart from that particular year there is a consistency in the proportions helped in the following years.

While it would be reasonable to suspect that Wakefield Prison may be a rather special case on account of an active committee and its particular interest in setting up the special arrangement with the Ministry of Labour, there is a similar situation if one examines those discharged from all the regional prisons to the care of NADPAS. When the liaison scheme with the Ministry of Labour was introduced in 1950, the initial enthusiasm and interest enabled

30 per cent of those discharged from all regional prisons to be placed in work by the Ministry of Labour. Even when the figure seems to stabilize about six years later, over one-fifth of the men were still placed in work by the statutory body. Surprisingly, therefore, Wakefield Prison is if anything a little below the average for the proportion of discharges from the regional prisons who were placed in work by the Ministry of Labour.

In presenting these figures in the various NADPAS annual reports there is never a clear definition of what exactly is meant by 'placed in work by Ministry of Labour', but one assumes that these were men given a pre-release interview by a Ministry of Labour official and subsequently found work by the local employment exchange. It is unlikely to include men who attend employment exchanges on their own initiative after release, for the research undertaken by the Ministry for the Pakenham-Thompson Report to include this aspect proved to be a most difficult task and it was clearly not a routine procedure to collect these figures.

The discussion till now has largely been about the impact of the Ministry of Labour pre-release scheme on regional prisons and, in particular, Wakefield Prison. However, it is the local prisons which contain the bulk of the prison population and it is easy to argue that the inmates of regional prisons are rather an elite group, and one cannot generalize from the impact of the scheme on these men. However, in the NADPAS annual report for the year ended 31 March 1960 there is an opportunity to compare figures from three types of prison, namely, a local prison, an open prison and a regional training prison. This evidence suggests that in the large local prisons a smaller proportion of men are seen by the placing officer of the Ministry of Labour. Only 13 per cent of the men discharged in 1959 from Birmingham were interviewed by the Ministry of Labour placing officer before discharge compared with 18 per cent at Eastchurch Special Open Prison and 20 per cent at Maidstone Regional Training Prison. Assuming that there is a similar success rate in the proportions actually placed in work at all the prisons (and it would be easy to maintain that at a local prison it would be lower in view of the probably lower calibre of the men involved), it seems likely that only about 5 per cent of prisoners discharged from a local prison were placed in work by the Ministry of Labour directly as a result of the pre-release interview.

The Pakenham-Thompson Committee, which was formed in 1960, was particularly interested in 'the present methods of assisting discharged prisoners to find and keep employment'[31] and produced some interesting information on the existing situation by following up one week's discharges from Pentonville. Of the 58 men in this analysis, only 4 saw the Ministry of Labour officer in prison; 2 of these were placed in work, while the other 2 were still unplaced after two months. This tends to indicate that the pre-release procedure of the Ministry of Labour was beginning to fall into comparative disuse, although it is relevant to record that after release almost half of the sample (in fact, 27) 'were traced as having reported to an Employment Exchange: 7 of these reported only once; 10 of those who kept touch were placed in jobs; the remaining 10 were not placed within two months'.[32]

The importance of considering the total service of the statutory employment agency is indicated in Martin and Webster's detailed study entitled *The Social Consequences of Conviction*.[33] They demonstrate that 'though many prisoners profess to despise the services of the Ministry and maintain they will get their own jobs, in fact about three-quarters of our ex-prisoners needing jobs registered with the Ministry'. Twenty-five out of 47, or 53 per cent of the ex-prisoners who registered at least once with the ministry, were placed during the follow-up year. In fact, 5 of the ex-prisoners were placed four or more times by the Ministry of Labour during their first year after release. More pertinent to our own experience is the evidence in Martin and Webster's work that ex-prisoners were rather more difficult to place than those who had been convicted but had not had custodial sentences.

All this evidence, however, refers to the period prior to the reorganization of after-care as a result of the ACTO report which was briefly discussed in the previous chapter. While altering the role of the voluntary organizations (including the eventual disbandment of CACA and NADPAS, although the National Association for the Care and Resettlement of Offenders emerged as a phoenix from the ashes of NADPAS) and almost certainly realizing that the direct involvement of the probation service in finding employment for discharged prisoners was neither theoretically nor practically so widespread, there was no fundamental review of the working of the special arrangement with the Ministry of Labour. It was rather assumed that the system was working entirely satisfactorily and the examination of such a practical matter as finding employment was perhaps somewhat anathema to the general approach of the ACTO report, which wished to emphasize that 'after-care is essentially a form of social casework'.[34]

The present arrangements by which the Department of Employment interviews men before release comprise substantially the same procedure as when the scheme was introduced twenty years ago. These are as follows.

> Arrangements agreed with the Prison Department provide for all offenders who are serving sentences of more than three months to be interviewed if they wish and registered for employment by an officer of the Department of Employment, about two months before discharge. Details are sent to the Employment Exchange nearest to where the offender will live on discharge and efforts are immediately made by that office to find work for the man to go to on release – in collaboration with the particular after-care organization or the probation service, as may be appropriate to the particular area.

> Those offenders serving sentences of less than three months are seen by the Prison Welfare Officer before discharge and advised to register for employment at an Employment Exchange if they need help in finding work. Placing action on the lines described above is taken in respect of any of these short-term offenders who attend at Employment Exchanges.

> Our instructions provide for all discharged offenders who seek our help to be interviewed in privacy and generally dealt with tactfully; thus a letter of introduction to his home local office is given to the offender if he wishes. The fact that a man has served a prison sentence is not disclosed to an employer without his consent.[35]

There was no significant change in policy or procedure adopted by the Department for dealing with ex-offenders over the three years covered by the present project. At the time of writing, however, the Department of Employment was about to introduce an extension for the pre-release interviewing of male borstal inmates. When the arrangements outlined above were agreed with the Prison Department, borstal boys were excluded because at that time responsibility for them was vested in another department of the Home Office. There is the difference, however, that whereas arrangements for interviewing offenders in prison are on a voluntary basis the Home Office asked the D.E. to arrange for all borstal boys to be registered for employment before release. It is understood that for borstal boys the interview will be conducted either by an employment officer of the D.E. or by a careers officer of the Youth Employment Service. So an arrangement which really started as a result of the problems of borstal girls on release being recognized has now twenty-five years later been adapted to try to encompass the employment of borstal boys on release.

THE PRESENT SITUATION

Since the implementation of many of the recommendations of the ACTO Report (1963), interest in the employment problems of discharged prisoners has somewhat waned. This has been partly because this is an area about which the Probation and After-Care Service is not directly concerned in the same way as were many of the voluntary societies which had the responsibility for after-care before the ACTO report, and partly because the market situation has been such that unemployment has not been (at least certainly not till the late 1960s) a central issue and the belief was widespread that any man discharged from prison who wished to find work could do so. One suspects that there was some truth in the assertion that practically any man could find some sort of work after release, but it was always a matter of a different order whether discharged prisoners were able to find work commensurate with their ability or experience.

Since the ACTO Report (1963) there have been some changes in the market situation. The figure of 1·6 per cent registered unemployed in Great Britain in 1964 rose to an average of 2·4 per cent during the time of the Apex project. This figure has since risen still higher, and it is relevant to remember that when Martin and Webster conclude from their study that the possession of a criminal record was, for most of their men, an inconvenience rather than a major obstacle to finding a job, they do emphasize that their study was in a period of full employment.[36]

Although this is only a relatively small shift in the market compared with the problems of unemployment encountered before the Second World War, and the social security schemes are more satisfactorily organized, even a slight change of this kind inevitably affects to a greater degree the most vulnerable and those who are only marginally employable, and ex-prisoners certainly figure in this group. One would suspect that the category of ex-prisoners who would suffer most would be those who normally lean heavily on the support of after-care agencies to find them work. As one of the effects of the probation service taking on the responsibility of all after-care was the lessening of the number of agencies directly concerned with the finding of work for their clients, it is an interesting conjecture whether as a result a heavier burden would fall on to the Department of Employment.

To investigate this possibility, and also to examine whether the introduction of another employment-placing service by a voluntary agency working in the prison setting seemed to affect the numbers who were helped by the D.E., the Department's London and South-East Region agreed to co-operate in supplying an analysis of the number of men in two samples from two London prisons who were seen at a pre-discharge interview by their employment officer and the outcome in terms of whether the men interviewed did report to the appropriate D.E. office after release and of the total number of these men placed in work by the D.E. within three months after release. One must emphasize that all subsequent discussion concerns the pre-discharge interview and hence there is no allowance whatsoever made for the quite considerable numbers who may attend an employment exchange on their own initiative after release.* Indeed it is important to realize that many men seem to opt deliberately for this latter procedure as they maintain that they are less likely to be identified as an ex-prisoner – one of the embarrassments that the pre-discharge procedure was actually designed to avoid!

There are three reasons for concentrating on the pre-discharge interview rather than trying to examine the comprehensive placing service that the D.E. offers, of which the pre-discharge interview is an extremely small part. The first reason is that it is an enormously difficult task to trace the amount of contact that any individual has with the D.E. if he registers only for employment. He can register at any number of exchanges he wishes and the amount of information he needs to divulge does not always make identification an easy task. However, even if the D.E. had agreed and it had been possible to follow up a reasonable number of men (as we have mentioned, enormous difficulties were encountered in trying to follow up the very small sample for the Pakenham-Thompson Report), the information would not be directly relevant to a discussion of the special provisions for discharged prisoners, although it might provide evidence as to why special provision may be unnecessary. On the other hand, the pre-discharge interview was introduced as a special arrangement which it was felt might help to solve the particular problem of men discharged from prison finding suitable employment, so it seemed reasonable to examine this provision in isolation from other facilities offered by the Department of Employment. Finally, the figures relating to the outcome of the D.E.'s pre-discharge interview seemed to be fairly comparable with the Apex experiment which is fully discussed in the subsequent chapters of the present report.

* The Pakenham-Thompson Report showed that only 4 out of 58 men saw the Ministry of Labour officer before release, but 27 men were traced as having reported to an employment exchange after release (see page 69).

Without anticipating all the details of the project, one must appreciate that the primary purpose of the research was to examine the effectiveness of a service provided by the Apex Trust of finding suitable employment for prisoners immediately on their release and to discover whether the provision of this service lowered the reconviction rate of those helped in this way.

It is perhaps not surprising that there was some anxiety at the outset of the Apex project as to whether the Apex service would in some way deprive the prisoner of his statutory entitlement to see the D.E.'s placing officer before release. This belief was easily fostered by the realization that Apex would be interviewing men for the first time at approximately the same time in their sentence that men were often referred to the D.E. by the prison welfare officer. The Department of Employment and the welfare departments of the two prisons concerned were assured that the Apex service was *over and above* the influences ordinarily brought to bear upon discharged prisoners and certainly was not intended to replace any existing service. Hence the welfare department was encouraged to act as it normally would in referring men to the placing officer of the D.E. without reference to whether they had been seen by Apex. Similarly, men seen by Apex who mentioned that they had intended to see the D.E. placing officer were encouraged to continue with this course of action. This policy naturally laid one open to the other objection that this possible duplication was a waste of resources, but, as Apex was an experimental rather than a permanent feature of the particular prisons involved, it was felt in the final analysis that one must do nothing to endanger the rights of men to see the statutory agency.

The two prisons involved in the experiment were Wormwood Scrubs and Pentonville. Both these contained local prison populations, but whereas the sample from Wormwood Scrubs consisted almost entirely of those serving their first term of adult imprisonment, Pentonville contained men who had served at least one previous prison sentence and in many cases many more. (The sample populations are discussed more fully in Part II.) The two samples from each prison consisted of a control group selected at random and a treatment group also selected at random. The control group was not interviewed and hence should indicate what normally happens to a group of men passing through the prison. On the other hand, the treatment group was interviewed and their responses to the offer of the Apex service were recorded in terms of Full Acceptance, Partial Acceptance and Rejection of the Apex service. (These categories are also discussed fully in Part II.) For reasons

c*

of confidentiality, the Department felt able to supply information only on various groups of men rather than the outcome for particular individuals. In consequence, those in the full acceptance, partial acceptance, rejection and control groups for each prison were submitted to the Department of Employment for analysis. Only the names of those who were actually discharged from the particular prison were submitted, for even if a man was transferred just a few days before release it is possible that the records were no longer held by the employment exchange responsible for the pre-discharge interview at the prison.

TABLE 2 *Comparison of treatment and control groups in terms of the use of the pre-discharge employment service offered by the Department of Employment*

| | Wormwood Scrubs sample | | Pentonville sample | |
| --- | --- | --- | --- | --- |
| | *Total No. interviewed by Apex* | *Apex control group (not interviewed)* | *Total No. interviewed by Apex* | *Apex control group (not interviewed)* |
| Total No. in each group | 216* | 150* | 214* | 167* |
| (A) Total No. interviewed by D.E. official while in prison | 45 | 44 | 9 | 6 |
| % of total group interviewed by D.E. official while in prison | 20·8 | 29·3 | 4·2 | 3·6 |
| (B) Total No. of (A) who reported to appropriate exchange after release | 21 | 28 | 4 | 2 |
| % of total group who reported to appropriate exchange after release | 9·7 | 18·7 | 1·9 | 1·2 |
| (C) Total No. of (B) who were placed in work by D.E. within 3 months after release | 4 | 9 | 1 | 0 |
| % of total group who were placed in work by D.E. within 3 months after release† | 1·9 | 6·0 | 0·5 | — |

* The names of men not actually discharged from either Wormwood Scrubs or Pentonville were not submitted to the D.E.

† No allowance made for the numbers found work by D.E. after reporting to an employment exchange on their own initiative after release.

The first question is whether the attempt to encourage the welfare officers and prisoners to act as normally as possible in their use of the D.E. actually worked out in practice. Table 2 compares the total of men interviewed by Apex, which is referred to as the treatment group (i.e. full acceptance, partial acceptance and rejection groups), with the men in the control groups who were not interviewed and can be said to indicate 'normal use'.

Comparing the two groups of the Wormwood Scrubs sample, it appears that the introduction of the Apex scheme did have some effect on the numbers interviewed and subsequently helped by the Department of Employment, for although the difference is not statistically significant, 29·3 per cent of the control group had a pre-discharge interview whereas only 20·8 per cent of the men interviewed by Apex were also seen by the Department of Employment. This difference between the two groups is similarly reflected in the proportion who were placed in work by the statutory body within three months after release. On the other hand, at Pentonville, where the numbers seen by Apex as a proportion of the prison turnover for the year were considerably smaller, the introduction of Apex appears to have made no noticeable difference to the numbers seen by the placing officer of the Department of Employment.

Table 2 demonstrates that the special arrangement of the pre-discharge interview has a fairly minimal impact on men serving sentences at Wormwood Scrubs and Pentonville. Using the control group as the measure, 6 per cent of the Wormwood Scrubs population serving sentences of between six months and three years were placed in work by the Department of Employment within three months after release as a direct outcome of the pre-discharge interview, while none of the Pentonville control group were similarly placed. Furthermore, one should recognize that the Department of Employment concept of 'placed in work' indicates that the employer has accepted the man in question rather than indicating that he has in fact started the job. Our experience at Apex in placing men suggests that probably about 10 per cent of men fail to start work although they have been accepted by the employer.

Although it would be possible to suggest that the effectiveness of the Department's service has deteriorated since the early 1950s when this special arrangement was first introduced, this may well be a too facile explanation. One must emphasize that the present figures are from local prisons and much of the early enthusiasm about the arrangement was the result of examining the effect in regional training prisons and other establishments which are not typical of local prisons. It is fair to say that the Department of Employment was surprised at the numbers seen and assisted from Pentonville, but this is not much of an indication as to whether the situation has deteriorated or has never been fully investigated. One suspects that always a much lower proportion of men in local prisons benefited from the special arrangement with the Department, but it further suggests that men with more than one sentence are less likely to avail themselves of the service offered. This is an interesting corollary to Martin and Webster's observation that:

> after a prison sentence men were more likely to seek the assistance of the Ministry of Labour. Such assistance was, on the whole, rather more effective with men registering for the first time than with those who had sought it before imprisonment. Help given to previous customers was marginally less effective than that which they had received on previous occasions.[37]

While we do not know how many of our Pentonville men registered with the Department after release, there is still some evidence that there is a certain career pattern in seeking the assistance of the Department of Employment; when a man comes into prison for the first time, the likelihood of his seeking help from the Department is at its highest together with the likelihood of the Department placing the candidate in work, but after the first sentence the likelihood of men approaching the Department and success with those that do diminishes quite dramatically.

There is one further point in interpreting the figures relating to the work of the Department of Employment in prisons, for they should be considered within the context of the resources made available to this aspect of their work. Within this context condemnation would be unreasonable and inappropriate, for one suspects that the resources available are nowadays spent with a slightly different emphasis. In the prisons of the present study one employment officer from the local exchange spends half a day a week at the prison to deal with all matters regarding employment. This is probably the same arrangement as was worked out about twenty years ago, but there have been certain changes in the prison system which increase the burden of these employment officers. In both prisons there were some men who were anxious for the employment officer to find work for them quickly so that they could take their place on a hostel scheme or out-workers' scheme attached to the prison. Inevitably these men (and possibly men who are being considered for parole) will take priority, for failure on these cases will be quickly open to examination whereas men who will soon be released are unlikely to upset the equilibrium. The Department of Employment officer quickly becomes identified as being particularly helpful only in these special cases, and the remainder of the prisoners soon do not bother to ask to see him, or the welfare officers perhaps do not bother to refer the general run of men who are to be discharged. There is only a limited amount that one man can do in one afternoon session every week and it is difficult to believe that such an arrangement could ever make much impact on a prison which has such a high turnover. One must remember that one interview per prisoner is sometimes as much as the staff of the welfare department can hope to achieve and there are perhaps half a dozen full-time welfare officers in each of the prisons concerned.

In contrast to the one employment officer from the local exchange who spends half a day a week at the prisons and, in theory at least, has a caseload of every inmate in the prison, Apex Trust employed one person full-time to try and find work for about a hundred or so men a year who had been selected at random from the discharge diary. One must bear in mind when comparing the two services the considerable disparity in cost, and that the purpose of the D.E. operation is to liaise between the prison and the D.E. office in the area where the man will be living on his release. In fact, much of the point of this project is to examine whether the extra effort which Apex took to place men in suitable employment is worthwhile on a cost basis. While the cost of placing an ex-prisoner in work is likely to be more expensive for the D.E. than the average cost per placement for the average client of the Department, it is unlikely to be as expensive as pursuing a policy of attempting to find a suitable interview for every man. The average cost per man will obviously increase as the placing effort required for each man increases.

Whereas Apex carried out a series of interviews before release, it is probably true to say that the D.E. had to rely on the fact that, as a result of one perhaps fairly brief prison interview, the prisoner would attend the appropriate employment exchange, and that the employment officers of the various exchanges would be able to find suitable work. The latter procedure appears to have many links that could break down and, within this context, a Placing Index computed for the work of the D.E. for the Wormwood Scrubs control group (which could be regarded as a measure of normal usage) comes out quite favourably. Of the 44 men in this group interviewed by the placing officer while in prison, 9 men (or 20·5 per cent) were placed in work by the D.E. within three months after release. A comparison can be made with those men in the Wormwood Scrubs sample who made a full acceptance of the Apex service (which theoretically would seem a more positive acceptance than what is often simply seeing the Department of Employment at the suggestion of a welfare officer). In this case, the placing index is 42·7 per cent – that is, the percentage in this group who were placed in work by Apex within three months after release.

The higher placing index of Apex expressed as a crude comparison with that of the Department of Employment may be a function of a different procedure rather than simply the result of a larger amount of resources invested per man in trying to find work. The men dealt with by Apex were placed within the first couple of weeks after their release, and practically all were notified of the interview arranged *before* their release, whereas with the D.E. procedure there is at best a suitable job awaiting the man when he reports to the appropriate employment exchange. However, the questions of resources and procedure outlined above are not distinct, for it is to a large extent the policy of finding a suitable interview *before* release that makes the Apex service a more expensive outlay. The ultimate value and effectiveness of this Apex procedure is a question to which we must return subsequently.

CONCLUSION

Whatever interpretation is placed on the figures, it is indisputable that the special arrangement with the D.E. has some sort of impact on only a minority of prisoners in the two prisons used in the present study. At Wormwood Scrubs with a sample of 'star' prisoners serving sentences which ranged from six months to three years, less than a third (29·3 per cent) were interviewed by the employment officer from the Department of Employment. Nine men (or 6 per cent) out of the total group of 150 were placed within three months by the D.E. as a direct result of the pre-discharge interview. At Pentonville with a sample of recidivists serving sentences of six to twelve months, only 3·6 per cent of the men were interviewed by the employment officer of the D.E. before release and none of these six men were placed in employment within three months after release by the D.E.

If one wishes to test rigorously the hypothesis that if a prisoner could be found suitable employment within but also up to his capabilities immediately on release there would be a reduction in his temptation to resort to crime, it is clearly necessary to set up a project which goes some way beyond what is at present being offered by the statutory service. It is for this reason that the Apex project described in Part II was set up.

## REFERENCES

1 Kahn, H. R., *Repercussions of Redundancy*, London, Allen and Unwin (1964).
2 Reid, G. L., 'The Role of the Employment Service in Redeployment', *British Journal of Industrial Relations*, Vol. 9, No. 2 (July 1971).
3 'Fifty Years of the Employment Exchanges (1910–1960)', *Ministry of Labour Gazette*, Vol. 68 (January 1960), p. 1. For this and other information on developments prior to the 1909 Act.
4 Loc. cit.
5 Loc. cit.
6 *Report of the Ministry of Labour*, London, HMSO, Cmd. 2481 (1923 and 1924), p. 14.
7 Martin, J. P., *Offenders as Employees*, London, Macmillan (1962), p. 27.
8 'Changing Role for the Employment Service', *Ministry of Labour Gazette*, Vol. 74 (II) (June 1966), p. 285.
9 *Report of the Commissioners of Prisons*, London, HMSO, Cmd. 7010 (1942–4), p. 8.
10 *Report of the Commissioners of Prisons*, London, HMSO, Cmd. 6820 (1939–41), p. 59.
11 *Report of the Ministry of Labour and National Service*, London, HMSO, Cmd. 7225 (1939–46), p. 234.
12 *Annual Report of the National Association of Discharged Prisoners' Aid Societies* (1949), pp. 16–17.
13 *Report of the Commissioners of Prisons*, London, HMSO, Cmd. 8088 (1949), p. 49.
14 *Annual Report of the National Association of Discharged Prisoners' Aid Societies* (1950), p. 16.
15 *Report of the Commissioners of Prisons*, London, HMSO, Cmd. 8356 (1950), p. 56.
16 *Report of the Ministry of Labour and National Service*, London, HMSO, Cmd. 8640 (1951), p. 51.
17 *Report of the Commissioners of Prisons*, London, HMSO, Cmd. 8356 (1950), p. 56.
18 *Annual Report of the National Association of Discharged Prisoners' Aid Societies* (1952), p. 16.
19 *Annual Report of the National Association of Discharged Prisoners' Aid Societies* (1953), p. 19.
20 *Report of the Committee on Discharged Prisoners' Aid Societies*, London, HMSO, Cmd. 8879 (1953), p. 18.
21 Ibid., p. 12.
22 Ibid., p. 13.
23 Loc. cit.
24 *Annual Report of the National Association of Discharged Prisoners' Aid Societies* (1961), p. 20.
25 *Report of the Committee on Discharged Prisoners' Aid Societies*, London, HMSO, Cmd. 8879 (1953), p. 13.

26 Loc. cit.
27 *Report of the Commissioners of Prisons*, London, HMSO, Cmd. 8948 (1952), p. 66.
28 *Report of the Advisory Council on the Treatment of Offenders. The After-Care and Supervision of Discharged Prisoners*, London, HMSO (1958), p. 31.
29 Ibid., p. 32.
30 *Report of the Ministry of Labour and National Service*, London, HMSO, Cmd. 9791 (1955), p. 52.
31 Pakenham-Thompson Committee, p. 9.
32 Ibid., p. 72.
33 Martin, J. P., and Webster, D., *The Social Consequences of Conviction*, London, Heinemann (1971), p. 142.
34 *Report of the Advisory Council on the Treatment of Offenders. The Organization of After-Care*, London, HMSO (1963), p. ii.
35 Personal communication from the Department of Employment.
36 Martin and Webster, op. cit., p. 147.
37 Martin and Webster, op. cit., p. 145.

# PART II

# The Apex Project

## Introduction

It is fairly evident from the discussion in Part I that attempts to place prisoners in suitable employment immediately on their release from prison have been numerous enough to give birth to a whole range of speculations regarding the importance of this sort of enterprise. Some attempts have been carried out with such vigour and enthusiasm that it would appear almost sacrilege to question the efficiency of such a policy. Other attempts, not necessarily carried out with less vigour and enthusiasm, have appeared less successful and certainly since the war there has been a tendency to relegate the job-finding agency from a primary to a subsidiary role in the concept of prison after-care. While there has been no dearth of speculation on the basis of scattered and often highly selective evidence, there has clearly been a lack of scientific examination to investigate the effectiveness of a policy of finding employment for prisoners immediately on their release.

Chapter 3 outlines the research design to test the hypothesis that finding employment for prisoners immediately on their release lowers the subsequent reconviction rate of these men compared with a group who are not helped in this way.

Chapter 4 indicates the response of men to the offer of an employment-placing service, and then describes the pre-release procedure of the Apex project.

Chapter 5 examines the reconviction rates of the two prison samples, comparing the treatment and control groups and the differences in terms of reconviction between the various Apex groups.

Chapter 6 begins to indicate that one has to go beyond a fairly superficial analysis, for it would be very misleading to believe that each group is comparable in terms of potential risk of reconviction. In an attempt to extend the analysis, the two prison samples are compared and further consideration is given to comparing on various dimensions those who accept and those who reject the offer of the Apex service.

Chapter 7 considers the employment plans of those who rejected the offer of the Apex service. This begins to indicate that men reject the Apex service for a variety of reasons and also that the variety of employment plans have a variety of outcomes.

## CHAPTER 3

# Research Design of the Project

'Tis well averred,
A scientific faith's absurd.
*Browning*

Although there has been some emphasis on the fact that the aim of the Apex propect was to test a hypothesis in a scientific manner, it is probably not appropriate at this juncture to consider all the attributes necessary for a piece of work to qualify as scientific. However, one can mention two interlinked aspects which seem particularly vital in this field. In summary these are a control group and a statement of criteria for judging effectiveness. A control group is necessary where there is no known base of expected behaviour. For example, if one in fact knew that everyone who had served a prison sentence returned to prison again within a stated period, then it would be reasonable to argue that this type of situation did not require a special control group designed for the occasion. However, this is far from the case in reality and a suitable control group with which one can compare the group one is trying to assist must be made an integral part of the research design. The use of a control group is the only way to avoid the valid criticism that the men one has apparently helped may well have made some sort of 'spontaneous recovery' of their own accord. This type of criticism could be levelled at all the proponents of the 'finding work for ex-prisoners is the vital factor' school, for one must recognize that they have up to now failed to substantiate the necessary link in their argument between an agency finding work for ex-prisoners and the subsequent rehabilitation of these men. This leads directly on to the question of the 'effectiveness' or 'success' of a rehabilitation policy. In a scientific study, it is important to state from the outset the particular criteria or measure of 'success' which one is using. Naturally several measures can be examined within the same research design but inevitably they will almost always be only a small proportion of possible measures. In the Apex project it was decided that the basic measure would be whether the employment service offered to prisoners managed to reduce the subsequent reconviction figure of these men compared with a group who were not helped in this way. It must be admitted that one of the reasons for choosing this measure was its possible availability, and this criterion of success is also an objective measure which is generally acceptable. However, the most attractive feature was that, if it were possible to demonstrate a significantly lower reconviction figure for the 'treatment group', then it could be fairly readily converted into a cost-benefit analysis, as the cost of further incarceration or some form of penal activity is possible to calculate. The possibility that the agency could put forward a case for expansion on the basis of scientific evidence that it is an economically viable concern in the national interest was perhaps the key reason for settling finally for the reconviction figure as the basic measure.

## THE RESEARCH DESIGN

The primary purpose of the research was to examine the effectiveness of the Apex service in finding suitable employment for prisoners immediately on their release. The basic measure is the reconviction rate of a 'treatment group' whom Apex has tried to assist and a 'control group' who have just experienced the influences ordinarily brought to bear upon a discharged prisoner.

As the research was to be designed to test an employment-placing service, the size of the sample was largely determined by the numbers it was estimated that the director of Apex* could handle in a year. It was decided that the director could deal with approximately 100 men in a year and that these men should be selected at random by the research officer. Any additional time available over and above that needed to place the men in the research programme was to be used to place men who were referred to Apex from other sources, such as probation officers and prison welfare officers. (There is no mention in the report of the effectiveness of any of this additional placing activity at Apex.)

It was further thought that the effect of a placing service might be considerably different for men serving their first term of imprisonment than for men serving at least their second prison sentence. This possible distinction seemed to link well with the way

---

* Throughout this report, 'the director of Apex' refers to the person who did all the employment-placing work of the men in the project. He could perhaps more appropriately be called 'placement officer' or 'placing officer' although he was always referred to as the director of Apex by prisoners, prison staff, personnel officers and other members of the Apex Trust, so this designation has been retained.

the penal system classified men into two basic classes† – 'stars' (who are normally serving their first term of adult imprisonment) and 'ordinaries' (who have been to prison at least once). One should perhaps emphasize from the outset that it is only the minority of 'stars' who are genuinely first offenders in the present sample (in fact, only about one in four 'stars' can be so regarded). In other words, most have committed previous offences and many have had previous institutional experience, such as approved school, borstal or detention centre. In addition, prison governors are in some circumstances empowered to regrade suitable 'ordinaries' who then become known as 'governor's stars' (or 'second stars'). In fact there is only a small proportion of men who are reclassified as stars and many of these have simply served their previous imprisonment as 'young prisoners', so they are actually serving their first term of adult imprisonment. However, the distinction between 'stars' and 'ordinaries' appears, in general terms, to correspond to what are loosely called 'first offenders' and 'recidivists'. It was therefore decided to spend one year examining the effect of the service on 100 'star' prisoners and a further period on a recidivist study.

## SELECTION OF THE PRISONS

While it would have entailed a fairly elaborate sampling procedure to obtain a random sample of all 'star' prisoners in England and Wales and then to repeat the operation for all the recidivists, the main objection was that it would be impossible within the resources available to set up the employment agency to cover the area involved, particularly in terms of finding suitable employment for the men on release. It was for this and other such administrative reasons that it was not considered possible to move the project away from the London area.

It was eventually decided to accept the compromise solution of selecting a prison which *a priori* seemed to contain a reasonably representative population of 'stars' and another prison for 'ordinaries'. In the circumstances, Wormwood Scrubs and Pentonville prisons respectively seemed the most suitable prisons located in or near the London area, although, as I shall mention, both have some shortcomings as useful sample populations.

† There is a further class of prisoner, namely civil prisoners, but these were disregarded in planning this research. In actual fact, a recidivist civil prisoner was included in the Pentonville sample by virtue of the fact that he was serving a sentence of between six and twelve months.

One problem was that Wormwood Scrubs accepted no prisoner serving a sentence of less than six months. In one way this could be regarded as an advantage in so far as it gave a good opportunity for contact to be established with the man well before release, but it should immediately be emphasized that one is excluding an important group, namely those in prison for the first time but serving a sentence of less than six months. An upper limit of sentence range of three years was also fixed because men serving sentences of over three years were likely to be considered for the hostel and 'working-out' scheme and, what was then on the horizon, the possibility of being considered for parole. Hence, it soon became a rationale at the time of planning the project that offenders serving sentences of between six months and three years were less likely to be affected by some of the provisions of the Criminal Justice Act 1967 that was then being discussed, and so it was hoped that any conclusions on an employment agency placing service based on this sample were more likely to be valid for some years to come.

The short- and medium-term offenders who spend the last three months of their sentence in Wormwood Scrubs are not (unfortunately for this study) a completely random sample of men serving their first adult prison sentence from the catchment area of South-East England. For adult prisoners serving short- and medium-term sentences, Wormwood Scrubs is essentially an allocation prison and perhaps ideally no man with this length of sentence would be discharged from the Scrubs unless he were receiving medical treatment at the prison hospital. However, we estimated that approximately 450 men a year are in fact discharged from the Scrubs after serving the last three months of their sentence there and it is from this population that the samples were selected at random.

Eighty-six per cent of these men had been allocated to closed prisons, either Stafford or Camp Hill, but it had not been possible to send them there. The remaining 14 per cent had been allocated to an open prison, usually Ford, Eastchurch or Springhill, and most of them had had the experience of an open prison regime at least for a while. However, the latter group could in practically every case be regarded as 'open prison' failures, for most of them had been returned to Wormwood Scrubs either as a result of attempting to escape or on account of a breach of discipline. In summary, the Wormwood Scrubs population from which the sample was taken contains a wide range of men (most of whom have been imprisoned for the first time), but does not contain men who have been allocated and have succeeded in 'open conditions'. In Mountbatten classification terms, therefore, they are men who would have been classified as security category 'C' and men who should have been classified as 'C' rather than 'D' category (i.e. the 'open prison' failures). Security category 'C' are those prisoners 'who cannot be trusted in open conditions, but who do not have the ability or resources to make a determined escape attempt'.[1]

The selection of Pentonville as a suitable prison for the recidivist study provided very similar problems regarding the bias of the sample population. Pentonville contains men who have served at least one previous prison sentence and have been committed to prison for a sentence of twelve months or less* by a court in the Home Counties area.[2] Many are transferred to other prisons, but there is a large number who serve their sentence at Pentonville and it is this latter group in whom we are interested. Again we decided to restrict the sample population to men serving sentences of at least six months but made an upper limit of sentence range of twelve months. Men serving sentences of less than six months are a major problem to the prison system and are the men who outside prison tend to be a nuisance to society, but they are perhaps not a category that one would readily expect to be helped by the simple provision of employment on release, so once again this 'stage army' is overlooked in an after-care experiment.

When we were working in Pentonville, the Mountbatten classification into security categories was already in operation. Of the men in our sample population, 68·3 per cent were classified at the reception interview as 'C' category and a further 31·4 per cent as 'D' category (the remaining 0·3 per cent is accounted for by one man originally given a 'B' category who came to Pentonville at a later stage of his sentence). In this case, the 'D' category men were not usually 'open prison' failures but rather men who remained at Pentonville because there were no suitable vacancies in an open prison or because the subsequent arrival of the record of their previous convictions revealed a reason for debarring them from open conditions. Therefore, in a similar way to the Wormwood Scrubs sample, this is largely a sample population of men who were or should have been classified as 'C' category. We estimated that approximately 1,450 men a year are in fact discharged from Pentonville after serving the last three months there of a sentence ranging from six to twelve months.

---

* Pentonville also operates an 'out-workers' scheme for men serving longer prison sentences, but these men were disregarded and, anyway, they are physically separate from the rest of the prison.

SELECTION OF PRISONERS

The procedure for obtaining a random sample of prisoners was virtually identical for each prison, and while the following description relates to the Wormwood Scrubs study the alternatives cited in brackets refer to the modifications necessary for the Pentonville study.

For the year from 6 January 1967 to 4 January 1968 (from 8 March 1968 to 6 March 1969), all the names of men who were both 'star' category prisoners and serving a sentence of six months to three years (both 'ordinaries' and serving a sentence of six to twelve months) were taken from the discharge diary at Wormwood Scrubs (Pentonville) prison. The discharge diary was inspected each Wednesday or Thursday and the names of those to be discharged in eleven weeks' (eight weeks') time were abstracted – for example, on 6 April 1967 a list was taken of the appropriate men to be discharged in the week 16–22 June 1967.

This procedure gave a total list of 590 (1,473) names, but 190 (219) men were eliminated *before* the sample was taken for the reasons shown in Table 3.

The remaining 400 (1,254) men constituted the sample for the study. A random sample of 1 in 3 (1 in 12 – but after week 30 the sampling fraction was changed to 1 in 10 to ensure that we interviewed the required number of men in the time available), was taken for the 'Apex treatment group'. If a man rejected the offer of the employment service, the man immediately above (below) him on the list was used as a substitute. (For the Pentonville study, if each man continued to reject the service or only partially accepted, a maximum of four substitutes could be used.) After week 30 for the Wormwood Scrubs sample, a sample of 2 in 3 was taken – that is, the first man selected for the 'Apex treatment group' *and* all the potential substitutes were interviewed and offered the service. The reason for this change was the delay in interviewing the substitutes and hence a potentially short time before their release in which to take the appropriate placing action. However, as there was an approximately 50 per cent rejection rate, this seemed a particularly suitable solution.

A further random sample of 1 in 3 (1 in 12 and then, after week 30, 1 in 10) was taken for the control group. The men in the control group were not interviewed, but their prison records were examined for comparison purposes. In the analysis, the 29 potential substitutes who were not used, i.e. before the change in procedure

TABLE 3 *Reasons for eliminating men before taking random samples for the control and treatment groups*

| | Wormwood Scrubs No. of men | Pentonville No. of men |
|---|---|---|
| The hall principal officer indicated to the research officer that these men will not be staying at Wormwood Scrubs for the rest of their sentence | 46 | — |
| Men who were in hospital or who had been specifically returned to or retained by the prison for medical treatment | 34 | — |
| Men transferred to Wormwood Scrubs from a prison outside the London area (excluded – except where they had been committed to Wormwood Scrubs in the first instance, as this usually indicated they were being referred for hospital treatment) | 29 | — |
| Men whose home address as shown in the discipline office was outside the London area (excluded from Wormwood Scrubs sample after week 36) | 34 | 172 |
| Men who were resident abroad or who were given a deportation order when sentenced | 15 | 27 |
| Men who were either serving soldiers or who had received a court martial (excluded from Wormwood Scrubs sample after week 12) | 14 | — |
| Men who were given an additional sentence beyond the end of prison interview period or who were awaiting further charges at CCC | 8 | — |
| Men who gave their occupation as 'retired' or as 'student' (excluded from Wormwood Scrubs sample after week 44) | 4 | — |
| Excluded on request of Principal Officer as the men were either on 'special watch' or on a particular outside working party | 6 | — |
| Men aged 60 and over at time of sentence | — | 20 |
| TOTAL | 190 | 219 |

at week 30, have been included in the control group. (Similarly, in the Pentonville study, there were 58 potential substitutes – who were not needed for interviewing purposes – who were included in the control group.)

This procedure gave a total of 162 men in the control group of the Wormwood Scrubs sample (a total of 173 men in the control group of the Pentonville sample). Of this total, seven men had to be disregarded as their prison records were not obtained – five men were transferred to another prison, another spent the relevant period in an outside hospital, and the remaining one was given a further sentence while in custody which put him outside the scope of this project. (Of the total of 173 men in the Pentonville control group, four men had to be disregarded – two were transferred to another prison before the prison record was obtained, one was discharged after his appeal was upheld and the remaining man was given a further sentence of eight years while in custody so putting him outside the scope of the project.)

A total of 238 men in Wormwood Scrubs were selected for interview to be offered the opportunity of the Apex service, but eleven of these men were subsequently excluded from the project. Three of the eleven spent the relevant period in hospital, a further six were transferred to other prisons before the first interview was arranged, and the remaining two were given further sentences which excluded them from the project. (Similarly, a total of 239 men in Pentonville were selected for interview, but sixteen of these men were subsequently excluded from the project. Eight were transferred to another prison before being interviewed, three were retained in the hospital wing throughout their sentence, and five were released from prison earlier than expected – either because of a successful appeal or because of a paid fine.)

COMPARISON OF THE TREATMENT AND CONTROL GROUPS

In the way described above, four basic groups were obtained, namely Wormwood Scrubs control group, Wormwood Scrubs treatment* group, Pentonville control group and Pentonville treatment* group. As the comparison of the control group and treatment group from each prison will be the basic measure when reconviction rates are examined, it is vital that these groups should be reasonably comparable. This can be done by analyzing the over-all distributions on some important variables to discover whether there are any significant differences between the control and treatment groups from each prison.

The groups have been compared on the following ten dimensions.

* 'Treatment group' is used here in a statistical sense to mean the group to be compared with the control group. In this case, as we shall see, the treatment group was offered the opportunity of being found employment on release, but the term does not imply that they all accepted the offer.

1. Age at time of sentence
2. Place of birth
3. Ethnic origin
4. Marital status as stated on prison record
5. Present offence – type of offence
6. Present sentence
7. Age at first conviction or finding of guilt
8. Previous convictions as an adult
9. Period from last release from custody to date of present sentence
10. Proportion of time from leaving school spent in custody.

It is reassuring that on these dimensions there are no statistically significant differences between the treatment and control groups at a higher level than 5 per cent and one can quite confidently assert that the treatment and control groups are perfectly acceptable as a basis for comparison. The fact that there are a few differences at the 5 per cent level should not be regarded as surprising, for the two groups have been compared on a large number of items within each dimension and one would naturally expect that at least one significant difference in twenty would occur by chance. The only difference worthy of note is that the Pentonville treatment group had 31 per cent who were recorded as married on the prison record compared with 22 per cent in the Pentonville control group. In contrast, the Wormwood Scrubs groups are in the reverse direction with 36 per cent of the treatment group recorded as married compared with 38 per cent of the control group.

## THE OFFER OF THE APEX SERVICE

Before discussing the actual procedure of offering the service to men selected at random from the two prisons, it is worthwhile to mention the sort of provision the Trustees of Apex had felt would significantly help the prisoner in settling down after release. This is summarized in a Foreword to the first Annual Report (1966–7) of the Apex Trust written by the Chairman of the Trustees:

The philosophy of the Apex Trust was conceived in 1965; it is based on the principle that the State accepts that it has an obligation to rehabilitate and train the handicapped – those who are physically and mentally sick. Legislation by means of the Disabled Persons (Employment) Act 1944 implemented the idea that it was in the interests of society and the disabled that they could and should work. As a result a number of training establishments have been set up and are working successfully. The concept behind Apex is that this principle should be extended to the socially sick: men and women who are socially and emotionally handicapped as a result of having served prison sentences.

There is a strong case on both humanitarian and economic grounds for the establishment of a central agency designed solely to assist ex-prisoners to find employment. Apex (X-Prisoners' Employment Agency) sets out to do exactly that, and in implementing this principle it is, perhaps, unique in that it attempts to find work for prisoners whilst they are still in gaol, so that jobs will be awaiting them as soon as they are released. To avoid continual change, we attempt to match the skills of the man with the jobs available. Thus one crisis period in an ex-prisoner's life is lessened – that is when he leaves the prison gates – often friendless, frequently separated from his family and almost certainly without belongings, accommodation, or a job. The difficulties at this critical moment in his life may well be insurmountable without help and may easily cause him to commit further offences. . . .

If the ex-prisoner can be helped at this vital juncture he may actually benefit the community, keep his family together and be able to maintain himself and his dependents. If on the other hand assistance is withheld, he is likely to find himself back in prison or at least living on Social Security Benefits.

This extract clearly indicates the context within which the agency was set up originally, for although the Trustees were keenly aware of all the other problems often confronting the prisoner on discharge it was hoped that the provision of a suitable job would somehow act as a panacea for all other ills. It must be emphasized, though, that the Apex service was not intended to replace any help already offered to prisoners, and so what amounted to the 'treatment' of Apex was something *over and above* the influences ordinarily brought to bear upon a discharged prisoner. In this way it could be argued alternatively that a job on release may perhaps be regarded as a catalyst to enable any other support available to have a more beneficial effect rather than that the job should have the effect *per se*.

The above extract from the Foreword of the 1966–7 Annual Report fails to acknowledge that the Trustees were anxious that the attempt of Apex to act as a job-finding agency should not be restricted to the first job after release, for their own previous experience in this field indicated that this first job often seemed to end quickly and disastrously. The Trustees felt that, if a series of job placements could be secured, if necessary, for a man, then eventually he might well find a niche in which he could settle down. There is no doubt that the Trustees hoped that complete concentration on this one aspect of after-care would result in a high proportion of men dealt with by Apex settling into jobs arranged by Apex. In fact during the preliminary discussions before the project was actually launched, it is fascinating to record that much thought was given to the possibility of charging fees either to the employer or to the client when Apex secured a suitable job. This particular topic was adjourned until more had been learnt about the outcome of placing work in practice and in the event has never been put into operation. As we shall see, the possibility of operating a fee-charging system was largely lost when the decision was made to offer the service to a random selection of prisoners for experimental purposes rather than allowing prisoners to select themselves with the knowledge that they were approaching a fee-charging agency. There is no logical reason why a fee-charging system could not be introduced, but the importance of indicating this particular aspect of the early discussions was to emphasize how enthusiastic the Trustees were to consider ways of getting the agency on a sound commercial basis.

APEX AS AN AFTER-CARE ORGANIZATION

While the philosophy of the Apex Trust was conceived in 1965, the agency was not fully operational until September 1966 when the director of the Trust, who also acted as the sole placing officer, was appointed. As we have hinted in Part I, the period from the publication of the ACTO Report (1963) was one of tremendous administrative upheaval and the responsibility of providing and organizing statutory after-care facilities both within and without the prison was entrusted to the probation service. For many voluntary organizations this was clearly the end of an era and, although they were encouraged with varying degrees of enthusiasm to direct their resources and goodwill into other spheres of activity such as the provision of hostel accommodation, there is no doubt that the reorganization shifted not only the responsibility but also the mainstream of the after-care problem on to the shoulders of the Probation and After-Care Service. Hence this may have seemed a strange time to set up a new voluntary organization when the existing voluntary organizations were desperately seeking new roles. Apex, however, was probably exactly the type of organization which the ACTO members hoped would emerge as a result of their recommendations, for Apex was not only anxious to concentrate on a specific activity but also keen to include a research design to measure the effectiveness of its work. One suspects that it was largely for these reasons that the Home Office felt able to give every encouragement in the form of facilities to carry out this project.

## REFERENCES

1 *Report on the Work of the Prison Department*, London, HMSO, Cmd. 3774 (1967), p. 4.
2 Ibid., p. 6.

## CHAPTER 4

# The Offer of the Apex Service

Every organization develops a procedure which will change deliberately or perhaps imperceptibly over time. Unless the process is observed closely, there is the possibility that one falsely believes one is still continuing the procedure as originally conceived. In a scientific experiment it is important to try to indicate as accurately as possible what one is doing throughout so that anyone else, if they wish, can replicate the experiment. With the Apex project we conscientiously tried to follow a set procedure for each man and, although there were slight modifications which we will indicate, the general procedure remained the same throughout. It is worthwhile to outline in detail how we offered the Apex service, for as well as the question of replication, this may be a fruitful source of developing a different approach. In other words, some may consider that the particular time at which we first interviewed the men was too late and that one should be planning a man's employment on release from the first day of his sentence; others may consider that we discussed employment plans too early and that a more profitable time would be when men were in the throes of 'gate fever' immediately prior to release. We do not know the extent to which a different procedure to ours would have produced different results, but we will now describe the context within which we made the offer of this employment-placing service.

The men selected for interview were called up by the research officer for an interview almost invariably five to eight weeks before their release. The research officer had a number of interviewing sessions arranged in the prison for each week and two or three men were usually seen at each session, which lasted a total time of just under two hours. The number of men seen depended quite obviously on the appearance of the men scheduled to be interviewed in a particular session. As an overall average, just over 10 per cent of the men failed to attend the initial interview with the research officer as arranged, but as this was a problem restricted almost entirely to the first interview this probably indicates a reluctance of the men to participate rather than any shortcoming in the organization of the prison. In fact, the prison staff co-operated even to the extent of trying on occasions to explain to men who had failed to appear what Apex was trying to do. In the end there were only four men in the Wormwood Scrubs sample and seven men in the Pentonville sample who refused several times to come to see the research officer at an interviewing session. However, it was established quite conclusively that they were all able to attend if they had wished to do so. As they had conveyed either to the welfare department or to a prison officer that they wished to have nothing whatsoever to do with the Apex project, it seemed quite appropriate to include these men among the group who rejected the Apex service. The prison staff at Pentonville felt that one particular man was so disturbed that even the discussion of the Apex project was probably quite sufficient provocation for the man to erupt into extremely violent behaviour. The research officer accepted their recommendation that this was an unnecessary risk and so this one man was the only person of those selected and available for interview who did not have the opportunity to attend.

The purpose of the initial interview was to explain what Apex was trying to do in the prison and the sort of help that we were offering. In Wormwood Scrubs the concept was always explained individually to each man, but in Pentonville the general outline was often discussed with the men in a group. Assuming that one insists that the men avoid, for reasons of confidentiality, discussing their own individual cases in a group setting, this latter procedure is particularly appropriate for a project of this kind, for it enables men to relax more easily and to hear the answers to questions put by other members of the group which may in turn help to resolve some of their own anxieties. In actual fact, the procedure did not save time for there was a more lively response from the group and it often developed into quite a reasonable discussion, whereas the usual response when the outline was given individually was silence!

The research officer always explained how the men had been selected for the project and emphasized that the purpose of the sampling procedure was to get 'a typical bunch of men' who were in prison. He went on to suggest that if the results proved successful then it might well be possible in a few years' time to offer this facility to all men serving a prison sentence, but at this stage the work was experimental. He further insisted that the offer of the Apex service was an extra facility and in no way affected their entitlement to anything else offered to other men in prison. The exact service that Apex was trying to offer was then outlined in some detail, and although, over the course of three years, a whole range of anxieties and attitudes about the motives and success of 'helping' agencies were expressed by the men, this outline generally provoked a fairly constructive attitude. Not unnaturally, the most usual question was what the research officer meant by the term 'suitable employment'. As this concept usually led to a profitable discussion about employment in general and also enabled the research officer to try to establish the correct expectations regarding the type of work likely to be arranged for different types of inmate, the research officer quickly learnt to programme this question from his opening remarks.

'Suitable employment' for each man obviously varied according to each man's abilities and qualifications, so it was necessary to give examples to explain how suitable employment could vary with the circumstances and background of each man. An accountant who was debarred from practising his profession owing to the nature of the present offence could not reasonably expect to obtain a job which was completely commensurate with the employment he had had before his present sentence. On the other hand, any man whose offence did not debar him in this way could expect Apex to try to find him work in which he had the experience or the aptitude. It was clear that most men expected that the interviews arranged would be for jobs as a cleaner or kitchen porter regardless of qualifications, but it was emphasized that this type of work would be arranged only if that was what a man desired.

A point that was always emphasized from the outset was that Apex did tell employers something of a man's past and the employer would certainly know that the man had recently been discharged from prison. On the other hand, we also emphasized that this was not simply an inventory of all his convictions, but usually amounted to the present sentence and offence and anything else that either Apex or the employer thought was relevant information for the particular job in mind. Furthermore, the research officer insisted that Apex tried to encourage the employer to limit the number of people who knew of these facts and that often the staff manager or director of the firm concerned insisted that this would be the case so as to facilitate the smooth running of his organization. Naturally enough, this policy of revealing some criminal background led to some expressions of anxiety from the men, but most seemed to be assured fairly readily that Apex would act in a sensible manner. Whether this stated policy did have a possible effect on the outcome of the Apex service must be considered, but there were only two men in the Wormwood

Scrubs sample and five men in the Pentonville sample who overtly refused the Apex service on the grounds that Apex would reveal some of their criminal history to a prospective employer. There is obviously no way in which an agency describing itself as an 'X-Prisoners' Employment Agency' could accommodate itself to the demands of these seven men.

After this general discussion which gave some of the background to the Apex scheme and also helped to alleviate some of the more easily expressed fears and anxieties of the men, the research officer then encouraged each man to consider his own case, and it was at this juncture that the men were always seen individually.

Originally it had been intended to administer a rigidly structured questionnaire to elicit fairly comprehensive information and also to conduct a series of interviews before asking whether the respondent wanted the sort of help that Apex was offering. Both these policies were abandoned during the Wormwood Scrubs pilot study for the following reasons. It is essential to emphasize that the aim of this initial interview – and indeed all the interviews in prison – was to attempt to strike a balance between evidently representing a businesslike and efficient organization likely to produce the results and producing an informal atmosphere in which the prisoner felt able to relax enough to state his circumstances fully and accurately. A rigidly structured questionnaire seemed to upset this attempted balance, for, apart from the fact that a questionnaire seemed to antagonize a proportion of the men, some of the questions could not be readily reconciled in the men's minds to a job-finding organization. It was felt that one of the strengths of the present study was that it was observing the actual behaviour of men being offered a job-placing service and it was unwise to introduce unnecessary bias by making the research aspect too evident. The result was that the research officer concentrated on trying to obtain information on items concerned with the men's job histories, such as their employment situation at the time of committing their present offence and the longest time ever spent at any one job, and their responses to this type of question were recorded immediately in their presence. This seemed totally acceptable to the men as it related in an obvious manner to finding employment. Other topics of interest, such as the family and domestic situation, accommodation plans, possible addiction problems, almost invariably came up in the course of the subsequent discussion and these were recorded as a form of case report afterwards. While this indirect method is likely to produce the more valid replies and possibly prevented some antagonism towards the project, there was the usual problem of coding this type of material in a useful form. (It is perhaps worthwhile to mention that our access to the prison records – of which the men were aware – did enable us to avoid almost entirely the sometimes delicate subject of their criminal record.)

The original plan had been for the research officer to have two or three interviews with each man before any placing action would take place. This was an attempt to get a full amount of information and perhaps also in the hope that a more suitable type of prisoner would somehow select himself for the Apex service. The pilot study soon demonstrated that this policy was not appropriate, for the main reason that the majority of men had no wish to go away to consider their decision after hearing the general outline of what Apex was prepared to do. Practically all the men were keen to express their immediate reaction to the offer and those who had decided to reject the offer were obviously unlikely to return to an appointment a few days later simply to try to explain their lack of interest in the service. It soon became the practice, except in cases where there was obvious indecision or other problems to be considered, for the research officer to accept this almost spontaneous reaction to the offer of the Apex service. One suspects with the benefit of hindsight that Apex was unwisely colluding with the prisoner in accepting these snap decisions and so encouraging the men to enter into a commitment of starting a job arranged by Apex without really attempting to give the matter much thought. One could imagine that in a more therapeutic setting the ready acceptance of an employment-placing service could be examined profitably in discussion with each man to try to assess exactly how he thought such an arrangement could benefit him. However, this approach rather presupposes that anxiety about work is perhaps symptomatic of some other underlying problems and the present study was primarily concerned with trying to examine the employment factor in isolation.

An avoidance of any therapeutic role was one of the reasons why the series of preliminary interviews for each man was abandoned. Not only did the pilot study at Wormwood Scrubs indicate that little further information was gained at subsequent interviews, but, more perniciously, the men began to appear less relaxed in a situation which seemed to develop into a psuedo-therapeutic relationship if there were several interviews before any job-placing took place. This was a development which we did not want to encourage, for the staff of Apex neither wished nor were equipped to operate within a therapeutic situation.

Although men were generally keen to state from the outset their interest in the offer to find them employment on their release, whatever their response they were all given the following letter at the end of the first interview and, if they had rejected the Apex service, it was also emphasized that they were quite free to contact Apex after release if they found it difficult subsequently to find suitable employment.

APEX TRUST*

2 MANCHESTER SQUARE,

LONDON, W.1.

Tel. WELbeck 5724/5

Dear

The Apex Trust has been allowed to start a new scheme for men on release from Wormwood Scrubs. The purpose is to find suitable jobs on discharge for men in 'C' Hall. Our staff, however, is such that we can only assist 100 men in a year, so we decided that the fairest way was to choose these men purely by *chance* from the discharge diary.

If you decide to use this new service offered to you (and in view of the present economic situation, we strongly advise you to do so), I will have some further chats with you in the course of the next couple of months. Apex then undertakes to find what we regard as a suitable job for you on your discharge. We try to arrange that the staff manager of the firm employing you is the only one who knows something of your past. As you can appreciate, you will then avoid the difficult problem of explaining away your unstamped insurance card.

The Apex Trust is not just trying to find you one job and then forgetting about you. If there are problems regarding the job we find you, let us know; we may be able to solve the problem; or if the first job we find you is unsuitable, we will then have to try again. We want to keep you in permanent employment, so we hope you will keep working while we are looking for other work on your behalf. Whatever happens, we want to keep in touch with you after release, and I will arrange to see you when you have been out for a couple of weeks to find out whether everything is working out satisfactorily.

Naturally, I will answer any further questions when next we meet, but I hope you will see what we can do for you as regards fixing up a job on release.

Yours sincerely,

Keith Soothill

* The Apex Trust has since moved to premises at 9 Poland Street, London W1V 3DG (Telephone: 01–734 4658).

A similar letter with appropriate amendments was given to each man interviewed in the Pentonville sample.

## THE RESPONSE TO THE OFFER

The ideal experimental situation would have been if all the men interviewed had accepted the full implications of the Apex service, and then the outcome for this group could have been compared directly in terms of reconviction rates with the control group who had not been interviewed. Not surprisingly, the responses of the men interviewed had a far wider range. Hopefully it had been anticipated that there would be a straightforward dichotomy between those who accepted the Apex service and those who rejected the Apex service, and indeed we operated on this assumption for the first three months. We realized that this was definitely an unrealistic assumption when we interviewed a coloured entertainer and dancer who simply wanted work for two or three weeks to earn enough money to advertise in *The Stage* and to book rehearsal rooms.* While this was quite a reasonable request, we felt that casual and stop-gap work of this nature could not be regarded as full acceptance of the Apex concept. From this point we decided to introduce three major categories of response to the Apex service, namely full acceptance, partial acceptance and rejection, and to define the categories fairly strictly.†

*Full Acceptance* is defined as those men who apparently accept the full implications of the employment service as outlined in the letter given to each man at the initial interview – that is, that Apex will try to find suitable interviews to attend on release, revealing to potential employers something of the men's criminal records, and that Apex is attempting to settle them in permanent employment after release. While it was agreed that Apex would try to find employment at the level and in the field desired by the client, we made it clear from the outset that, if prevailing market conditions made the request impossible to fulfil, then we would arrange an

---

* He eventually did this after release, causing comment from a Sunday newspaper when the following advertisement appeared in *The Stage*. '. . . required female singers, dancers and striptease for England and abroad. Write to Church Army Hostel, Great Peter Street, S.W.1. (No coloured artistes, please)'.

† The men interviewed before this point had been divided into acceptance or rejection of the Apex Service; these have been included in the full acceptance and rejection groups respectively, although it is possible that the partial acceptance group may have been more appropriate for one or two men if it had been introduced earlier.

interview which we regarded as appropriate and discuss the change of arrangement before release. However, there were a group of men who would not accept this latter condition and emphasized that if we did not satisfy their first and only choice, these men did not want any further action on their behalf. When one considered that these were extremely specific jobs, such as fireman or deep-sea diver, then it is not unreasonable to classify these men as making a *Partial Acceptance – Specific Request*. We also included in this category men who wanted Apex to contact one particular firm only or who made a specific request for employment of a casual nature, intending to stay at the job only a short period.

A further category was introduced of *Partial Acceptance – Limited Interest*. This category contains those men who showed a limited interest in the Apex service, but were definitely not interested in Apex trying to find them suitable work immediately on release. Although, as we have mentioned, all men interviewed were told that they could come to the Apex offices after release if they desired, these particular men were those who seemed to want more assurance than this. For this reason they were either called up again or sent an individual letter to endorse the sentiments of the stencilled letter. There is no doubt that this is somewhat of a residual category including all those who cannot bring themselves, or are unable, to state in a straightforward manner that they are not interested in the Apex service. In particular in the Pentonville sample, this category includes men who are obviously totally unclear about what they are going to do on release but the possibility of needing help with employment is one of the alternatives they mention.

The *Rejection Group* is a much more clear-cut group, for it is defined as those men who state that they do not wish Apex to find them suitable work and, although this is not a necessary condition for inclusion in the Rejection Group, they usually state their reasons for this decision fairly categorically.

Finally, there is a *Miscellaneous Group* comprising those men who were not offered the Apex service. In the Wormwood Scrubs sample there were two men in this group – one seemed too disturbed to send to any employer while the other man seemed too disturbed by his offence and sentence for it to be possible to conduct the necessary preliminary interviews in the prison. In the Pentonville sample there were also two men in this type of condition – one was too disturbed to be interviewed while the other man had deteriorated to such an extent that he seemed totally unable to comprehend what Apex was trying to do. There was a further group of seven men who had plans to move right away from the Greater London area, and as they made this clear from the outset of the interview, the Apex service was not offered to them. Several of this latter group seemed fairly disturbed characters and their plans were often extremely vague. For example, one suggested that he was going either to Hastings or to Liverpool with no apparent reasons for either choice, while the remainder suggested destinations which probably had only a remote link with reality.

Apart from the men in the Miscellaneous Group, all the others had the opportunity of making their own response to the offer of the Apex service. The research officer tried not to influence any man's choice and, as we have stated, the majority of the men seemed fairly definite almost from the outset what their decision was to be. However, there was a small number who did change their mind between the time of their first interview and the time of their release from prison. The convention we adopted to decide in which category to place a man was the situation immediately at the conclusion of the joint interview with the director of Apex. In other words, if a respondent initially accepted the Apex service but then rejected it during the course of the joint interview with the director and research officer, he was regarded as a member of the rejection group. On the other hand, if the respondent changed his mind and rejected the service *after* the joint interview had taken place, then he was still regarded as a member of the full acceptance group. The criterion, therefore, was whether the director could have started work in trying to find a suitable job interview for the respondent, and this could happen only after the joint interview.

Table 4 shows the numbers and percentages in the various categories for both Wormwood Scrubs and Pentonville samples.

The table shows a remarkably similar distribution for both samples and fails to support any hypothesis that 'stars' will accept the Apex treatment more readily than recidivists; in fact, there is a slight tendency in the opposite direction. This is perhaps surprising, in view of the much higher proportion of those in the Wormwood Scrubs sample compared with the Pentonville sample who were interviewed by the placing officer of the Department of Employment (see Chapter 2), tending to suggest that recidivists were not interested in any placing action being taken on their behalf. There is some suggestion in Table 4 that a lower proportion of the Pentonville sample tended to reject the Apex service completely, but this difference is not significant. It is perhaps important to stress that this apparent difference may in fact be an artefact. There

TABLE 4   *Response to the offer of the Apex service*

| Apex groups | Wormwood Scrubs sample | | Pentonville sample | |
|---|---|---|---|---|
| | No. | (%) | No. | (%) |
| Full acceptance | 112* | 49·3 | 117 | 52·5 |
| Partial acceptance (specific requests) | 9 | 4·0 | 7 | 3·1 |
| Partial acceptance (limited interest) | 17 | 7·5 | 23 | 10·3 |
| Rejection | 87 | 38·3 | 67 | 30·0 |
| Miscellaneous | 2 | 0·9 | 9 | 4·0 |
| TOTAL | 227 | 100·0 | 223 | 100·0 |
| Control group (not interviewed) | 155 | — | 169 | — |
| GRAND TOTAL | 382 | — | 392 | — |

* This group includes seven men who would have fully accepted the Apex service, but the director had to restrict the offer to a few enquiries on their behalf as they all resided well outside the London area. They are included subsequently when there is any discussion of the characteristics of men who are likely to accept the Apex service, but they are excluded when the outcome of the Full Acceptance Group is analysed, for they could not be given the full service.

was a slightly larger group of men in Pentonville who could not state their decision clearly even after two or three interviews, and the research officer interpreted this as 'partial acceptance – limited interest': furthermore, the somewhat extraordinary responses of some of the men in the miscellaneous group of the Pentonville sample may in actual fact be simply their way of rejecting the offer of the Apex service.

However one interprets the small differences in Table 4, it is clear that the broad classification into 'stars' and 'ordinaries' is not a good discriminating factor between those who accept and those who reject the Apex service. It is not possible to develop this point further until the characteristics of the two sample populations are analyzed in greater detail.

## THE WORK OF THE DIRECTOR OF APEX

The general procedure in both prisons was for the research officer to ascertain whether the director needed to be involved in any particular case. If it seemed that some action was required of the director, the particular man was called up again on a Thursday and was interviewed by the director with the research officer also present to introduce the man and to give a summary of what he understood the position to be. The director tried to establish and assess the man's abilities and agree with him the possible job, its area, wage, etc.; he wanted to know all details which could perhaps be of interest to personnel officers; he wanted to know what a man's reaction was to shift-work, night-work, factory work or anything else which may be relevant to a particular field of employment. Obviously there was a danger of a stalemate from the outset if the prisoners and the director failed to agree what was 'suitable employment', but this was in reality not a problem. On some occasions there seemed to be more of a danger that the director was willing to aim too high for a man rather than too low; for example, men who had spent some time convincing Apex of their vast experience as skilled tradesmen changed their tune when they realized that the director was in earnest and the man himself sometimes suggested that he should, for example, perhaps 'get his hand in again' by returning at an improver level for a while. The only major issue was the wage for which men maintained they were willing to work. This is an area which needs clarifying, for there was often confusion over this matter; in fact, genuine misunderstanding was difficult to distinguish from deliberate misinterpretation.

Some men were often convinced from the outset that Apex – or any other agency for that matter – could obtain interviews only for jobs which were extremely badly paid. This is the basic stereotype which any placing agency in prison has to combat. As many of the men do not know or do not want to know the average wage that men with their qualifications and experience do actually earn, an agency which invariably gets 'suitable employment' may reinforce the stereotype that it gets only badly paid jobs. A complicating factor is that when a man asks about the wage that he is likely to earn in a particular job (if he does not know, this is perhaps the surest indication that he has not been working in the industry recently!), one is usually able to state only the basic rate after deductions. In fact, though, probably very few men take home this basic amount, for there is usually overtime available which is reckoned as part of the wage packet in factory work or bonus schemes which operate quite extensively in the building industry. However, it was felt that the director must never promise higher wages than might be available by the time the prisoner was able to take up the job, for obviously bonus schemes and the availability of overtime do fluctuate. Eventually, this matter was largely resolved by emphasizing to each man that he would get the rate for a job 'which you know from your own experience probably more accurately than I can tell you'. Before telling any man about an interview offer, Apex tried to ensure that the employer was in fact offering the rate for the job.

The original plan was that, if the director felt that he had been able to satisfy the job requirements specified at his interview, he would simply send a letter before the man's release explaining the details of the interview arranged and also giving the time and date of the interview. If there was any particular difficulty about arranging a suitable interview, the man was called up and the situation was explained. This was in fact the arrangement for just under half the Wormwood Scrubs sample, but there were several defects in this procedure. It assumed in the first place that the prisoner was perfectly happy with what had been apparently agreed at his only interview with the director and, further, the prisoner was given no opportunity to discuss the subsequent interview arranged by the director. He was unable to state whether or not the interview measured up to his expectations and, if not, to indicate the particular shortcomings. At the same time, there was much concern about the poor attendance of interviews arranged by Apex and it was thought that perhaps the lack of contact shortly before release was the weak link. Therefore, a further interview taking place within eight days of release was gradually introduced specifically to discuss what had been arranged for a man on his release.

To complicate the matter further, the first director of Apex left the organization around the time of this change of procedure and two part-time workers operated as placement officers in the three-month period before a suitable replacement was found. When another full-time director was appointed the procedure was subsequently very consistent for the rest of the project. It was as follows. The research officer saw each man to introduce the Apex service. The director then interviewed those men who accepted the service to discuss with them their main employment requirements and later saw them again within eight days of their release to discuss the arranged interview. A letter which was normally sent to each man before the last interview before his release contained full details of the employment arranged, so that he would have time to consider it prior to being asked at the final interview whether it was suitable and acceptable.

To summarize the scope of the prison interviewing schedule, 438 men were interviewed at least once by the research officer; of these, 99 men had one further joint interview with both the research officer and the director present, while a further 143 men had two or more joint interviews as well as the initial one with the research officer. It is now interesting to consider whether the change of personnel and the slight changes in procedure had any appreciable effect on the numbers who accepted the Apex service.

## ACCEPTANCE OF THE APEX SERVICE

All the men selected at random from the discharge diary to be offered the Apex service were called up for interview by the research officer. As we have seen, all except twelve of the 450 men were in fact interviewed and the intention of the research officer was to make the same offer to all the men. In the event there were eleven men (two from Wormwood Scrubs and nine from Penton-ville) who have been classified in the previous section as miscellaneous and who were not offered the Apex service; these eleven men are disregarded in the following analysis.

The purpose of this present section is to examine whether the proportions of men who accepted or rejected the service changed during the time the studies were being conducted. If the proportions did change, then this could perhaps be the result of one of at least three factors or the interaction of these factors. In the first place, the research officer may unwittingly have been the source of increased acceptance or rejection by the men even though he intended to make an identical offer to each man. For example, if some of the initial enthusiasm for the project wore off, this may have affected the response of the men. Alternatively, the research officer may have used the same form of words to explain the Apex service but by practice may have speeded up the delivery to such an extent as to make the concept unintelligible to his audience. The second type of factor that could have made a difference could be summarized as a change in the expectations by the men of what the service was likely to do. For example, what had been arranged for the first few men could feed back to the rest of the prison (including the prison staff) and the proportion of those accepting could increase or diminish dramatically as a result. Finally, there was the possible effect of the change of director during the life of the project.

As a test for any change resulting from any of the above possibilities, the responses of the first hundred men interviewed in Wormwood Scrubs were compared with the responses of the second hundred and a similar exercise was carried out for the Pentonville sample. The most suitable test is to consider the numbers rejecting the Apex service, for there was never any conscious change in the definition of those included in the rejection group. Thirty-seven men out of the first hundred of the Wormwood Scrubs study rejected outright the Apex service, while 40 men out of the last hundred made a similar response. For the Pentonville sample, 29 men out of the first hundred interviewed rejected the offer of the Apex service and 32 men of the last hundred interviewed made this response. Clearly there is no indication in either prison that there was any significant change in the response to the Apex offer, apart from a very slight tendency for a higher proportion to reject the longer the study went on. Generally, though, the figures indicate that in the course of the study Apex failed to make a dramatic impact on either prison to the extent of resulting in wholesale acceptance or, more disastrously, rejection of the service. This is perhaps not surprising, as there was a tremendous turnover of men in both prisons and, anyway, Apex was interviewing only a minority of men, so it was not an ideal situation for either universal approval or disapproval to occur. However, the fact that approximately the same proportion felt able to accept throughout both studies tends to endorse the feeling of the research officer that there was no substantial body who felt strongly about the intrusion of the Apex project on the scene. The project had been initially explained to a general meeting of the prison officers, and although some expressed the opinion that it was likely to be work done and money spent in vain others felt strongly that this was the type of after-care they could understand and wanted in the prison. Some of the men had obviously asked prison officers what Apex was doing in the prison when they knew they were to be interviewed. Indications were that prison officers gave a reasonable account of Apex and tended if anything to encourage the men to opt for the Apex service, but more generally it is true to say that the work of Apex was not an issue that raised tremendous passions within either prison. Hence, one can reasonably suppose that each man interviewed tended to make his own decision and was not responding in answer to definite pressures in the prison either for or against the Apex project.

## CHAPTER 5

# The Effectiveness of the Apex Service in Reducing the Number of Offenders Committing Further Offences

While we have discussed in the previous chapter how we aimed to put into practice the basic philosophy of the Apex Trust to find suitable employment for the men to take up immediately on their release, it may seem an enormous jump to consider next the effectiveness of this service in terms of the reconviction measure before we have even examined whether we were able to fulfil our aim of finding suitable employment for all the men who accepted the Apex service. Indeed, perhaps there is much to be said in terms of dramatic impact in retaining the chronological order of events so that the reconviction of the various groups could be revealed as some kind of final *dénouement*. While this approach could perhaps produce a more exciting narrative, it may be less useful in an attempt to explain the relative success or failure of the project. This chapter, therefore, should be compared to the antics of those avid readers of detective stories who turn to the last few pages to find out the villain, and then happily read the earlier pages to find out how everything worked out in that way. For convenience – and this innovation may or may not appeal to future 'whodunit' writers – material suitable for a conclusion has found its place before what may be the beginnings of an explanation.

We have pointed out that the basic measure in examining the effectiveness of the Apex service is the reconviction rate of a 'treatment group' whom Apex has tried to assist and a 'control group' who have just had the influences ordinarily brought to bear upon a discharged prisoner. In a slightly different context, Hammond and Chayen point out that:

> the success of any treatment of offenders can, in theory, be assessed from the number of offenders undergoing that treatment who cease to commit any further offences, compared with the number of comparable offenders who do not receive treatment and who do not offend again. In practice, this is impossible to realize since all offenders receive some 'treatment' (even if

the offender is given an absolute discharge there is the effect of the appearance in court and the stigma of being found guilty).[1]

The problem for Hammond and Chayen was to find a suitable control group for a group of offenders sentenced to preventive detention, but the problem in the present case is that the control group who were not interviewed contains men who would have responded in various ways to the offer of the Apex service. In other words, the control group contains men who would have been categorized with responses of full aceptance, partial acceptance or rejection, while we can probably expect only that the Apex service would have a beneficial effect on those who fully accepted or at least partially accepted the Apex service. The present problem is that the treatment group contains men who rejected the Apex service, or, alternatively, the control group contains a proportion of men who would have rejected the Apex service if they had been given the opportunity to do so! On the other hand, can we definitely maintain that men who reject the Apex service do not gain from the offer? It is possible to conceive that an employment offer which is rejected may prompt some men at least to consider whether their own arrangements are in order. For example, it may prompt some to contact the employer whom they maintained would be willing to re-employ them and by this action may secure a vacancy which was perhaps not so definite as they had imagined. Equally one could argue that a discussion about future plans could prompt a man who was uninterested in the actual Apex offer of finding employment to consider more positively what he is going to do about, say, accommodation on release. Even the response 'I certainly don't want a job until I've got a roof over my head' may have assisted the man in deciding exactly what his priorities are on release.

As a first measure, therefore, it would be interesting to compare all those who were selected for interview and offered the Apex service (i.e. the treatment group in its widest sense) with the men in the control group who were not interviewed and did not have the opportunity of the Apex service. Before this is done, though, one must consider what we mean by a comparison of reconviction rates.

Obviously, two of the important factors in examining reconviction rates are the length of time one should allow to elapse before checking reconviction and, secondly, the criterion of what one should regard as a reconviction.

If one attempts to compare reconviction rates after too short a period 'at risk', then the number of men reconvicted during this period will not begin to reflect the proportion of men who will eventually be reconvicted. On the other hand, if one tries to get a completely accurate picture of the numbers of men who are reconvicted after a long period 'at risk' there is the danger that the research will be of only historic interest. Inevitably, some form of compromise is necessary. Hammond and Chayen show in their study of preventive detainees how the proportion of men reconvicted cumulates over the years. Twenty-one per cent were reconvicted in the year of release (the average period at risk being only six months), but as many as 51 per cent had been reconvicted up to one year after their year of release. They indicate that the number of reconvictions occurring during each year after release decreases progressively and the ultimate failure rate of these men can be expected to be about 80 per cent. Even if one allows for the fact that 'one reason for the progressively smaller number of additional reconvictions as the interval from release increases is that, in such vulnerable groups, there are fewer offenders still at risk', it is still evident that 'the year of release and the year following are the most dangerous for these offenders as for any others'.[2] Although men serving their first term of adult imprisonment should not be as vulnerable as a group of preventive detainees, it is fairly likely that they would have similar reconviction patterns in that the greatest danger period is probably in the first year after release. For this reason, the total sample from each prison was submitted to the Criminal Record Office when every member of the particular sample had had an opportunity of being at liberty for one complete year. In consequence, as each study was a year at the particular prison involved, some men were at risk for two complete years while some had just completed one full year. The average period at risk for the total sample, therefore, was eighteen months.

In order to make a strict comparison between the treatment and control groups, it is necessary to take an identical period at risk for each man in each group; in this case, the period of time for which this is possible is one year. One must emphasize that, if there is a statistically significant difference between the two groups in favour of the treatment group after this period of time, then this, of course, would not be conclusive proof that the Apex service is effective over a long term. For example, one could argue that the Apex service results in fewer breakdowns during the early stages after release, but may simply delay the time of breakdown rather than produce a state of affairs in which there are no subsequent reconvictions. This situation would be somewhat comparable to the findings of Hammond and Chayen in their study of preventive detainees that 'significantly fewer offenders who were released after two-thirds of their sentence were reconvicted in the year of release than was the case with offenders released after five-sixths of their sentence',[3] but after about two years an almost identical proportion had been reconvicted in the two groups. If this phenomenon occurred after one year in the present study, then one could see in general terms what the trend was after eighteen months, although as we have explained this cannot be regarded as such a rigorous comparison because this period is simply the average time at risk of each group as a whole.

On the other hand, if there is no significant difference between the two groups after one year, it is still worth examining the differences after eighteen months, for it may support the finding of Berntsen and Christiansen. The effect of their treatment seemed particularly strong during the second and third year after release which, as they point out, 'is surprising as, for most of the prisoners, the period of treatment was very short'.[4] They describe their treatment as 'socio-psychologically oriented supporting therapy combined with relatively comprehensive welfare measures',[5] but felt that their work 'did not by any means reach the extent or achieve the intensity which was necessary to ensure the entire success of the experiment'.[6] In spite of their reservations about the effectiveness of their treatment, the recidivism was significantly higher in the control group than in the experimental group, particularly after the second year. Their suggestions to explain this 'delayed reaction' is that:

> in both groups there is a hard core of criminals, unaffected either by the short-term sentence served under ordinary forms or by the treatment given in the E–group (experimental group), who continue their criminal careers immediately after their release. The less persistent types whose relapse into crime occurs at a later stage are presumably those who are most favourably in-fluenced by the attempts to resocialize them.[7]

This is an attractive explanation, and naturally one would wish to see whether there is any indication of this phenomenon in the present study. There is the severe limitation, however, that the Scandinavian study eventually had a follow-up period of seven years, so we can simply try to indicate whether there is the beginning of a trend in the same direction. Apart from the problem of a suitable time interval to measure the reconviction rate, another problem is to assess what is to count as a reconviction. Every time a person is convicted in a criminal court could quite reasonably count as a reconviction, but there is the danger that the gravity of subsequent offences will be completely disregarded. In fact one could conceive of a situation in which two groups had an equal number of reconvictions, but one group committed all serious offences while the other group committed all trivial offences. In reality a situation is not likely to be so clear-cut, but the point remains valid. The famous Cambridge–Somerville study indicated the value of examining this possibility for, though the boys in the treatment group committed, on the whole, more offences in the aggregate and in fact more boys in the treatment group than boys in the control group committed 'serious' offences, 'there is some evidence, though slight, that the *most* serious offenders are in the control group'.[8] An allied problem is the difficulty of measuring possible improvement in the behaviour of each individual. A bank robber whose subsequent conviction is larceny by finding would appear to be much less of a threat to society and one could reasonably suggest that an improvement in behaviour has taken place. On the other hand, the man who had served his last prison sentence for larceny by finding and who subsequently committed a similar offence represents a similar threat to society but one could not say that his behaviour had apparently changed in any way. By taking a simple reconviction count after a stated time-interval, all these kinds of distinction are lost.

Inevitably one must also emphasize that no reconviction during a certain period does not necessarily mean that there has been no criminal activity during that time. If a rehabilitation programme inadvertently made a significant proportion of ex-prisoners more competent criminals, in the present state of research techniques it is likely that we would be demanding more of these types of programme! In the present sample, there was one young man aged 22 who fully accepted the Apex service but was subsequently shot dead in a gun fight. The *Guardian* briefly but faithfully reported:

CASE AGAINST DEAD MAN DROPPED. Proceedings on a charge of stealing £325 against . . . (22) who was shot dead at Fulham, were ordered to be withdrawn at the Inner London Sessions yesterday.[9]

By the criterion of reconviction, he would be regarded as a 'success' although in fact he never even attended the interview arranged by Apex. Two other men were known to have died during the year after release – one who had been reconvicted and one who had not by the time of his death – and for a completely accurate assessment of reconviction one should consider the number of men who were in fact genuinely at risk during the period in question. This point is particularly relevant for long-term follow-ups, but was not considered worthwhile in the present case when the follow-up was only one year. These familiar reservations, however, should be borne in mind when one is examining the results of this study.

The present study uses reconviction data supplied by the Criminal Record Office which records all indictable offences and the more important non-indictable offences. Information on any offence where the conviction has occurred within the sample period of one year is considered relevant in the present analysis.* First of all, we will examine the crude reconviction figures for each group with the result that an offence for which the punishment is an absolute discharge has the same value for this simple measure as a fifteen-year prison sentence. Next, however, we will examine the proportion in each group who received a prison or custodial sentence and this will resolve some of the shortcomings of the crude reconviction rate. Obviously, men can be sent to prison for very trivial offences, particularly if this has been a part of a consistent criminal pattern, but if one group has significantly fewer custodial sentences imposed then it is almost certain that this group will be costing the community much less money, at least in terms of penal expenditure.

ANALYSIS OF SUBSEQUENT RECONVICTIONS

There was no trace of a criminal record for four men in the Wormwood Scrubs sample (two were from the full acceptance group and two men from the rejection group), so these men have not been included in the subsequent reconviction analysis in any way. Table 5 shows the number and percentage reconvicted for the treatment and control groups from Wormwood Scrubs.

It indicates that for the strict test where the observation period

* In stricter terminology we are in fact considering court appearances after release rather than convictions. Separate occasions of adjudication only are counted, so if someone is convicted on one occasion of several separate charges with others 'taken into consideration', this still counts as one conviction.

TABLE 5 *Number and percentage of Wormwood Scrubs sample reconvicted during observation period (one year after release)*

|  | Treatment group (interviewed by Apex) | | Control group (not interviewed by Apex) | |
| --- | --- | --- | --- | --- |
|  | No. | (%) | No. | (%) |
| No subsequent convictions | 144 | 64·6 | 106 | 68·4 |
| Conviction during first year after release | 63 | 28·3 | 40 | 25·8 |
| Known conviction after one year | 16 | 7·2 | 9 | 5·8 |
| TOTAL* | 223 | 100·0 | 155 | 100·0 |

* Throughout this report percentages do not always add to totals because of rounding errors.

was set for exactly one year after release computed separately for each man, 25·8 per cent of the control group and 28·3 per cent of the treatment group were reconvicted within that year. Not surprisingly, there is no significant difference between the two groups in terms of whether or not they were reconvicted during the first year ($x^2 = 0.27$; 1 d.f.; N.S.).* If one then adds the men who are known to have a conviction after one year (as we have explained, this averages to a period at risk of eighteen months), there is certainly no indication that the treatment group is improving compared with the control group – in fact, if anything, the reverse is the case!

Table 6 giving the Pentonville results demonstrates a remarkable similarity with the pattern of Table 5, except that whereas a quarter of the men released from Wormwood Scrubs were reconvicted within one year this is the case for half the men released from the recidivist prison of Pentonville. The similarity between the two samples is in the marginal difference between the treatment and control groups, for 53·8 per cent of the former group and 50·9 per cent of the

* In every case where comparisons have been made between groups of prisoners, tests of significance have been performed; the results of the tests are placed in brackets in the text. The symbol $\chi^2$ refers to the chi-square distribution: the letters d.f. refer to the degrees of freedom of the distribution. The significance of the result is shown by $p < 0.01$ (significant at the 1 per cent level), $p < 0.05$ (significant at the 5 per cent but not the 1 per cent level), and N.S. (not significant at the 5 per cent level).

TABLE 6 *Number and percentage of Pentonville sample reconvicted during observation period (one year after release)*

|  | Treatment group (interviewed by Apex) | | Control group (not interviewed by Apex) | |
|  | No. | (%) | No. | (%) |
|---|---|---|---|---|
| No subsequent convictions | 86 | 38·6 | 71 | 42·0 |
| Conviction during first year after release | 120 | 53·8 | 86 | 50·9 |
| Known conviction after one year | 17 | 7·6 | 12 | 7·1 |
| TOTAL | 223 | 100·0 | 169 | 100·0 |

latter group were reconvicted within the first year of release. Once again, there is no significant difference between the two groups. (Reconvicted during first year v. Not reconvicted during first year: $x^2 = 0.35$; 1 d.f.; N.S.). Clearly this is not an encouraging start in an attempt to demonstrate the effectiveness of Apex, for although we have not begun to compare the type of reconvictions for both groups, the distribution at this stage looks remarkably similar.

The next step is to consider the extent to which the treatment group is weighted by the inclusion of men who completely rejected the Apex service. However fanciful one may become about possible ways by which the rejection group may have been indirectly helped by participation in the Apex project, it is obvious that the Apex project was designed to help men who fully accepted the concept of finding men work immediately on release. We have not yet discussed the success of Apex in finding suitable employment, but whatever the outcome of each individual acceptance it is still the overall result of this group which is nearer the real test for the success of the Apex project. For the various groups in the Wormwood Scrubs sample, there is a surprising similarity in the proportion of each group who were reconvicted in the first year after release. The full acceptance, rejection, partial acceptance and control groups in the Wormwood Scrubs sample had reconviction rates of 28·2 per cent, 27·1 per cent, 31·4 per cent and 25·8 per cent respectively and these slight differences are well within the limits of chance fluctuations.

The fact that a quarter of the Wormwood Scrubs sample were reconvicted whatever their responses to the Apex service is remarkable, for even if the Apex service was totally ineffective in terms of lowering the reconviction rate one would have perhaps hypothesized that the reason why men responded to the offer would identify groups with different risks of reconviction after release.

There is a similar pattern for the Pentonville sample, for the full acceptance, rejection, partial acceptance and control groups had reconviction rates of 57·3 per cent, 55·2 per cent, 41·0 per cent and 50·9 per cent. Whereas in the Wormwood Scrubs sample the partial acceptance group had a slightly higher reconviction figure, the situation is reversed for the Pentonville sample as this category has the comparatively low reconviction figure of 41 per cent. There is some evidence to suggest that the partial acceptance category tends to contain men who are perhaps more socially distressed than criminally disposed. The fact that a higher proportion seem to have lost contact with their families means that they have a slightly worse prognosis compared with the rest of the Wormwood Scrubs sample, but in the Pentonville sample the slightly less serious criminal record of the men in this category helps to explain to some extent the lower reconviction rate.

TIME OF SUBSEQUENT RECONVICTION FOR THE VARIOUS GROUPS

Although there are no differences at the end of the first year in the proportions of the various groups who were reconvicted, one could argue that the Apex service may be delaying slightly the date of the first conviction after release. The time-interval before a criminal's first relapse into crime after release cannot be measured very accurately with the present information, for we have available only the date of conviction, but it may give some indication whether it is worth pursuing this particular line of thought.

While there are obvious reservations about using the date of conviction as a measure of a criminal's first relapse into crime after release – apart from anything else, the date of conviction may in fact be some time after the arrest (which in turn may be some time after the offence) – there is for the Wormwood Scrubs sample a slightly different effect than might reasonably be expected. Of those who are reconvicted within one year, 65 per cent of the Apex treatment group are reconvicted in the first six months compared with only 53 per cent of the control group. This difference does not reach statistical significance, and the probability that it is a chance factor is strongly endorsed by the fact that there is an opposite trend for the Pentonville sample. Of those reconvicted within one year, 79 per cent of the control group are reconvicted within six months, but this is the case for only 63 per cent of the treatment group. This difference is, in fact, significant. (Reconvicted within 6 months v. Reconvicted from 6 months to 1 year: $x^2 = 5.92$; 1 d.f.; $p < 0.05$), so providing tentative evidence that at least the onset of recidivism is delayed for the treatment group of the Pentonville sample. It is not, however, as simple as that, for one must bear in mind that a higher (though not significant) proportion of the Pentonville treatment group were reconvicted within one year compared with the Pentonville control group (see Table 6). If there had in fact been the same proportion reconvicted in the control group as in the treatment group, namely 53.8 per cent, this would have meant that 91 instead of 86 of the control group would have been reconvicted within one year. If one made the assumption that all these five extra reconvictions took place within the six months to one year period, the difference between the treatment and control groups would no longer be significant. To a large extent this argument tends to nullify the suggestion that the relapse into crime of the Pentonville treatment group is delayed somewhat, for one should take into account the different reconviction rates of the two groups.

However, even if there were no doubt that the men in the Pentonville control group were reconvicted earlier, one still must consider the matter further. For instance, one could even make the paradoxical suggestion that the men interviewed by Apex (i.e. the treatment group) may be committing more serious offences and hence, because they would tend in consequence to appear before higher courts, their date of conviction may be somewhat later!

An indirect way of examining the seriousness of an offence is to examine the severity of the sentence or sanction imposed. (It is indirect because among other considerations the man's previous record is usually taken into account in deciding an appropriate sentence.) Analyzing the most severe sanction during the first year after release for both samples, there is a similar pattern to that described in considering the time-interval before the man's first reconviction after release. The Wormwood Scrubs treatment group seemed to do less well than the Wormwood Scrubs control group, for whereas of those reconvicted just over half the control group received prison sentences, two-thirds of the treatment group received prison sentences or hospital orders. On the other hand, the Pentonville treatment group seemed to have marginally less severe sanctions than the Pentonville control group, but this is nowhere near being statistically significant.

One can pursue this further, for within the category of imprisonment there is obviously still a tremendous range of lengths of sentence from a tramp's lagging to the possibility of permanent incarceration. The cost of keeping a man in prison is so high that, if it were possible to show that the treatment group were imprisoned subsequently for significantly shorter periods, this could be a basis for indicating some effect of the Apex service and could fairly easily be translated into a demonstration of how it reduces penal expenditure.

An analysis of the lengths of prison sentences imposed largely explains some of the apparent discrepancy between the treatment and control groups for the Wormwood Scrubs sample when it rather appeared that the treatment group was receiving severer sentences than the control group. The treatment group included four men who were given a prison sentence of less than three months and two men who were given a compulsory hospital order, while the control group had no one in these categories. With the Pentonville sample, however, the treatment group showed up less favourably, for a higher proportion of the treatment group received sentences of one year or more than was the case with the control group, but this difference is not significant.

It is perhaps relevant at this stage to consider once again whether a reconviction check after one year would be sufficient to reveal the subsequent criminal activity of the men. This chapter should have given sufficient evidence that in an experiment of this kind there are plenty who fall by the wayside in reconviction terms even within one year. Twenty-seven per cent of the Wormwood Scrubs sample were reconvicted within one year, and of those reconvicted, three-fifths received prison sentences. Not unexpectedly, the Pentonville sample performed even more poorly, for 53 per cent were reconvicted within one year, and of these, over two-thirds received prison sentences. There is plenty of scope for a reduction in reconviction rates to be revealed, but the crucial issue remains whether those who are reconvicted within the first year after release are in fact the men whom one expects to respond favourably to an employment-placing service. Certainly, there is not really any indication that the Apex service has any definite effect in reducing the proportion of men who are reconvicted within one year after release. In fact, the treatment group seems to do marginally poorer in both prisons although this is almost certainly a chance fluctuation. In the Wormwood Scrubs sample, 28·3 per cent of the treatment group were reconvicted within one year compared with 25·8 per cent of the control group. In the Pentonville sample, 53·8 per cent of the treatment group were reconvicted within one year compared with 50·9 per cent of the control group. Even when one examines the reconviction rate of those who fully accepted the Apex service, there is no evidence that they have a significantly lower reconviction rate than any other group.

The only tentative suggestion that the treatment group did perform more satisfactorily than the control group in terms of reconviction was the indication that the date of the first conviction after release of a significantly high proportion of the Pentonville treatment group tended to be in the second six months after release rather than the first six months. It may seem surprising that the only evidence of a slightly more favourable outcome should come from the Pentonville rather than the Wormwood Scrubs sample, for there tends to be the inherent belief in after-care work that you are rather more likely to get positive results by concentrating on those who have arrived in prison for the first time. While no one would doubt the apparent plausibility of this approach, we should not too readily assume that those with less criminal experience will always respond more favourably to a particular type of after-care. If one considers once again the findings of Berntsen and Christiansen concerning the resocialization experiment with short-term offenders, they suggest that 'the less crime-loaded categories, where the rate of recidivism was low, seem to have profited very little or not at all from their participation in the project'.[10] Until one considers the matter in more detail, one can perhaps assume that this group is equivalent to many in the Wormwood Scrubs sample. On the other hand, Berntsen and Christiansen suggest that 'the treatment had the greatest effect in an intermediate group whose previous career was relatively heavily crime-loaded',[11] and perhaps at this stage one may be allowed to speculate whether this group is equivalent to some in the Pentonville sample. Although this is speculation, this does serve the purpose of suggesting that one cannot generalize too glibly about the appropriateness of a particular type of after-care for a particular group of prisoners. It needs not merely a personal impression of who is likely to respond but a more rigorous and objective technique of identifying those likely to benefit from a particular approach.

## REFERENCES

1 Hammond, W. H., and Chayen, E., *Persistent Criminals*, London, HMSO (1963), p. 89.

2 Ibid., p. 91.
3 Loc. cit.
4 Berntsen, K., and Christiansen, K. O., 'A Resocialization Experiment with Short-Term Offenders' in Christiansen, K. O. (ed.), *Scandinavian Studies in Criminology*, Vol. 1, London, Tavistock (1965), p. 48.
5 Ibid., p. 35.
6 Ibid., p. 43.
7 Ibid., p. 48.
8 Powers, E., and Witmer, H., *An Experiment in the Prevention of Delinquency: The Cambridge–Somerville Youth Study*, New York, Columbia University Press (1951), p. 334.
9 The *Guardian*, 12.3.68.
10 Berntsen and Christiansen, op. cit., p. 53.
11 Loc. cit.

# CHAPTER 6

# Acceptance and Rejection of the Apex Service

When the selection of prisons for this study was discussed, we pointed out that the resulting samples of 'stars' and 'ordinaries' from Wormwood Scrubs and Pentonville respectively would not be totally representative of these two classes of prisoners throughout the country. In addition to the bias of taking particular prisons with a particular catchment area, we introduced the further constraint of limiting the sample to men with certain lengths of prison sentence, namely, six months to three years for the Wormwood Scrubs sample and six to twelve months for the Pentonville sample. Within these limits, however, it is reasonable to maintain that the two samples are reasonably representative of men from the Home Counties catchment area who are classified as 'C' category men.

The purpose of taking samples from two prisons was to examine whether the effect of a placing service was any different for men serving their first term of adult imprisonment from men serving at least their second prison sentence. One could hypothesize, for example, that a man who has had one lapse for which he has been imprisoned may need only the provision of suitable employment after release, for he may have retained sufficient links with the community for everything to fall satisfactorily into order with one effective employment placement acting as a catalyst. Alternatively, one could argue that the man serving his first prison sentence may not fully appreciate the potential problems on release and so reject the offer of a placing service, while a man with several previous prison sentences may grasp the opportunity offered and re-establish himself after being given this 'flying start' compared with his previous experiences on discharge. This present chapter, however, indicates that the two samples of Wormwood Scrubs and Pentonville do not provide two homogeneous groups for a straightforward analysis on these lines. The tendency over the years to discourage the judiciary from imprisoning men for the first offence has resulted in many men arriving in prison for the first time after several previous clashes with the law; similarly, the introduction during this century of institutions for young offenders, namely borstals and detention centres, has meant that a higher proportion of offenders reach prison for the first time after some previous penal institutional experience.

A prison officer at Wormwood Scrubs summarized precisely the position by pointing out to the research officer that 'the star is now tarnished'. The question of the value of the conventional distinction between 'stars' and 'ordinaries' has not gone unnoticed in other studies. Dr Pauline Morris, in her study of *Prisoners and their Families*, noted the overlap between 'stars' and 'ordinaries' in terms of their previous criminality, for she commented that 64·8 per cent of her sample of 'stars' had had at least one previous conviction. Even more noteworthy is the fact that 18·6 per cent of 'stars' had been in prison before, while 13 per cent of the recidivists in her sample had served only one previous prison sentence.[1] Hence, this produces an overlap of approximately 15 per cent on the dimension that is the main basis of the distinction.

The origin of the star class system for local prisons was contained in the Report from the Departmental Committee on Prisons (1895). The Prison Commissioners published a statement in 1898 outlining the action they had so far taken to carry out the recommendations of the 1895 Departmental Committee and stated that:

The Star Class System, previously in force in Convict Prisons only, under which first offenders are separated from other prisoners, has now been extended to all Local Prisons throughout the country, and the Commissioners have every reason to be satisfied with its operation.[2]

In actual fact, the relevant passage in the 1895 report foresaw some of the difficulties of the distinction and emphasized that:

while it is desirable to devote special treatment to [first offenders] as a class, it should be recognized that many 'first offenders' have probably been convicted more than once, and that several of those who are convicted for the first time have been to a greater or less extent engaged in criminal practices. We do not therefore think it desirable to lay down a hard and fast rule under which all 'first offenders' . . . should have the privilege of any special treatment.[3]

The flexibility of the system recommended by the Gladstone Committee has in fact been used in the opposite direction than the one suggested, for there has been a tendency to tarnish rather than polish the 'stars'! While not wishing to raise in this context the age-old question of the dangers of contamination, the amount of overlap is relevant when one wishes to examine differences between the two samples.

Even disregarding the matter of previous prison sentences among the Wormwood Scrubs sample, there is still a tremendous range of previous penal experience among this group. There are men in Wormwood Scrubs, who, apart from many non-custodial punishments, have 'graduated' through approved school, borstal and detention centre (15 men in the Wormwood Scrubs sample had been to all three types of institution, while a further 55 men had been to at least two). In contrast, there are 58 men for whom the present offence appears to be their first conviction of any kind. Similarly, among the Pentonville sample, there is a wide range of previous penal experience. There are 73 men who have had only one previous prison sentence and, for a small minority of these, this is also their only other offence. At the other extreme, there are 147 men who have either served five or more previous prison sentences or have had at least one sentence of seven years or more.

These examples begin to indicate the danger of regarding the samples from the two prisons as two homogeneous groups. One could reasonably argue that the overlap between the two categories is so large and the within-group differences so great that the distinction is more of a hindrance than a help in examining the results of this project.

In terms of the acceptance of the Apex service we have already shown that a very similar response to the offer of the Apex service is given by both samples – 49·3 per cent of the Wormwood Scrubs sample and 52·5 per cent of the Pentonville sample fully accepted the Apex service. Eventually we suggest that it is more meaningful to combine the two samples and to consider instead three risk groups of which the 'low risk group' would comprise men from Wormwood Scrubs, the 'high risk group' men from Pentonville, and the 'medium risk group' men from both Wormwood Scrubs and Pentonville samples. One could conceive of a situation where the simple dichotomy of the two prison samples obscures a significant result. There may in fact be a U-shaped curve with the high and low risk groups tending to reject and the medium risk group tending to accept the Apex service. This possibility could reasonably be explained by suggesting that the low risk group have sufficient contacts with the outside world to re-establish themselves (or at least believe they have) while the high risk group (even assuming they wish to be rehabilitated in some way) appreciate that they have such a wide-ranging set of problems on release that finding employment in isolation is of little use; the medium risk group, on the other hand, may be well on the route to a criminal career but perhaps see this as an opportunity to change the pattern before the situation becomes irretrievable. It is not uncommon to hear young men in Pentonville remark that they are certainly not going to end up like some of the derelict old men who surround them in the prison. Although they do not specify that the alternative to this fate is a non-criminal career, it still suggests that the hypothesis is worth investigating. One must emphasize that at this juncture we are still simply considering the initial acceptance and rejection of the offer and that the outcome of accepting the Apex service will be discussed in subsequent chapters.

THE SAMPLE

We have already described the selection of the two prison samples and their response to the offer of the Apex service (see Table 4, page 104). In the last chapter we followed the rather laborious procedure of analyzing the samples from Wormwood Scrubs and Pentonville separately. In fact, if one considers those reconvicted in more detail, it is clear that the relevant feature is not the prison but the previous experience of the subject. A familiar item which illustrates the importance of the overlap between the Wormwood Scrubs and Pentonville samples is the number of previous convictions as an adult.* Three-quarters of the Wormwood Scrubs sample have up to three previous adult convictions and the reconviction rate within one year of this group is 21 per cent. The remaining quarter of the Wormwood Scrubs sample have four or more previous adult convictions and for these men the reconviction rate within one year rises to 47 per cent. Similarly, one in ten of the Pentonville sample have only up to three adult convictions and their reconviction rate is 28 per cent (i.e. fairly similar to the Wormwood Scrubs group, bearing in mind that this group is weighted favourably by men who have had no previous convictions at all). The remaining 90 per cent of the Pentonville sample have a reconviction rate of 55 per cent; this is higher than the Wormwood Scrubs sample because of the presence of a group of fifty-eight

---

* As the records of juvenile offences seemed in some cases to be incomplete and there was a danger that a high number of minor juvenile offences might produce a misleading weighting, it was decided to consider only previous convictions after the seventeenth birthday in calculating the item. More strictly, this is a record of previous occasions of adjudication, for if a man is convicted of several separate charges on one occasion, this counts as *one* previous conviction.

men with fifteen or more previous adult convictions. With this number of previous convictions, the reconviction rate within a year rises to 79 per cent.

The irrelevance of the present prison is even clearer when one considers each man's period in freedom since his last penal custodial sentence. Of the total Wormwood Scrubs sample, fifty men had been in freedom for less than a year when they received their present sentence and the reconviction rate for this group after one year was in fact 62 per cent. Those in the Pentonville sample who had previously been in freedom for less than a year had a reconviction rate after one year of 64 per cent. For men in the Wormwood Scrubs sample who had had some form of penal custody, but not in the year before their present sentence, the reconviction rate was 32 per cent, while the comparable figure for the Pentonville sample was 37 per cent. For completeness one should perhaps add that those men with no previous custodial experience at all have a reconviction rate of 18 per cent.

In considering the differences between those accepting and those rejecting the Apex service, clearly it is not worthwhile to continue discussing the two prison samples separately. In addition, the categories of 'partial acceptance – specific requests' and 'partial acceptance – limited interest' have been combined and the eleven men in the miscellaneous group have been disregarded. This means that, combining the two prison samples, there are 229 men in the full acceptance group, 56 in the partial acceptance group and 154 in the rejection group. We will use the abbreviations FA, PA and R to refer to the various groups. The term 'Apex groups' refers to the FA, PA and R groups.

THE SCHEDULE

The schedule was largely composed of items which were available from the prison record, or, where this was incomplete, from the Criminal Record Office. A larger number of items were coded than are discussed here. The information on the remainder was either seriously incomplete or the validity or reliability of the data was in question. As an example, the pattern of offence most characterizing a subject's behaviour seemed of possible interest, but after several attempts no code was worked out which could provide even personal reliability in the re-test situation. It must be pointed out that the items on the employment record of the subject were taken from the interview schedule. There was no thorough attempt to make any independent check on this information, although sometimes the responses were clarified by reference to information on the police record.

The following are the items which are used in this analysis:

*A. Basic items and social circumstances*
1. Age at time of sentence
2. Place of birth
3. Ethnic origin
4. Religion
5. School and education standard
6. Marital status
7. Domicile

*B. Present offence and sentence*
1. Present offence
2. Present sentence

*C. Previous criminal record*
1. Age at first conviction or finding of guilt
2. Previous convictions as an adult
3. Penal institutional experience
4. Length of criminal career
5. Period in freedom since last custody
6. Experience of probation

*D. Employment*
1. Job at time of committing last offence – how long held
2. Longest period in any one job
3. Longest period in any one job – field and level of employment
4. Time since longest job
5. Employment offences

*E. Interest in other services*

A. BASIC ITEMS AND SOCIAL CIRCUMSTANCES

*1. Age at time of sentence*
The age distribution of the FA, PA and R groups was very similar with 65·9 per cent, 67·9 per cent and 64·3 per cent of each group respectively being under 30 years of age.

*2. Place of birth*
There is a tendency for a higher proportion of men who reject (46·8 per cent) than of those who fully accept (37·4 per cent) the

Apex service to have been born in the Home Counties, but this is not statistically significant.

Although not strictly relevant to the present study, it is of interest to note the lower reconviction of those born in the West Indies compared with the rest of the sample. In Wormwood Scrubs, only 5 out of the 35* men (or 14·3 per cent) born in the West Indies were reconvicted within one year, while the rate for the total Wormwood Scrubs sample was 27·2 per cent; similarly, in Pentonville, 9 out of the 24 men (or 37·5 per cent) born in the West Indies were reconvicted within one year, while the rate for the total Pentonville sample was 52·6 per cent.

### 3. Ethnic origin

The categories used were those defined by T. and P. Morris in *Pentonville:*

> The term 'full negro' was applied to men with the normal combination of negro features, viz., hair type, nose, lips and dark skin colour. 'Mixed' negroes were those with clear indication of miscegenation in their ancestry, e.g. dark skin with Caucasian nose and lips . . . 'Levantine' were those of clear Mediterranean origin, with distinctive features, e.g. skin colour and hair type. Asians included those of mongoloid stock. . . .[4]

The judgements were made visually at the interview or by examination of the prison photographs. The distinction between 'full negro' and 'mixed negro' was particularly difficult to maintain, so these categories have been combined. There is a slight tendency for negroes to accept and Levantines to reject the Apex service, but this is not statistically significant.

### 4. Religion

There is no evidence of any significant differences in stated religious affiliation between the Apex groups.

### 5. School and education standard

This item was limited to the Wormwood Scrubs sample and was taken from the assessment made at an allocation interview by prison officials. The education standard of 22·9 per cent of the FA group (n = 105) and 27·0 per cent of the R group (n = 74) was assessed as either indifferent, poor or illiterate. Not one of the PA group was described in this way.

* There were two further men born in the West Indies whom CRO could not trace.

6. *Marital status*

The marital status recorded in the prison record may be about as misleading as the stated religion. While accepting the inevitable limitation of this source of information, this item produces the first significant difference between the groups. 49·8 per cent of the FA group, 67·9 per cent of the PA group and 53·2 per cent of the R group are described in the prison record as single. There is a significant difference between the FA and PA groups ($x^2 = 5.87$; 1 d.f.; $p < 0.05$). Assuming that the married state is indicative of some degree of social integration, this result gives some support to the impression that the men in the PA group had fewer contacts with the community, and this was further reflected in their apparently vague pre-release plans when sometimes they had no idea of even the area in which they intended to settle.

From the prison interviews it was possible to make another assessment of the marital situation at the time of sentence. It appeared that 59·4 per cent of the FA group, 45·5 per cent of the PA group and 51·0 per cent of the R group were married, had been married or at present had a reasonably stable relationship with a common-law wife. None of these differences was significant. The fact that the difference between the FA and PA groups is not significant ($x^2 = 3.53$; 1 d.f.; N.S.) suggests that some of the difference is explained by the presence of a subgroup in the PA group who had been married but now described themselves as single.

7. *Domicile*

Accommodation is the area apart from employment which most concerns the ex-prisoner.[5] It was mentioned several times by men that a more beneficial action would be to find suitable accommodation for men on release rather than for Apex to concern itself with employment.

As the possession of satisfactory accommodation could have a bearing on the interest of an employment-placing service, it would have been interesting to make some estimate of the quality of accommodation before and after release. Experience, however, suggested that it was misleading to rely too heavily on the response of the men. For example, 'flats' and 'flatlets' seemed to cover an enormous, and eventually meaningless, range of accommodation. Hence, we limited the analysis to whether a man had been living with his own family (either of birth or marriage) before his sentence and whether or not he intended to do so after release. Even the responses to this apparently straightforward question may be misleading, for some of the follow-ups after release suggested that

E

some 'family households' seemed little more than a *poste restante* address.

Approximately half the men in both the FA and R groups seemed to be living at a 'family household' at the time of sentence, while this was true of only 40 per cent of the PA group. While this marginally supports the tendency of the PA group to be more isolated from close contacts with their family, this is even more apparent when one examines release plans. Whereas 59 per cent of the FA group and 56 per cent of the R group had plans to live in a household with other members of their family, only 35 per cent of the PA group had similar ideas.

While the evidence is slender, there is some suggestion that while some in the FA and R groups had made efforts on occasions to renew contacts with their family, for some in the PA group this present sentence had tended to break even further any residual family ties.

## B. PRESENT OFFENCE AND SENTENCE

### 1. Present offence

The present offence was coded on the basis of the principal offence proved following the convention in the Criminal Statistics.[6] Unlike the Criminal Statistics, though, there was no double-counting for indictable and non-indictable offences and we just considered one principal offence for each person. The major categories of stealing and breaking and entering have almost identical proportions in the three Apex groups. There is a slight, but statistically not significant, tendency for those convicted of violence against the person or of sexual offences to reject the service. The men convicted of drug offences tended to accept the Apex service – 17 (or 7·4 per cent) in the FA group, 4 (or 7·1 per cent) in the PA group and 4 (or 2·6 per cent) in the R group. There is some indication that these fragile personalities turn to Apex in the desperate hope that the comparatively simple remedy of finding suitable employment will solve their more severe and intractable problems.

In Wormwood Scrubs, the present offence is a simple guide to the likelihood of reconviction. Only 7·8 per cent of the sexual offenders were re-convicted within one year compared with 54·2 per cent of the drug offenders. Paradoxically, in Pentonville, the drug offenders had the lowest proportion of reconvictions within one year, namely 44·4 per cent, while the greatest risks were those convicted of stealing, where there was a reconviction rate of 58·3 per cent.

## 2. Present sentence

The design of the project restricted the range of possible prison sentences. There was a slight tendency for those with sentences of over twelve months to reject the Apex service, but this was not significant.

### C. PREVIOUS CRIMINAL RECORD

#### 1. Age at first conviction or finding of guilt

It was thought that it may well be relevant to an interest in an employment-placing service to consider at what age a man had started his official criminal career. There is a slight tendency for those who accept the Apex service to be convicted earlier than those who reject the service. 67·5 per cent of the FA group, 60·7 per cent of the PA group and 58·4 per cent of the R group were first convicted before the age of 21, but none of the differences is significant.

There is, however, a significant tendency for men who were first convicted between the ages of 21 and 34 to reject the Apex service ($x^2 = 5\cdot55$; 1 d.f.; $p < 0\cdot05$). We will suggest subsequently that the more important factor is the question of previous custody and that men in the sample who had had no previous penal custody were often first convicted at this age. When those with no previous custody are disregarded, there is no longer a significant difference between the FA and R groups.

#### 2. Previous convictions as an adult

Although there was a slight tendency for the R group to have none (14·3 per cent) or one previous conviction (13·6 per cent), compared with the FA group of whom only 11·4 per cent had no previous and only 9·6 per cent one previous conviction, this difference is not significant.

#### 3. Penal institutional experience

One of the more important milestones in the process of stigmatization is whether a person has had institutional experience. In the present case we are interested in whether a person has been to a penal institution, for these may provide experience of particular problems of adjustment after release which in turn may influence the reaction to the Apex offer. Perhaps surprisingly, as many as 38·3 per cent of the total Wormwood Scrubs sample had some prior penal institutional experience. In fact, 16·3 per cent of the Wormwood Scrubs sample had been to approved school (46·8 per cent of these were reconvicted within one year), 24·1 per cent had been to borstal (45·7 per cent reconvicted) and 16·3 per cent had been to detention centre (43·5 per cent reconvicted). Fifteen men in Wormwood Scrubs had in fact been to all three young offender institutions and their reconviction rate was higher still, namely 53·5 per cent. In contrast, the men for whom there was no evidence of previous custody had the much lower reconviction rate of 18·4 per cent.

This is very relevant when one considers the response to the offer of the Apex service, for a significantly higher proportion of the men who reject the Apex service had had no previous experience of penal custody ($x^2 = 5.84$; 1 d.f.; $p < 0.05$). 29·3 per cent of the FA group, 30·4 per cent of the PA group, but 40·9 per cent of the R group had had no previous experience of custody.

This finding has two important implications. In the first place, remembering that those men who have had no previous custodial experience are less likely to be reconvicted in the future, the fact that there is a higher proportion of these men in the R group helps to explain the puzzling feature that the R group has a lower overall reconviction rate than the acceptance groups. Secondly, it begins to shatter any belief that those likely to respond to the offer of this particular type of after-care are necessarily the 'good bets'. It suggests that there is a tendency for those likely to need help the most to be those likely to accept it, but this is still far removed from the question whether the men respond favourably to the help which is offered.

After indicating that some experience of custody is a relevant feature, it is of interest to discover whether the type or amount of previous custody is a significant factor in examining the responses to the offer of the Apex service. For this part of the analysis we have disregarded the 147 men who have had no previous experience of penal custody.

There seems to be no evidence that the age when penal institutional experience began is of any significance. Similarly, the type of penal institution experienced seems to have little bearing on the response to the Apex offer, for similar proportions of the Apex groups had experienced approved school, detention centre, borstal or only imprisonment. In terms of amount of institutional experience, there is a slight indication that the PA group has a higher proportion of men with less than three years' previous penal institutional experience, and a slight tendency for the FA group to have had a higher proportion of men with three but less than six years' penal institutional experience, while the R group has a slightly higher proportion of men who have had six or more years' previous custodial experience. While none of these differences reaches statistical significance, they do support a general impression that the PA group includes more disturbed men who have recently crept into the penal circuit and are so perplexed by their whole predicament that they cannot even make a decision whether to accept or reject the offer of help from Apex. Then there appear to be those who have had a fair amount of custodial experience, more than three years but less than six, and who have decided to try to make a break from this pattern, so accounting for a higher proportion of these men among the FA group. Finally, there are those who have had a considerable amount of custodial experience, more than six years, who have given up hope, and for whom even a gesture towards rehabilitation is not worthwhile, so accounting for the higher proportion of these men among the R group.

### 4. Length of criminal career
Another way of considering which men are likely to accept a particular type of after-care is in terms of a man's criminal career. While there was nothing to suggest that a person's age at his first conviction or finding of guilt was relevant to his response to the Apex offer, this does not take into account how long ago this first event took place. For example, if two men were first convicted at the age of twenty, this fact has a somewhat different bearing if one of the men is now aged twenty-two and the other is now aged, say, fifty-two. To some extent an estimate of the length of a man's criminal career begins to consider these differences. A rough measure of the length of a man's criminal career can be calculated by subtracting a man's age at first conviction or finding of guilt from his age at the date of the present sentence.

When one considers the response to the Apex offer for those interviewed, it is interesting that a significantly high proportion of the combined FA and PA groups have a criminal career of between seven and ten years, as shown in Table 7 ($x^2 = 7.27$; 2 d.f.; $p < 0.05$).

These figures tend to support the view that there may be a watershed after a man has been criminally active for just short of a decade and that at this juncture he may be more willing to consider ways of getting out of his predicament. Of the 80 men interviewed who had a criminal career of between seven and ten years, 48 fully accepted and 14 partially accepted the Apex service while only 18 rejected it.

TABLE 7  *Response to Apex offer in terms of length of criminal career*

| Length of criminal career to date of present sentence | Full acceptance (%) | Partial acceptance (%) | Rejection (%) |
|---|---|---|---|
| Under 7 years | 42·5 | 37·5 | 50·0 |
| 7 years and under 10 years | 21·1 | 25·0 | 11·7 |
| 10 years and over | 36·4 | 37·5 | 38·3 |
| TOTAL | 100·0 | 100·0 | 100·0 |
| No. of prisoners | 228* | 56 | 154 |

* For one man in the full acceptance group there was insufficient information to calculate a length of criminal career.

### 5. Period in freedom since last custody

One measure which may be useful in attempting to estimate the success of a rehabilitation programme is to compare the length of the present period with the period in freedom before the last custody, although, of course, one may simply be measuring a period of more successful criminal activity. Of those who had previous custodial experience, 52·5 per cent of the FA group, 52·6 per cent of the PA group and 46·2 per cent of the R group had been at liberty for less than a year. Although none of these differences is significant, this is a further indication that there was a slight tendency for the FA group to contain proportionately more of the higher risk categories.

### 6. Experience of probation

Apart from periods in custody, most of the men in both samples had experienced other types of penal sanctions. In fact, nearly half (47·3 per cent) the Wormwood Scrubs sample had had some experience of probation, while this is the case with two-thirds (65·1 per cent) of the Pentonville sample. This discrepancy between the two prisons is partly explained by the presence of approximately 15 per cent in the Wormwood Scrubs sample for whom the present offence is the first conviction and partly by the fact that the Pentonville men are much older and have had more opportunity of experiencing all types of sanctions at one time or another.

One would perhaps have expected that those who had experience of probation might tend to react against another offer of support, as almost by definition they must have failed to some degree after their period on probation. In fact, the opposite is the case, for those men who have had previous experience of probation accept the Apex service to a remarkably high and significant extent. 62·0 per cent of the FA group, 58·9 per cent of the PA group, but only 44·2 per cent of the R group had had previous experience of probation. Alternatively one can say of the 245 men who had experience of probation, 142 fully accepted and 35 partially accepted the Apex service and only 68 rejected it.

Of the total interviewed, 51·7 per cent of those with previous probation experience were reconvicted within one year whereas this was the case in only 27·5 per cent of the cases with no probation experience. This apparently disturbing result simply reflects the longer criminal record of those who have had experience of probation as well as often a vast variety of other sanctions in the past, but the fact that the FA group is once again weighted towards having a higher proportion of these higher risk cases will inevitably have a bearing on the overall reconviction rates of the Apex groups.

While there is no evidence that it is the probation experience *per se* which is the important factor, it is still worth noting that former probationers tend to favour this type of further assistance. If one couples this finding with the fact that previous experience of probation seems to have little link with opting for voluntary after-care provided by the probation service, this provides tentative evidence that there is a need for a range of facilities in the after-care field which are provided by various types of organization, both statutory and voluntary. It should perhaps be regarded as encouraging that former probationers are willing to try an entirely different kind of help.

D. EMPLOYMENT

*1. Job at time of committing last offence – how long held*
Of the Wormwood Scrubs sample, 37·9 per cent stated they were unemployed at the time of the offence, compared with 61·0 per cent of the Pentonville sample. This is in agreement with Blackler's study where a significantly higher proportion of the primary recidivists than of the first sentence men were unemployed at the time of committing their present offence[7] and with Morris's work where 22·2 per cent of 'stars' and 43·5 per cent of recidivists were unemployed at the time of the offence.[8] The fact that the percentages in Dr Morris's sample are 15 per cent lower in each case

is probably explained either by the different sampling procedure or by a slight deterioration of the employment situation since her study; however, the important feature is that the ratio of unemployed 'stars' and recidivists is somewhat similar.

There are a significantly higher proportion of unemployed men who tend to accept the Apex service. 54·4 per cent, 52·8 per cent and 36·7 per cent of the FA, PA and R groups respectively were unemployed at the time of committing their last offence:

FA v. R    : $x^2 = 11·35$; 1 d.f.; $p < 0·01$
FA v. PA  : $x^2 = 0·05$; 1 d.f.; N.S.
PA v. R   : $x^2 = 4·20$; 1 d.f.; $p < 0·05$
(FA, n = 228; PA, n = 53; R, n = 150; there was no information on 8 men for this item).

In fact, whereas 42 men out of 150 (or 28·0 per cent) in the R group had been at their present job for over a year, this was the case for only 23 men out of 228 (or 10·1 per cent) in the FA group.

This is a further category where the worst risks are tending to accept the Apex service and so will have the effect on the overall reconviction rate of the various groups. Of those who were unemployed at the time of committing their last offence, 111 men out of 207 (or 53·6 per cent) were reconvicted within one year; 54 (or 36·5 per cent) out of the 148 men who stated that they had been at the job for up to one year at the time of the offence were reconvicted within one year; finally, only 8 (or 11·1 per cent) of the 72 men who maintained they had at that stage been employed at the job for over a year were similarly reconvicted. Although when using the interview technique one cannot rely too heavily on the accuracy of an individual response, there is no doubt that there is a close relationship between the recent employment record prior to custody and the subsequent reconviction pattern. When the length of time at the last job is controlled, the comparable reconviction rates of the Apex groups are very similar, although the PA group tends to emerge with slightly more favourable results.

## 2. Longest period in any one job

The longest period of employment in any one job (excluding national service but including the regular forces) was recorded. 51·4 per cent of the Wormwood Scrubs sample compared with 46·3 per cent of the Pentonville sample maintained that they had worked in at least one job for longer than two years. Although there was a significant tendency for the period to be longer for men in the R group, this rather reflects their better employment position at the time of the present offence.

*3. Longest period in any one job – field and level of employment*
The fields of employment in which men spent the longest period are almost identical for the two prison samples. In fact it is worthwhile to combine the two prison samples and indicate in order the proportion of men involved in each field. The two clear leaders are 'manufacturing and extraction firms' with 24·8 per cent and 'civil engineering and building' with 18·2 per cent. Self-employed situations of various kinds occupy third place with 9·1 per cent. The remainder are: transport work (8·6 per cent); service industries (8·2 per cent); catering industry (7·0 per cent); professional groups and public bodies (5·6 per cent); Armed Forces (4·7 per cent); Merchant Navy (4·4 per cent); shops (3·0 per cent); agricultural and fisheries (2·3 per cent); entertainment and communications (2·1 per cent); commerce and selling (1·9 per cent).

In terms of the response to the Apex offer, there is a significant tendency for the R group to have a higher proportion of men who have been in self-employed situations for their longest period in any one job ($x^2 = 6·50$; 1 d.f.; $p < 0·05$).

The important feature of these men is that they managed to be self-employed for a reasonable length of time. If one examines the response to the Apex offer in terms of those who have been self-employed at some time, there is no significant difference between the Apex groups. Although there was no specific question on this point, one can estimate from all the information available that 25 per cent of the FA group, 23 per cent of the PA group and 34 per cent of the R group could be regarded as having been self-employed at some time.

In assessing the level of occupation, those whose longest job was in the Merchant Navy, Armed Forces or in a self-employed situation have been disregarded. Of those interviewed, only three men (two in Wormwood Scrubs and one in Pentonville) could be regarded as holding high administrative or senior managerial posts as their longest job. A further five men had had inspectorial, supervisory or other higher-grade non-manual jobs (e.g. catering manager, teacher, etc.). Eleven men had had medium-grade non-manual jobs (e.g. specialized clerks, sales representatives, trainee ground surveyor). Fifty-nine men had been in skilled manual or routine grades of non-manual occupations, 130 in semi-skilled manual occupations and 143 in unskilled manual occupations.

E*

Although a higher proportion of the FA and PA groups (42·1 per cent and 41·9 per cent respectively) had their longest period in an unskilled manual occupation compared with only 35·8 per cent of the R group, there were no significant differences between any of the groups.

### 4. Time since longest job

Although the two samples have very similar proportions in terms of the various fields and levels of occupation, there are highly significant differences when one considers the time which has elapsed since working at this longest job. Whereas for only 16·7 per cent of the Wormwood Scrubs sample has six years or more elapsed, this is the case for 52·3 per cent of the Pentonville sample.

When one considers the Apex groups, for nearly a quarter (or 23·3 per cent) of the R group the longest job was the job in which they were engaged at the time of the offence, whereas only 7·1 per cent of the FA group were in this position. This difference is highly significant ($x^2 = 18·74$; 1 d.f.; $p < 0·01$).

Only 10 per cent of the R group for whom the present job was also the longest were in fact reconvicted within one year – as we shall subsequently show, some were actually able to return to the same jobs – so, once again, there is evidence that the R group had a higher proportion of low risk cases.

### 5. Employment offences

One matter of speculation is how men with a record of offences in which employers have suffered materially would regard an employment agency for discharged prisoners. One suspected that men who intended to carry on such activities would not wish their future employers to know of their criminal past.

The criminal records were inspected for offences where an employer suffered, but often there was not enough information to make a judgement – the cryptic statement 'larceny', for instance, may in fact have referred to the offence of 'larceny as a servant'. Using the available material, however, there was evidence of some abuse of trust as an employee on a past occasion by 14·8 per cent of the FA group, 7·1 per cent of the PA group and 18·1 per cent of the R group. It is clear that the FA group is not over-represented by men with a record of employment offences, even allowing for the crudity of the measure. In this context it is interesting to note that the only man in the sample placed by Apex whom the employer did subsequently suspect of taking money from a cash till had no previous record of a similar offence. As the employer did not pursue the matter, he still has not!

## E. INTEREST IN OTHER SERVICES

The present project was designed to examine the effect of finding employment for men immediately on release without being concerned directly in trying to resolve any other of the problems which often beset a discharged prisoner. In other words, it is an attempt to examine employment in isolation from other factors. However, one cannot assume simply that because Apex is not offering any additional services, the men in the sample do not receive other sorts of help (or even the same sort of help) from other sources. One can only hope to estimate the effect of one particular type of 'treatment' within the context of something *over and above* the influences ordinarily brought to bear upon a discharged prisoner. The purpose of this section is to indicate the varying interest that the Apex groups take in two of the main statutory services which participate in the after-care of discharged prisoners.

The two statutory bodies which kindly co-operated in supplying relevant information were the Department of Employment and the Probation and After-Care Service. The former offers a pre-release interview procedure by one of the D.E. officials with the purpose of speeding up the process of placing discharged prisoners after release by the appropriate local employment exchange (this procedure has been described more fully in Chapter 2). The Probation and After-Care Service, which shortly before the start of this project had taken over statutory responsibility for the after-care of all discharged prisoners, had begun a scheme by which the prison welfare officers interviewed all men before release and tried to encourage the men to opt for voluntary after-care offered by the probation service for all those who were not already obliged to have some form of statutory supervision.

The other main statutory body involved in trying to assist discharged prisoners is the Department of Health and Social Security (DHSS). Many prisoners would quite rightly and understandably regard the DHSS as the only tangible help they receive. The DHSS is concerned with material aid but, although one should not underestimate the real and potential importance of the DHSS in contributing to the satisfactory rehabilitation of the prisoner, the administration of the discharge grant system has been fairly successfully delegated to the prison authorities. The more serious question is whether the failure to peg the discharge grant to the cost-of-living index means that the effectiveness of the system is being eroded. Unless this matter is examined, the procedure will degenerate into something comparable to the days of the discharged prisoners' aid societies when the amount of money given was inadequate to do any of the things which every ex-prisoner needs on release. On the other hand, on the credit side, an impression at present is that there is no attempt to distinguish between the 'deserving' and 'undeserving' cases, as often happened with an enthusiastic case committee of a discharged prisoners' aid society.

In concentrating discussion on statutory agencies, there is a danger of overlooking the work of voluntary agencies. Pauline Morris noted that 'prisoners' wives tend to under-estimate the assistance they receive from voluntary welfare agencies, partly because they normally regard only material aid as helpful'.[9] For some voluntary agencies, work with ex-prisoners is just a proportion, sometimes a very small proportion, of their total referrals, while others concentrate exclusively on the needs of the ex-prisoner. In theory the work of the voluntary agencies is beginning to be channelled through the prison welfare office, but in practice this varies from prison to prison and from case to case.

It needs a separate study to examine all the possible influences brought to bear upon a discharged prisoner before release. However, the present section is largely concerned with the question of whether there is any indication that men who tend to accept the Apex service also tend to accept other after-care facilities to a greater extent than men who reject the Apex service or whether in fact the opposite is the case. We also wish to examine whether those who opt for voluntary after-care as well as accepting the Apex service seem to settle down any more satisfactorily than the other groups, so raising the question whether there is any possible value in a combination of the two services.

## THE PLACING SERVICE OF THE DEPARTMENT OF EMPLOYMENT

One of the points that we wish to examine is whether in general terms the same type of prisoner is attracted to the D.E. service as accepts the Apex service and, more particularly, which group is helped by the D.E. There are two possible arguments. One could maintain that the men who may be deterred by the official and statutory nature of the D.E. service may be attracted by the voluntary and rather more informal nature of the Apex service. On the other hand, one could also argue that the procedure is not the important matter, but that those who need employment on release will be attracted to both services. In examining this, we will first use information from the Wormwood Scrubs sample.

Although the difference between the treatment and control groups in terms of the numbers seen by the D.E. was not quite significant, the fact that there were approximately one-third fewer seen in the treatment group suggests that the arrival of Apex had some effect on the numbers seen by the D.E. (see Table 2, page 74).

Of the men interviewed by the research officer in Wormwood Scrubs, the D.E. also saw 23·3 per cent of the full acceptance group, 27·6 per cent of the partial acceptance group but only 15·5 per cent of the rejection group; none of these differences is significant. However, one could quite reasonably argue that, if there are fewer men who see the D.E. because of the advent of Apex (and the evidence suggests that there is a fall from 29·3 per cent to 20·8 per cent), this is because these have either fully accepted or partially accepted the Apex service: it is difficult to see how rejection of the Apex service would tend to make men not see the D.E. officer in cases where they normally would. Assuming, therefore, that in the absence of Apex, 29 per cent of the treatment group would have seen the D.E. rather than the present 21 per cent and assuming that all the additional men were in the acceptance groups, then this would produce quite a significant difference between the acceptance and rejection groups in terms of the proportions who would normally be seen by the D.E. in a pre-release interview ($x^2 = 12·47$; 1 d.f.; $p < 0·01$). ˙

If one moves from considering the proportions accepting the D.E. to the proportions placed in work by the D.E. within three months after release, we have already shown (see Table 2, page 74) that there are proportionately fewer placed in the 'treatment' group compared with the control group, for less than 2 per cent of the former group are found work by the D.E. compared with 6 per cent in the control group. The four men of the treatment group who were given a pre-discharge interview and were subsequently placed in work were all in the full acceptance group. It is possible to use a similar argument that those who would normally be placed by the D.E. were dealt with by the Apex service. In other words, using the 6 per cent of the control group as a norm, one would have normally expected that 13 out of 216 of the treatment group would be placed by the D.E., but because of the intervention of Apex, the D.E. placed only 4 men in the treatment group.

To sum up, there is no clear-cut evidence that a significantly higher proportion of the men who see the D.E. official tend also to accept the Apex service. However, if one makes some assumptions, there is a suggestion that men who normally opt to see the D.E. are more likely to accept than to reject the Apex service. There is an even stronger suggestion that the men who are actually placed in work by the D.E. come from within the category who would fully accept the Apex service. Therefore, it is fair to say that the Apex service is not helping an entirely new group of men from those who tend to opt for a pre-release interview by the D.E., but rather increasing the number in this group. One can assume that in the normal course of events in Wormwood Scrubs the D.E. would place approximately 13 men out of 216 as a direct result of the pre-discharge interview. We shall indicate later that the number Apex seems to place in work out of a random sample of 216 is 39 men (disregarding those helped in the partial acceptance group). The Apex procedure, therefore, seems to result in about three times as many men being placed in work from Wormwood Scrubs compared with the pre-release procedure of the Department of Employment. However, this rather crude comparison does not take into consideration the important and complex problem of the comparative cost of the two procedures.

When one considers the Pentonville sample, a slightly different pattern emerges. There is the same tendency for the men who opt for the Department's pre-release interview to be the ones who tend to accept the Apex service if they are given the opportunity. In fact, only one man in the Pentonville rejection group opted to see the Department of Employment before release – he was also the only man who was placed within three months by the Department as a direct consequence of the pre-release interview. With these figures in mind, Apex made a quite dramatic impact, for 26 men started in the work arranged by Apex (again disregarding those helped by Apex in the partial acceptance group). At Pentonville, of a random sample of 214, therefore, Apex can claim to have placed about 12 per cent in work, whereas it would appear that the D.E. places less than 0·5 per cent as a direct result of the pre-release interview. One should point out once again that many of the Pentonville sample may well use the offices of the D.E. after release, but this is not the question at issue, for we have been concerned in the present project with considering the value of making pre-release arrangements. On present evidence, it would appear that the Apex procedure is considerably more effective than the D.E. in dealing with men being released from Pentonville. The turnover at Pentonville is many times more rapid than the turnover at Wormwood Scrubs, and the potential market in terms of numbers is obviously much larger at Pentonville, but the D.E. seems to apportion a similar amount of resources to each prison. This is the reason which may well explain the apparent discrepancy between Wormwood Scrubs and Pentonville. Using the Apex experience, which indicates that the percentage who start work falls from 18 per cent of a random sample at Wormwood Scrubs to 12 per cent of a random sample at Pentonville, this would suggest that the D.E. must raise the percentage placed from Pentonville as a result of the pre-discharge interview to 4 per cent to compare with the present figure of 6 per cent at Wormwood Scrubs.

## VOLUNTARY AFTER-CARE BY THE PROBATION AND AFTER-CARE SERVICE

The body which now has the statutory responsibility of concerning itself with the after-care of discharged prisoners is the Probation and After-Care Department. It is difficult to describe in a few sentences the more comprehensive facilities that the probation service is trying to develop, but there is certainly a clear distinction from the very specific service of employment-placing offered by Apex Trust. The present report, however, is not concerned with an evaluation or even a description of the work of the probation service. Anyway, it would be particularly inappropriate to consider the working of the prison welfare department during the period of the project, for the probation service had only recently taken up the responsibility for administering this aspect of after-care. We are interested in the specific question of the extent to which the same men who opt for voluntary after-care also accepted the Apex service. We wish in addition to examine whether the men who opt for voluntary after-care have any significantly different characteristics from those who do not opt for voluntary after-care.

The effectiveness of the welfare department will naturally vary, sometimes quite dramatically, from prison to prison. Even when exact standards are laid down, there will still be variations within certain limits, often as a result of the varying enthusiasm and ability of the staff. While the Trust was working in Wormwood Scrubs we were fortunate that two active and able welfare officers were responsible for the hall in which we were working. They understood how the Apex project was designed and accepted the fact that they were unable to refer to the project men who had not been selected by the random sampling procedure. As they were seeing the majority of men for the first time at a pre-discharge interview held a few weeks after the men had decided whether or not to accept the Apex service, there was little possibility of their own views having any direct effect on the responses to the Apex offer. The research officer submitted a list periodically to the welfare department, giving the names of the men we were trying to help and of those who had rejected the offer. If the matter arose subsequently during their own pre-discharge interview, the welfare officers probably just tried to encourage the men to make use of any employment opportunity being offered. There seemed to be a perfectly satisfactory relationship between Apex and the welfare department although there was fairly minimal face-to-face contact. The arrangement probably worked well because from the outset the welfare department and Apex Trust seemed to understand clearly and accept each other's role. There were no demarcation disputes and the only question is whether closer communication would perhaps have been more beneficial to the men in planning their discharge from prison. There was one case where Apex was arranging work in one area of London, while the welfare officer was arranging accommodation in another area, simply because the prisoner concerned gave two different versions of his release plans.

At the time of the present study, there were six welfare officers in Pentonville who were dealing with the total prison intake. As the number interviewed by Apex was only a small minority of the total receptions, our work had less impact on the daily routine of these officers, for during the year we interviewed only between 30 and 40 men in whom one particular welfare officer was interested. However, it is pleasant to record that the administrative arrangement of informing the welfare department of the response of each man interviewed to the offer of the Apex service worked equally well in Pentonville. The present information on the response to the offer of voluntary after-care, however, is confined to the Wormwood Scrubs sample because there was no comparable data available in the Pentonville files.

While we have suggested that there was little opportunity for the welfare department to influence the responses of the men to the offer of the Apex service, it is still conceivable that men interviewed by the research officer of Apex might make a different response to the offer of voluntary after-care as a result of the Apex interview. It is possible that men who had accepted the Apex service might be encouraged to go the whole hog and opt for voluntary after-care when in normal circumstances they would not even have considered the matter; alternatively, one could argue that men who would perhaps opt for voluntary after-care simply in the hope that a probation officer could help with finding employment on release would no longer be interested when the offer of Apex answered this need. These possibilities can be examined by comparing the 'treatment' group (men interviewed by the research officer) and the control group (men not interviewed). Of the total Wormwood Scrubs sample, a total of 125 men (32·7 per cent) opted for voluntary after-care, 192 men (50·3 per cent) did not opt for voluntary after-care, a further 47 men (12·3 per cent) were under some form of compulsory supervision after release, and there was no information on the remaining 18 men (4·7 per cent). Disregarding those under statutory supervision (i.e. still on borstal licence, Y.P. licence or continuing a probation order after release) and those for whom there is no information, 39·2 per cent of the treatment group and 39·7 per cent of the control group opted for voluntary after-care after release. Quite clearly, for the Wormwood Scrubs sample at least, the arrival of Apex on the scene did not have any effect either one way or the other on the numbers who opted for voluntary after-care. This is in contrast to the tendency (which, though, was not statistically significant) for some of those interviewed by Apex not to accept the similar service offered by the Department of Employment.

The next step is to discover whether there is any difference in the proportion who opted for voluntary after-care in relation to their response to the Apex offer. Table 8 indicates that a significantly higher proportion of those who fully accept the Apex service also opt for voluntary after-care ($x^2 = 6·23$; 1 d.f.; $p < 0·05$. For this calculation, those men under statutory supervision were disregarded).

While Table 8 shows that compared with the rejection group a significantly high proportion of those who accept the Apex service also opt for voluntary after-care, one must emphasize that there is still a sizeable group (in fact, over half of those who have any choice in the matter) of the acceptance group who did not opt for voluntary after-care.

In other words, there are at least two points which should be recognized. Firstly, there is evidence that a significantly high proportion of those who accept one kind of service are also likely to accept any other offers of help as well. By offering further types of assistance one is partly widening the range of prisoners attracted into the sphere of after-care, but at the same time making a somewhat more comprehensive provision for the others who would also accept whatever else is available. This leads on to the further point of how difficult it is to assess what actually may be helping in a particular situation. While the Apex project was designed to try to demonstrate the effect of finding employment on release

TABLE 8  *Comparison of the Apex groups in the Wormwood Scrubs sample in terms of opting for voluntary after-care*

|  | Full acceptance (%) | Partial acceptance (%) | Rejection (%) | Total (%) |
|---|---|---|---|---|
| Yes – opted for voluntary after-care | 39·3 | 23·1 | 25·3 | 32·0 |
| No – did not opt for voluntary after-care | 41·1 | 57·7 | 59·8 | 50·2 |
| Statutory supervision – borstal licence | 8·0 | 7·7 | 4·6 | 6·7 |
| – y.p. licence | 0·9 | 3·8 | 1·1 | 1·3 |
| – probation | 5·4 | 3·8 | 4·6 | 4·9 |
| No information | 5·4 | 3·8 | 4·6 | 4·9 |
| TOTAL | 100·0 | 100·0 | 100·0 | 100·0 |
| No. of prisoners | 112 | 26 | 87 | 225* |

* The two men in the Miscellaneous group have been disregarded.

without offering other types of support after release, one must acknowledge that the men Apex tried to help do not live in a vacuum and are in fact assisted in other or even similar ways by other agencies. Within the present research design it is impossible to assess very accurately whether these other facilities had any effect on the Apex service, but the fact that there was no attempt to co-ordinate with the efforts of other agencies probably meant that the project came fairly close to examining the effect of finding em-ployment for men immediately on release *over and above* the various other influences ordinarily brought to bear upon a dis-charged prisoner. On the other hand, one must recognize in this sort of situation that a favourable outcome in a particular case might still be the result of an interaction with one of these other influences rather than the effect of finding employment in isolation. Sometimes one suspected that this is what in fact happened, for when in one case a probation officer advanced a loan for a man to secure suitable accommodation one's impression after the event was that the probation officer had been inclined to do this because he knew that his client had started work and financial assistance seemed useful and meaningful in a context when the employer held two weeks' money in hand. Normally one considers in experiments of this kind whether there is the possibility of a 'Hawthorne effect' whereby participants in an experiment perform more efficiently simply because they are in an experiment. Unfortunately, there were no significant differences between the treatment and control groups, so there was no necessity to consider this possible explanation. However, there is a variation of the 'Hawthorne effect' of which one should also be aware, for an impression was that the Apex project had a most favourable effect on other workers who were also trying to assist the participants in the Apex experiment. It should not be regarded as a cynical conclusion if one begins to wonder whether the Apex project may have helped after-care workers rather more than the participants in the experiment. Without pressing the analogy too far, prison after-care may have at least one similarity to the treatment of cancer. It is easy for the feeling to intrude that everything is lost and that so much more could have been done for the patient at an earlier stage. One suspects that staff morale could get very low in dealing with terminal cancer cases, but the perseverance of research has the dual purpose of providing the opportunity for a breakthrough and demonstrating to the staff that there is still public interest in their work. While in so many other ways the 'cancer model' is most inappropriate, there seems to be the same desperate desire on the part of both workers and clients for research to provide an answer and the same feeling of hopelessness about the likelihood of success.

## FURTHER DISCUSSION ON THE ACCEPTANCE AND REJECTION GROUPS

Acceptance of a service is clearly one large step towards the service fulfilling its stated function, for it needs an elaborate explanation to indicate how those rejecting a service can be substantially helped by the service in question. As a result it would be ideal if one could identify accurately the group who accept a particular service, for apart from the possibility of producing a more appropriate control group to assess the effectiveness of this approach, it would also obviously isolate those who reject the service and one could begin to consider whether there were alternative ways by which this latter group might be helped.

Although the analysis has shown that there are some significant differences between the acceptance and rejection groups on some of the dimensions examined, it is not possible to state definitely that men with certain characteristics will almost always accept the service while men who have another set of characteristics will almost invariably reject the Apex service. Even if one considers, for example, the group of 54 men for whom the job at the time of committing their last offence was also their longest job ever (note that there was a highly significant proportion of these men in the R group compared with the FA group), it is by no means clear-cut that they all reject the Apex service. While 31 men in this group did so, 15 men fully accepted the Apex service and a further 8 men partially accepted. The other significant differences between the groups could be considered as even less helpful in deciding categorically whether a particular individual is likely to accept or reject the offer of the Apex service.

Much of this problem is undoubtedly the result of the bluntness of the chosen instruments. We have not, for instance, tried to demonstrate how far the acceptance or rejection of the service is due to a prisoner's personality structure. However, some of the bluntness may be overcome by going beyond the simple dichotomy of, say, employed or unemployed at the time of the offence. For example, if one examines those employed at the time of the offence* in terms of how long they had held the job, the proportion accepting the Apex service progressively falls as the period in that job increases. The high point of acceptance comes from those who are actually unemployed at the time of the offence, of whom 73·4 per cent (n = 207) accept the Apex service. Those for whom the job at the time of the offence was up to and including six months had an acceptance rate of 69·1 per cent (n = 110); over six months and up to one year, an acceptance rate of 50 per cent (n = 38). Over one year and up to four years, there was still an acceptance rate of exactly 50 per cent (n = 52); over four years, the acceptance rate fell to 30 per cent (n = 20).

Another approach is to try to improve the discrimination between the acceptance and rejection groups by combining several of the factors which indicated a significant difference between the groups. For ease of presentation, the analysis will be limited to only three

---

* There were 8 men for whom there was incomplete information on one of the items for the subsequent analysis and a further 4 men could not be traced by CRO. These men have been disregarded in the subsequent analysis. The FA and PA groups have been combined and this analysis concerns 279 men in the acceptance group and 148 in the rejection group.

of these items, namely, previous experience of custody, previous experience of probation, and employment at the time of the last offence. To simplify the matter further, we will consider the items only in terms of simple dichotomies although we have seen above that a refinement of these items, such as the length of time at the last job, may well be worthwhile. In fact the three items were chosen mainly because one could produce straightforward and understandable dichotomies, and, furthermore, the information is virtually complete on these items.

## 1. Characteristics of those who accept the Apex service

The present exercise is concerned with estimating the extent to which combining the items is helpful in compiling a profile of the person likely to accept and the person likely to reject the Apex service. Table 9 lists the eight possible combinations of the three items we are considering and places them in an ascending order in terms of the acceptance rate.

TABLE 9    *Acceptance or rejection of Apex service in terms of a combination of the items*

| Combination of items | No. who accepted Apex service | No. who rejected Apex service | Acceptance rate* |
|---|---|---|---|
| A. No custody – no probation – employed | 34 | 42 | 44·7 |
| B. Custody – no probation – employed | 19 | 18 | 51·4 |
| C. No custody – probation – unemployed | 12 | 8 | 60·0 |
| D. Custody – probation – employed | 57 | 31 | 64·8 |
| E. Custody – no probation – unemployed | 35 | 15 | 70·0 |
| F. No custody – no probation – unemployed | 19 | 8 | 70·4 |
| G. Custody – probation – unemployed | 86 | 24 | 78·2 |
| H. No custody – probation – employed | 17 | 2 | 89·5 |

* The acceptance rate is the percentage of the total in a group who accepted the Apex service.

At first glance Table 9 would appear to show a somewhat random result, but closer examination reveals an almost consistent internal logic. Holding the items of probation and employed constant, the factor of previous custody raises the acceptance rate on two occasions (A and B, C and G), makes no difference on one occasion

(E and F) and actually lowers it on another occasion (D and H). Holding the items of custody and employed constant, the factor of previous probation experience raises the acceptance rate on three occasions (A and H, B and D, E and G) but lowers it on another (C and F). Finally, holding the items of custody and probation experience constant, the factor of unemployment at time of offence raises the acceptance rate on three occasions (A and F, B and E, D and G) and lowers it on another (C and H). In each case, it is either combination C or combination H which seems to destroy a simple pattern, so any explanation must try to accommodate these apparent anomalies.

Disregarding the two combinations of C and H for a moment, one can indicate something of a profile of men who tend to accept and men who tend to reject the Apex service. If one assumes that probation experience is shorthand for experience of non-custodial sanctions and that being employed at the time of offence suggests a better employment record (this is a fair assumption when one considers present job time and longest period ever in a job), one can perhaps generalize along the following lines. Men who have never had previous experience of custody and in fact have had few, if any, previous non-custodial sentences and were also employed at the time of the offence will more often than not tend to reject the Apex service. If one goes further and adds a fourth item, namely when the job at the time of the offence is also the longest job ever held, the acceptance rate falls even lower to 32 per cent (n = 25). One could suggest that all these men are likely to have more roots in the community, for they have had little or no previous disruption to their lives on account of criminal activities. We will indicate when we discuss the rejection group that many of these were quite justified in rejecting the offer of an employment-placing service as they had already made satisfactory arrangements regarding employment on release.

In contrast, men who tended to accept the Apex service had had previous experience of custody and previous non-custodial sentences and were unemployed at the time of committing their present offence.

It is important to emphasize, in preparation for the next section, that the most typical characteristics of the rejection group outlined above contain all the assets when considering likelihood of reconviction – no previous custody, few (if any) previous convictions and being employed at time of offence – whereas the most typical acceptance group had all the liabilities in predicting likelihood of reconviction – namely, previous custody, previous convictions and unemployed. In other words, if one compares the reconviction rates of the two groups, these factors should be taken into account by a form of weighting system.

Finally, one must consider the apparently anomalous group of C (no custody; probation; unemployed) and H (no custody; probation; employed) where one might perhaps have expected their acceptance rates to be reversed. While one must acknowledge that the numbers are small and that the explanation is extremely speculative, it is important to note that the difference between the two combinations is whether the person is employed at the time of the offence, for otherwise both groups have had no previous custody and are probation-failures. It may be reasonable to suggest that combination H contains probation-failures who have been trying (i.e. employed at time of offence) and are willing to try again (i.e. accept the Apex service), while combination C contains a higher proportion of men who reject the Apex service because they are already committed to a criminal career. This latter point will be pursued in the next chapter which discusses the rejection group in greater detail, for we will then suggest that the rejection group dichotomizes into two groups – those who probably intend to take normal employment after release and have made some arrangements to do so and those who probably intend to follow a criminal career and have made no arrangements about normal employment.

*2. Readjustment of the reconviction rates of the acceptance and rejection groups*

Using the eight possible combinations, Table 9 has already shown that the most frequent combination for the acceptance group is 'custody; probation; unemployed' (i.e. combination G), which is the highest risk group in terms of reconviction, and the most frequent combination for the rejection group is 'no custody; no probation; employed' (i.e. combination A). If one takes the eight combinations in turn and computes the reconviction rate for the acceptance and rejection groups separately, it would be reasonable to assume that the reconviction rates of the two groups would be comparable for each combination. However, Table 10 shows that this is not the case – for combinations A and B the reconviction rates are virtually identical, for combinations C and D the reconviction rates of the rejection group are markedly better, and for combinations E, F, G and H the reverse is the case and the reconviction rates of the acceptance group are markedly superior. It is clear that one must consider not only the different proportions of the acceptance and rejection groups in the various combinations but also the difference of performance of the groups within each combination.

One way of eliminating the importance of the varying proportions of the acceptance and rejection groups in each combination is to

TABLE 10   *Reconviction rates of the acceptance and rejection groups by each combination of items*

| Combination* | No. | Acceptance group No. of reconvictions | (%) reconvicted | No. | Rejection group No. of reconvictions | (%) reconvicted |
|---|---|---|---|---|---|---|
| A | 34 | 2 | 5·9 | 42 | 2 | 4·8 |
| B | 19 | 7 | 36·8 | 18 | 7 | 38·9 |
| C | 12 | 7 | 58·3 | 8 | 3 | 37·5 |
| D | 57 | 28 | 49·1 | 31 | 13 | 41·9 |
| E | 35 | 16 | 45·7 | 15 | 9 | 60·0 |
| F | 19 | 5 | 26·3 | 8 | 4 | 50·0 |
| G | 86 | 50 | 58·1 | 24 | 17 | 70·8 |
| H | 17 | 1 | 5·9 | 2 | 2 | 100·0 |
| TOTAL | 279 | 116 | 41·6 | 148 | 57 | 38·5 |

\* For full list of combinations, see Table 9.

assume that each combination has equal numbers from the acceptance and rejection groups. By retaining the original proportion who were reconvicted within each cell, one can begin to see more clearly that the apparently higher reconviction rate of the acceptance group compared with the rejection group (see Chapter 5) is simply a reflection of the fact that a higher number of the poorer risks accept the Apex service.

Re-calculating the acceptance group on this basis and assuming a unit of 100 men in each cell would result in an overall reconviction rate of 35·8 per cent while re-calculating the rejection group in a similar manner would result in an overall reconviction rate of 50·5 per cent. While this quite dramatically reverses the earlier, rather surprising, suggestion that the rejection group seemed to do somewhat more favourably than the acceptance group after release, at least in terms of reconviction, and shows that when the different characteristics of the two groups are taken into account the opposite is probably the case, one is reluctant to pursue the argument too far as the actual numbers in some of the cells are rather small. To counter this quite reasonable argument, one can indicate what seems to be happening by taking just one of the items. Table 11 takes the simple dichotomy of employed or unemployed at the time of committing their present offence and then calculates the reconviction rate for the acceptance and rejection groups in terms of this item.

TABLE 11 *Reconviction rates of the acceptance and rejection groups in terms of employment at time of offence*

|  | Acceptance group | | | Rejection group | | | Acceptance rates (%) |
|---|---|---|---|---|---|---|---|
|  | No. | No. re-convicted | (%) re-convicted | No. | No. re-convicted | (%) re-convicted | |
| Employed | 127 | 38 | 29·9 | 93 | 24 | 25·8 | 57·7 |
| Unemployed | 152 | 78 | 51·3 | 55 | 33 | 60·0 | 73·4 |
| TOTAL | 279 | 116 | 41·6 | 148 | 57 | 38·5 | 65·3 |

Well over half of the men in the acceptance group compared with just over a third of the men in the rejection group were *unemployed*. These men are generally poor risks in terms of re-conviction and the acceptance group is heavily weighted with these potentially poor risks. However, what should not pass unnoticed is that the members of the acceptance group perform somewhat better after release in terms of reconviction. In contrast, for those *employed* at the time of the offence (and among the rejection group there are proportionately more of these men), the men in the rejection group perform marginally better after release.

What this begins to indicate is that we should perhaps be much more sensitive to the context within which a particular response to an offer of help is made.* When the acceptance rate of a particular group is comparatively low, the reconviction rates of the acceptance and rejection groups are either virtually identical or show a slight tendency for the rejection group to have a lower reconviction rate (this is the case in Table 11 for those employed where the acceptance rate is 57·7 per cent), so suggesting that the rejection group has a higher proportion of men who have more competently arranged their affairs after release – possibly these men rejected the Apex service because they had already arranged

* This is developed a little more fully in the Ph.D. thesis (University of London) 1971, but it is too detailed to reproduce here.

their employment plans after release. As the acceptance rate rises, this almost certainly reflects the fact that a much lower proportion of men are able or willing to help themselves satisfactorily after release. The corollary to this is that those who reject the service from a group with a generally high acceptance rate perhaps tend to be those who are more definitely set upon a criminal career and this becomes reflected in a higher reconviction rate (this is the case in Table 11 for those previously unemployed where the reconviction rate and the acceptance rate are comparatively high, and the rejection group perform somewhat less well after release). It is more likely that the lower reconviction rate for these members of the acceptance group reflects the fact that they had a more constructive attitude on release compared with the appropriate rejection group rather than the attractive possibility that the Apex service particularly helped these groups. If it had been the case that the Apex service had substantially helped in these cases, this should have been reflected at least to some extent in a slightly lower reconviction rate in the treatment group compared with the control group, but there was no evidence that this happened.

Men of particular interest are those in the rejection group when the acceptance rate is at its highest. In the present case this was the combination of 'no previous custody, previous experience of probation, and employed at the time of the offence' when all but two men accepted the Apex service in this category (see combination H, Table 9). We have already indicated that both men in this combination of items who rejected the Apex service were in fact reconvicted. Both these men had had quite remarkable criminal careers in managing to avoid previous custodial sentences, although they had suffered various other penal sanctions including probation. One was serving a nine-month sentence for 'demanding money with menaces and malicious damage' and was reconvicted for an 'assault occasioning actual bodily harm'. The other was serving a sentence for 'stealing lead fixtures from the roof of a warehouse' and an 'assault occasioning actual bodily harm', and within a year he was reconvicted on three separate occasions. The second offence within two months of release was another 'assault occasioning actual bodily harm', and the brief offence description simply says that he 'kicked employer in his private parts after being dismissed from his job'. The director of Apex should perhaps be rather grateful that he preferred to find his own work on release rather than accept the Apex service, for one cannot retain the sympathy of employers for long with that type of outcome!

SUMMARY

Although men who accept the Apex service seem *prima facie* to have a poorer reconviction record compared with men who reject the Apex service (41·6 per cent of the former group compared with only 38·5 per cent of the latter group were reconvicted within the first year after release), the analysis in this chapter suggests that this difference is explained by the fact that the acceptance group has a higher proportion of poor risks than the rejection group. However, when factors such as previous criminality and previous employment history are taken into account, there is evidence to suggest that overall the acceptance group performs more favourably than the rejection group. Naturally, though, this does not indicate that the Apex service was having a beneficial effect on the acceptance group, for otherwise this would have been reflected to some extent when the treatment and control groups were compared in Chapter 5.

Further analysis suggests that the relationship in terms of reconviction rates between the acceptance and rejection groups is somewhat more complex. It would appear that when there is a category where a comparatively low proportion of men accept the Apex service, *ceteris paribus* there is very little difference between the reconviction rates of the acceptance and rejection groups. However, when the acceptance rate of a category rises to around 60 per cent, *ceteris paribus* men in the acceptance group seem to be somewhat more vulnerable in terms of subsequent reconviction. This may perhaps indicate that men who are rejecting the service are doing so for the sound reason that they have organized their own employment plans satisfactorily. On the other hand, when the acceptance rate rises to 70 per cent and above, *ceteris paribus* men in the acceptance group seem to perform comparatively better in reconviction terms than the men in the rejection group. This finding perhaps suggests that very few of the men in these categories have much arranged on release (so accounting for the high acceptance rate) and that those who reject the service are doing so for the less commendable reason of intending to follow a criminal career (so accounting for the comparatively high reconviction rate of these men). This interpretation is put forward in the hope of encouraging a more sophisticated consideration of the context in which a person accepts or rejects a particular service. The present analysis suggests that on some occasions acceptance of a service may indicate a comparatively good prognosis (probably regardless of the effectiveness of the service offered), while on other occasions acceptance may indicate a comparatively poor prognosis.

## REFERENCES

1 Morris, P., op. cit. (1965), pp. 53–4.
2 *Statement by the Prison Commissioners of the Action which has been taken up to January 1898 to carry out the Recommendations in the Report of the Departmental Committee on Prisons, 1895* (C. 8790, 1898), p. 15.
3 The Gladstone Committee (1895), p. 29.
4 Morris, T., and Morris, P., *Pentonville*, Routledge and Kegan Paul, London (1963), p. 63.
5 *Report of the Advisory Council on the Treatment of Offenders. The After-Care and Supervision of Discharged Prisoners*, London, HMSO (1958), p. 27.
6 *Criminal Statistics, England and Wales*, London, HMSO, Cmd. 4398 (1969), p. ix, para. 6.
7 Blackler, C., 'Primary recidivism in adult men: differences between men on first and second prison sentence', *British Journal of Criminology*, 8 (1968), p. 142.
8 Morris, P., op. cit. (1965), p. 47.
9 Morris, P., op. cit. (1965), p. 300.

## CHAPTER 7

# Employment Plans of Those Who Rejected the Offer of the Apex Service

Before launching into a full discussion of the outcome of the Apex service for those who accepted the offer, it is worthwhile to make one final digression. When one is describing or even evaluating a particular service, a familiar pattern is to concentrate exclusively on the men who accepted the service and neglect the men who rejected the service. Sometimes too-ready assumptions are made that men who refuse to be involved in a new and glittering project have obviously poor prognoses because they are 'uncooperative' and so clearly represent the 'hard core' of recidivists or potential recidivists. It is perhaps too much of a bitter pill to consider that some men may not be in need of the universal panacea that one is introducing so enthusiastically. To some extent this happened with the present project, for the study was designed on the assumption that the vast majority of men would accept this seemingly wonderful offer of trying to find a suitable interview on release, and so it was something of a surprise to discover that over one-third of the men interviewed had no interest whatsoever in the wares which were being offered. An initial feeling of disappointment that men could be so foolish as to reject a possible opportunity to settle down in work after release soon gave way to an interest in whether or not these men were justified in rejecting an offer which *prima facie* was so reasonable. A further incentive to gather information on the rejection group was the realization that men who reject offers of help from statutory or voluntary agencies are the men we probably know least about. Unfortunately the resources available gave no opportunity to make much more than a foray into the subject of how the plans of these men seemed to work out after release without the help of the Apex service.

When a new and specific service is introduced, it is reasonable to consider whether men are rejecting it because there is an existing arrangement which retains their loyalty. In the present context, the obvious possibility is that the men who reject the Apex service tend to rely on the Department of Employment to a greater extent. However, only 9 per cent of those who rejected the Apex service saw the Department's placing officer before release and, almost paradoxically, it is the men who accept the Apex service who still tend to opt to see the Department of Employment before release to a greater extent than men who reject the service. Clearly, therefore, to establish reasons for rejecting the Apex service we have to probe further than the simple explanation that the statutory body is solving all employment problems on release.

It is important to point out that all the men were of course entitled to contact their local employment exchange after release even if they had not attended a pre-discharge interview, but, although there is no definite information on this matter, a general impression was that this was rarely a part of their intended programme at the time of their release.

Apart possibly from the discharge grants made to appropriate discharged prisoners, one suspects that the majority of the men in the rejection group are not in fact interested in any of the few facilities which are being offered to ex-prisoners. This often produces on the part of administrators and social workers a range of reactions from dismay to feelings of resignation about the hopelessness of the situation. Sometimes figures which seem to indicate an apparent apathy among prisoners towards what is available serve only as a basis for further promotional activities to get more widespread use of facilities which simply may not be appropriate. Before getting too concerned about and aggressive towards individuals who reject what is available 'for their good', we should consider whether they are quite so in need of these services as we sometimes imagine. To use a more medical term, perhaps there is a category which can be documented as 'spontaneous recovery'.

The view that noting rejection of a helping service is a good way of finding out the villains can be refuted by an examination of the reconviction figures of the various groups in the project. As we have seen, for the Wormwood Scrubs sample, the similarity between those who fully accepted the Apex service and those who rejected it is quite remarkable, for slightly over a quarter of the men in both groups were reconvicted within one year of release. For the Pentonville sample, the situation is very similar except that in both groups over half the men were reconvicted within one year.

Such a similarity is perhaps even more difficult to explain than a difference between the groups – whatever the direction of the difference! The similarity of the reconviction figures cannot be explained by the straightforward assertion that the men in the various groups share similar background characteristics, for we have already demonstrated that the men who rejected the offer of the Apex service after an interview in prison have as a group certain significantly different characteristics compared with the men who accepted the Apex service. For example, a significantly higher proportion of the rejection group had had no previous experience of custody and a similarly significant proportion were in some sort of employment at the time of the offence. On the other hand, within the rejection group there is still an extensive range on each dimension. Although a significantly lower proportion of men in the rejection group had no previous experience of custody before the present sentence, it is as well to remember that there were still nearly sixty per cent of the men who had. In a similar way, there were still over one-third of the rejection group who were in fact unemployed at the time of the offence, although this was much lower than the proportion unemployed in the full acceptance group. This leads one to consider whether it is possible to analyze the rejection group into more meaningful subgroups, for certainly on a common-sense level it is likely that men will reject an employment-placing service for a wide variety of reasons. In fact, we have already hinted that different reasons for rejecting the Apex service may well be a contributory explanation of some of the different reconviction rates we encountered in the last chapter. One could contrast men who are not interested because they have already arranged to return to their previous employer with men who are not interested because they may seriously intend to pursue a life of crime. A sexual offender in the Wormwood Scrubs sample who was serving a sentence for his first offence had already arranged with the employer that he was able to return to the same bench where he had been working for the past twenty years and for this reason pointed out that he had no need to use the Apex service. On the other hand, the young man of twenty-one who had graduated through approved school, borstal and dentention centre may spend most of the interview explaining that he is serving this prison sentence on account of one careless slip and when the question of future employment plans is raised he emphasizes confidently that he is always able to find his own work.

This chapter attempts to examine the reasons men gave for rejecting the Apex service and to relate this where possible to the outcome after release. There are two types of discrepancy likely to occur when comparing stated plans and actual outcome. In the first place, men might deliberately attempt to mislead or give a false impression of their plans after release. One suspects that this type of information is given in particular when the respondent feels he is forced to give some sort of 'suitable' reply. In this study, however, the reasons were given with little or no prompting, and if there was any reluctance, then the matter was not pursued and the respondent was coded as being 'reluctant to discuss employment plans'. On the other hand, there are certain responses which one suspects are a statement of hopes and aspirations rather than representing any planned activity; in particular one should perhaps regard with caution any plans to arrange one's own work in a sub-contracting field or to become self-employed. However, the general impression was that even the most outlandish plans were probably believed at some level by the men concerned and were rarely attempts simply to mislead the research officer.

The second type of discrepancy is when the plans so carefully or carelessly thought out while in prison fail to mature after release. There is little doubt that a successful outcome is largely a function of how carefully the plans were formulated before release, but there is some evidence that, in the words of Robert Burns, 'the best laid schemes o' mice an' men gang aft a-gley'. As we shall note in a later chapter, less than 10 per cent of the rejection group contacted Apex after release for assistance and it is difficult to estimate the extent to which the remainder fulfilled their original plans. However, the one measure that we can apply to all men is whether or not they were reconvicted within one year after release and this is at least an indication of whether there is a possible relationship between their stated employment plans and subsequent reconviction.

EMPLOYMENT PLANS AFTER RELEASE

There were a total of 87 men in the Wormwood Scrubs sample and a further 67 men in the Pentonville sample who seemed to reject outright the offer of any help from Apex with regard to finding employment after release. Although eleven of these men refused to be interviewed by the research officer of Apex, four of them did indicate to a prison officer or a prison welfare officer what they intended to do after release, so these are included in the present analysis.

Table 12 gives an assessment of the employment plans after release of the men who rejected the offer of the Apex service in the two prisons. It indicates that approximately one in five of the

TABLE 12   *The reconviction rates of the rejection group in terms of the various categories of employment plans after release*

| Group | Employment plans after release | Wormwood Scrubs No. | Wormwood Scrubs (%) reconvicted | Pentonville No. | Pentonville (%) reconvicted | Total No. | Total (%) reconvicted |
|---|---|---|---|---|---|---|---|
| A | Intends to start government training course or college course | 3 | 0 | 2 | 0 | 5 | 0 |
| B | Believes that he will be re-employed by former employer | 21 | 9·5 | 8 | 37·5 | 29 | 17·2 |
| C | Plans to work in relative's or friend's business | 9 | 33·3 | 3 | 33·3 | 12 | 33·3 |
| C | Intends to be self-employed | 15* | 21·4 | 8 | 50·0 | 23 | 31·8 |
| C | Plans to arrange own work in sub-contracting field | 3 | 0 | — | — | 3 | 0 |
| D | Relatives/friends arranging to find work | 3 | 66·7 | 1 | 0 | 4 | 50·0 |
| D | Plans to get specific type of job (skilled or semi-skilled work) | 7* | 16·7 | 10 | 60·0 | 17 | 43·8 |
| D | Confident of finding own work (unskilled or type of work not stated) | 14 | 35·7 | 13 | 53·8 | 27 | 44·4 |
| D | Intends to rely on Dept of Employment | 1 | 100·0 | 1 | 100·0 | 2 | 100·0 |
| E | Reluctant to discuss employment plans/no plans | 11 | 54·5 | 14 | 64·3 | 25 | 60·0 |
| F | No information | — | — | 7 | 85·7 | 7 | 85·7 |
| | TOTAL | 87 | 27·1 | 67 | 55·2 | 154 | 39·5 |

* There was one man in each of these categories for whom there was no reconviction information, so the reconviction rate has been calculated on the reduced total.

F

rejection group had plans to return to their last employment. Sometimes, though, no definite decision had been reached as to whether this was in fact possible at the time of the Apex prison interview, but in all cases there seemed a reasonable possibility that the employer would allow the respondent to return. This category also includes two men who had arranged to return to a job on a full-time basis where previously they had been working on a part-time basis as barmen.

A further 20 per cent stated that they intended to become self-employed or to arrange their own work as sub-contractors. These men implied that they were using their own initiative to set up businesses although the proposed structure was almost invariably a travesty of the term 'business'. Although in fact there was a certain similarity in the type of business involved for the twelve men who stated that they were entering either a friend's or a relative's business, these are considered as a further category, for none of these men were planning to set up something on their own initiative.

Apart from the small group who were intending to start a government training course or to attend a full-time educational course, the remainder were divided among those who had specific job plans, those who were confident that they would have no difficulty in finding work but appeared to have no particular job in mind, and those who were reluctant to discuss employment plans or had no plans whatsoever about finding employment.

Specific job plans usually refer to a particular skill or experience for which the men believe there would be enough demand in the market situation for there to be no need of an employment agency to act as intermediary. In certain skilled occupations this is a very reasonable belief, and, assuming that the gap in their employment record is not too long, then it is most unlikely that any reference to their present period in prison would be made. Similarly, there are certain areas in the unskilled field where, as Dr Martin has pointed out,[1] there is a practice on the part of employers of deliberately asking no questions about a man's past. Many of the men who stated that finding employment had never been a problem were clearly aware of this market situation and were quite realistically facing the future. In contrast, though, the category who stated that they were reluctant to discuss their employment plans had probably not formulated any plans at all.

These assessments of the employment plans after release of the rejection group were made at the time of the prison interview and it is interesting to consider whether the categories have any relation to the subsequent reconviction during the first year after release. Table 12 indicates that they are clearly relevant, for even bearing in mind that a few of the numbers are small, one can still see a pattern beginning to emerge. If one considers the percentage reconvicted for the total of each category, there is a range from 0 to 100 per cent. At one extreme, none of those who intended to start a government training course or a college course or planned to arrange their own work in sub-contracting was reconvicted within one year of release; then with a reconviction rate of 17·2 per cent there are those who hope to be re-employed by their former employer; next come those who intend to be self-employed (31·8 per cent reconvicted) and those who plan to work in a relative's or friend's business (33·3 per cent reconvicted); then come those who felt confident that they would be able to find work on release either by their own efforts or with the help of friends or relations (44·7 per cent reconvicted); next come those who were reluctant to discuss their employment plans (60·0 per cent reconvicted) followed by those who refused to be interviewed in Pentonville (this reconviction rate of 87·7 per cent clearly demonstrates that they were not a random group of men!). Finally, both the men who had stated specifically that they intended to rely on the services of the Department of Employment were reconvicted – in fact both were sentenced to further prison sentences about a month after release and it is doubtful whether either of them would have tried to seek employment in the interim period. In spite of certain shortcomings, this analysis begins to indicate that there are various groups beginning to emerge and that it is by no means a homogeneous group of men who reject the Apex service.

For the purpose of further analysis, the rejection group is divided into the following six categories.

A. Those intending to start government training course or college course (5 men – none reconvicted)
B. Those who intend to return to their former employment (29 men – reconviction rate of 17·2 per cent)
C. Those who have self-employment or sub-contracting plans (38 men – reconviction rate of 29·7 per cent)
D. Those who intend to seek employment in the open market (50 men – reconviction rate of 46·9 per cent)
E. Those with no apparent employment plans (25 men – reconviction rate of 60·0 per cent)
F. Those for whom there is no information (7 men – reconviction rate of 85·7 per cent).

We have already demonstrated in Chapter 6 that the rejection group differs significantly from the full acceptance group on several dimensions. The aim of the present analysis is to discover whether each of the categories (A, B, C, D, E and F) conforms to the R group norm or whether a particular category contributes the major amount of the difference from the full acceptance group.

Table 13 examines the proportion of working life spent in custody by the six R group categories. It demonstrates that the

TABLE 13    *The proportion of working life spent in custody by the various rejection group categories compared with the full acceptance group*

| Proportion of Working life spent in custody | *Rejection group categories* | | | | | | | *FA group* |
| | A (%) | B (%) | C (%) | D (%) | E (%) | F (%) | Total (%) | (%) |
| --- | --- | --- | --- | --- | --- | --- | --- | --- |
| Nil | 60 | 62 | 49 | 37 | 25 | — | 42 | 29 |
| Some but less than 10% | 20 | 10 | 22 | 27 | 25 | 14 | 21 | 26 |
| 10% but less than 25% | — | 17 | 14 | 18 | 13 | 43 | 17 | 19 |
| 25% or more | 20 | 10 | 16 | 18 | 37 | 43 | 21 | 26 |
| TOTAL | 100 | 100 | 100 | 100 | 100 | 100 | 100 | 100 |
| No. of men | 5 | 29 | 37* | 49* | 24* | 7 | 151 | 229 |

* There was incomplete information on one man in each of these categories and the percentages have been calculated on the reduced base.

profile of each rejection category is likely to be somewhat different, for whereas around 60 per cent of the men in categories A and B had no previous experience of custody, this is the case for only a quarter of the men in category E. Table 13 further suggests that the full acceptance group has a similar composition to categories D and E, for the men seem to have comparable experience of custody. If one considers the other differences between the full acceptance group and the rejection group in a similar manner, there is evidence that it is categories A, B and C which contribute the major differences in the characteristics of the rejection group as compared with those of the full acceptance group.

Table 13 also indicates why categories A to F are in ascending order of reconviction rates, for categories A to F are clearly in ascending order of risk – with 60 per cent of the men in category A having no experience of custody but none of the men in category F being in this promising position.

Even without developing a more sophisticated analysis, there is some support for the view that the rejection group can most usefully be divided into two. On the one hand, those who reject because they have other fairly definite employment arrangements (categories A, B and C have what one could perhaps call 'a satisfactory basis for the rejection of the Apex service'). On the other hand, those who reject with no stated alternative plans although they *prima facie* intend to compete on the open market (categories D and E, and possibly F, make what one could call 'an unsatisfactory basis for the rejection of the Apex service', for, with nothing definite arranged, Apex would seem a potentially useful organization for them). Whereas those in the former group who make a reasonable rejection have a reconviction rate of 22·5 per cent, those in the latter group who make a somewhat surprising rejection of the service offered have a reconviction rate of 54·3 per cent. The overall reconviction rate of those who fully accepted the Apex service is 43·2 per cent, so indicating once again that it is fairly meaningless to compare directly the reconviction rates of the total full acceptance group with that of the total rejection group. If it is compared with those men who maintained they were seeking work in the open market, then the full acceptance group seems to perform more satisfactorily after release. An impression was that some members of categories D, E and F (of the rejection group) had never considered for a moment finding employment on release, while even the worst members of the full acceptance group were fooling themselves on this score for at least some of the time.

In considering reconviction rates one should constantly be aware that 'no reconviction = satisfactory rehabilitation' is too simple a formula. In the present case the reconviction follow-up period of one year is very short, so there is every possibility that no reconviction may on occasions just reflect a period of successful criminal activity. There are also likely to be cases of men who have not committed any crime but nevertheless have since release been suffering tremendous hardship as their employment plans failed to work out as satisfactorily as they might have hoped. There was a limited follow-up of some of the men in the rejection group, so that some impression could be formed as to whether their proposed plans did come to fruition. However, one must establish from the outset that by no means all the rejection group was followed up and those that were should be regarded neither as a random group nor necessarily as completely representative of a particular category.

On the other hand, this exercise indicates that just as there is a vast range of outcomes for men who accepted the Apex service this is also the case for men who rejected the Apex service.

### A. Men intending to start a course of some kind

There were only five men in this category but none was reconvicted. There was some subsequent information on only two of the men, but there is an interesting contrast in the two cases. It is sufficient to indicate that one cannot too readily assume a simple causal relationship between starting a course and no subsequent reconviction.

The West Indian aged 24 who planned to study for his 'A' levels certainly started his course satisfactorily and at a later stage Apex was able to help him to find part-time work which assisted him financially. The other young man aged 26 lasted only two days at the government training course for hairdressing but wrote:

> I have a good job at the moment at a local factory, just as odd job man keeping the place tidy and sweeping the factory floor. The money is £18 per week with overtime and after tax, etc. I have £14 left. I have been working now for the past two weeks and I am getting on just fine.

He was still at the same job three months later and still seemed content.

### B. Men who believe that they will be re-employed by the last employer

There were 29 men in this category and as a group they tended to have had less criminal experience than other men who rejected the Apex service. By definition they were men who were working at the time of their present offence and because they had at least some hope of returning to the job it is unlikely that they were absolutely hopeless employees. Eleven of the men had been in skilled manual or non-manual occupations, 12 had been in semi-skilled work, and only 6 men could be regarded as unskilled workers. Quite clearly these are men who are slightly above the average of the prison population in terms of occupational skill, for although the level of skill needed to qualify for the semi-skilled category is fairly low, it is still true that 23 out of the 29 men in this category were doing particular tasks which could be identified rather than unskilled work of a general nature. Eight men intended to return to manufacturing or extraction firms (4 men were in either non-manual or skilled occupations, 2 were semi-skilled, and

2 were unskilled). Seven men intended to return to firms in the civil engineering or building industry (3 men were in skilled occupations, namely carpenter, painter and plumber, 1 semi-skilled as an asphalter and 3 unskilled site labourers). Six men had plans to return to some form of transport undertaking either as driver (2), docker (3) or lengthman (1). Six other men were in a variety of occupations, namely cinema projectionist, catering manager, aerial rigger, newspaper vendor, service engineer (working in a shop), and window cleaner (working for a commercial firm). Finally there were two men who had been working full-time as a currency stock cashier and a council maintenance labourer respectively and both of these men hoped to work full-time as barmen where they had previously had only part-time evening work.

Naturally there may be a tremendous difference between aspirations to return and whether these plans are realized. Indeed, although they all maintained that they were returning to their last employer, the extent of their negotiations to effect this varied tremendously; they ranged from expressions of faith that 'I feel fairly certain that I will get my job back' to having obtained a definite offer to return and in at least one case an employer had paid a social visit to the prison to reassure the prisoner of his intention to re-engage him.

Attempts were made to contact the 21 men in the Wormwood Scrubs sample who hoped to return to their former employer, but we obtained some sort of information on only 14 men. Interestingly, the men who were not contacted were almost exclusively either unskilled workers or of the managerial level. Neither the factory manager nor the catering manager could be located at their former address while the unskilled tended to have no address on release. Although in most cases we knew the firm to which they said they were returning, any contact with the firm after their release would obviously be an unjustified intrusion and a possible danger to their interests.

We had information on 6 men who were returning to manufacturing firms. In all cases they had contacted the employer before release and in all except one the situation had seemed to work out quite satisfactorily. The chemical compounder wrote that 'I have completely settled down and work is very interesting indeed'; the laboratory technician noted, 'Yes, I still like the work' and, three months later wrote, 'everything fine! I have been given a rise at work, in pay and grade'; the tyre layer was equally content – 'Glad to be able to tell you that everything is OK – I have settled back into the job, and feel as though I have never been away from it';

the welder simply said, 'Yes, I still like the job'; while the dental mechanic was taken back by a false teeth manufacturer who had employed him for nearly twenty years. Finally, the young man aged 23 who had been working as a factory labourer before his sentence decided not to return. He had already fluctuated in his life between work as a shop saleman and general unskilled work and in addition he felt that his present offence (indecent assault on young boys) made it difficult to settle back into a normal life, as he believed he was too well known in the local community. He expresses much of the problem in his own way in the following letter.

I was going to return to Smith of Blankshire. But two friends who did work there advise me against it. They said that the firm had gone from very good to terrible. And they had both left there. As one of them really sticks to one and I knew would give it much thought before changing his job I decided to take there advice.

The local Employment Exchange were not very helpful or encouraging. Before I told them that I just come out of prison they gave me a green card to go to Jones Ltd. But when I told him, he took the card back and tore it up. They didn't have much else to offer. I also tried [another] Labour Exchange but they couldn't offer me anythink.

So I had to relie on the local papers. I found that everytime I went for an interview as soon as I told them I just come out of prison. They wanted to know what I was in for. It was very difficult to have to tell these people that it was Attempting to commit Buggery.

When I finally went to where I'am working now. The Personal Office Mr. Brown said that there was no need to hide anythink as he reads the local papers and knows all about me. After a long interview he said he go and see the Stores Foreman. To ask him if he would have any objections. He came back and said Mr. Robinson said that it was alright with him. But then Mr. Brown said he have to check with the stock controller but he was out at the moment so he let me know by post the next morning.

When I didnt get a letter I thought I hadnt got the job. But at Teatime that evening Mr. Brown called personly to say that Mr. Black didn't mind and could I start Monday Morning.

The money is not as good as I know I could earn only 5s 7¾d. a hour. But the first two weeks there was a hour overtime each night and a Saturday morning. But only this Wednesday I was told that starting from that day there be no-more overtime for the time being.

To be honest I would like to change my job. But there are no really good jobs going and also a fair amount of unemployment. So, I just have to stay at my job and be thankful that I have got one.

Usually this time of year [July] you could be able to leave one job and walk straight into a good choice of jobs. But differnantly not this year.

I'am going to have medical treatment. I told Mr. Brown this when I was having my interview. But he said that alright he doesn't mind people having time off for a Bonfide reason. . . .

. . . I have now work three full weeks and no-one at work as tried being funny or made any snide remarks. . . . I though one was bound to get one or two trouble makers's. But I'am very please to say that so far no-one has made trouble for me. . . . I find it [the job] rather boring. But it might improve when I start doing more proper work.

Although there were seven men who hoped to return to firms in the civil engineering or building industry, only one man was in fact contacted after release. He simply stated that he had been able to return to work as a carpenter and he still liked the job.

Possibly the most unsatisfactory state of affairs was found with the men who hoped to return to either the docks or British Rail. The wife of one of the men who worked in the docks as a plumber said that he had been able to go back satisfactorily, but he seemed to be the fortunate exception. One other stevedore had believed firmly that he would get his job back on release, for while he had been in prison, the prison welfare department had heard from the National Dock Labour Board that he could fill in an application form to work as a stevedore again and that he would after a while come in front of the Board when a decision would be made. While in prison he found it easy to convince himself that this was a mere formality and his future was assured. However, two months after his release he replied to a general enquiry from Apex:

I am writing to you to let you know I received your letter and I thank you for writing to me. Sir I am out of work and I have been since I was released from prison. . . . Sir I have been looking for work but I cannot get a gob [sic] so if you could help me I would be very grateful. Sir if you could reply to this letter and let me know if you can help I would be very pleased to visit

F*

you at your office at your convenians if it was possible. Thank you.

In spite of a set-back owing to his baby's illness, everything seemed to work out rather more satisfactorily after he was found a comparable job at a brewery. He was still working there over three months later when the employer was contacted about another matter.

Another stevedore had been just as confident of reinstatement. He had been visited by a union official who, he maintains, assured him that it was '99 per cent certain that he would be able to go back'. He was subsequently sent a letter saying that 'Your Union card must be up-to-date and then immediately you are released you must contact Brother Blank at our Blanktown office who will advise you how to make an Appeal for your reinstatement'. He phoned Apex a few weeks after release to say that he had been 'unlucky'. He was now buying a tipper lorry but unfortunately could not find any work. The director of Apex suggested possible contacts but no more was subsequently heard of him.

A negro who had been employed as a lengthman had to go through a similar time-consuming procedure with British Rail. When he contacted Apex he was obviously disturbed that he was still awaiting a decision and had begun to make tentative enquiries about alternative employment. Although contact was lost before the outcome of his case was finally known, he obviously found the period awaiting the decision somewhat distressing and un-settling.

The point of these particular comments is not to question the procedure of British Rail or the National Dock Labour Board (nor to imply that the outcome is always unfavourable, for we have knowledge of others not in the present sample who have success-fully appealed and subsequently been reinstated) but rather to suggest that a more desirable practice would be for men to attend the appropriate board during the early part of their sentence while on employment parole. If the outcome is unfavourable, the man has the opportunity of making alternative preparations for his release and the possibility of accepting appropriate after-care.

There were three other men contacted who had hoped to return to their former employment. The projectionist had been able to return but soon afterwards the cinema had closed down and he was unemployed at the time of the follow-up interview. He did not seem distressed about this and the interviewer noted that 'it was obvious from his manner that he was not in too much of a hurry to return to work'; he felt that he would not need the help of Apex to find alternative employment when he wished to do so. The two men who had arranged to return as full-time barmen had somewhat contrasting results. In one case the young man was in hospital at the time of the follow-up with an infected arm owing to the use of a dirty syringe. His mother was very reluctant at first to give any information, but the interviewer explained that she was simply interested in whether her son had managed to start work after release. The mother suddenly broke down saying that her son would never be able to work again. If one accepts her account of his recent work history, it seemed that he had never worked part-time as a barman before sentence and one wonders to what extent he had been romanticizing about his future prospects when he had been interviewed in prison. A Catholic priest was closely in touch with this young man and he maintained that the letters sent by Apex had been a tremendous help to the man on the basis that they did show that someone was still interested in him. It is salutory to realize that this young drug addict who had not responded in any way to the fairly impersonal research follow-up letters should even bother to mention the receipt of these letters to a Catholic priest. In contrast, the other previously part-time barman who planned to become full-time on release seemed to have graduated to relief manager in a fairly short time and the fact that arrangements were going ahead for his marriage to a relative of the owner seemed to consolidate his position!

There is information on only one of the eight men in the Pentonville sample who hoped to return to their former employment. He had apparently settled into his work as an asphalter but added in his letter some gratuitous comments on after-care:

I have been working for Blank Asphalt since a matter of days after release, but Sir you can take it from me there is no such thing as Rehabilitation, nor can a man Rehabilitate himself because he is not allowed to do so. A phone call to XXX 0000 Ext. 00 would confirm that I have been working full time all over the country. I feel that your organisation and all like organisations are a forge [sic] and waste of public, or whomevers money it is.

To sum up, it would appear that in general those who had bothered to contact their former employers and had been promised work on release had not subsequently been let down. This is particularly the case with skilled workers. Men who had to go before industrial boards were usually in a less happy situation immediately after release, for the outcome of their case was some-times not known for some time and if the result was unfavourable, this appeared to be a serious set-back. For many of these men, the most useful activity would be to encourage them to make definite enquiries to discover the true situation on release and to try to make arrangements so that they could attend reinstatement boards before release.

*C. Those who plan to be self-employed or have sub-contracting plans*

There were 38 men for whom this was an appropriate category with regard to their stated plans for release. Twenty-three of these men maintained that they ran their own businesses, but in almost every case it seemed of a very small-scale nature if it had existed before the prison sentence and almost invariably the business had lapsed while they had been in prison. While they are a fascinating group who generally seem to be living on their wits rather than running a business, we have little information on their subsequent careers. In terms of subsequent reconvictions within a year after release, it is probably fair to say that fewer were reconvicted than might perhaps have been expected. The area of self-employment is worthy of much further study and is relevant to the whole question of the possible opportunity structure for ex-prisoners. The only comment one can offer here is that, as Table 12 indicates, plans to be self-employed are not necessarily or closely associated with immediate disaster if one's measure is subsequent reconviction.

The following brief account gives some indication of the type of enterprises in which men were interested and the outcome when this is known. Not surprisingly, there is likely to be a much greater discrepancy between aspirations and outcome than is the case for the other categories.

Two men described themselves as scrap metal dealers, but neither had business premises apart from their own back yards. Two more were car dealers of whom one had quite a large second-hand car business but had tried to solve a financial crisis by making an extraordinarily inept attempt at robbing a post office with two other men. Although he originally had plans to set up in business immediately on release, he seemed to be making much steadier progress than one had expected for he was working as a contracts manager a couple of months after release and wrote saying that 'I have taken this position, so that I can clear my existing debts, and commence business on my own again'. It would seem that he had modified his illegitimate way of sorting out his financial affairs before his prison sentence to a remarkably legitimate approach on release. The other car dealer had been doubling as a doorman at a West End club before the present sentence, but after release he made a complete break with the past and returned to Scotland where he worked for a while for a coal merchant before hurting his back and giving up the job. Two others worked as self-employed in the motor trade but on the repair side as bodybuilder and mechanic.

Another man who had treatment for heroin addiction maintained in a prison interview that he had met three other men who shared his interest in racing cars. They had decided to form a company for the manufacture and specialist tuning of racing cars and maintained that each had already put a share of £12,500 into the company and that this had already been deposited with a solicitor and a company formed. Although his story was that he acquired the money by drug trafficking from Morocco, one suspects that he was going beyond the normal 'no-man's land' between fact and fiction which one often encounters when such possible ventures are described.

A coloured prisoner maintained that he was self-employed in so far as he lived off the rent of two houses but his side-line of drug peddling resulted in another prison sentence within a year of release.

There were two men who maintained that they were self-employed bricklayers, while another two said that they were self-employed painters and decorators, but they all seemed rather haphazard enterprises and probably each could more appropriately be classed as an 'odd-job man'. One who had in fact planned to work as a decorator wrote from hospital where he was suffering from nervous depression adding that:

I should like you to be able to find me a job as a semi-skilled radial driller in a New Town where it would be possible to obtain a council house or an exchange for the house we live in now. If this is possible it may lead to a reconciliation. My wife has agreed to a change.

He failed to contact Apex as arranged and no more was heard of him until he was reconvicted on an assault charge.

The remaining men were interested in being self-employed on release in a range of activities – gardener, house-to-house photographer, club photographer, window cleaner, cafe owner, coffee stall proprietor, coal merchant and two in white-collar self-employment as an accountant and a photo-journalist respectively. Although not all these men were contacted after release, one suspects that they would continue in these fields after release, for, in practically all these cases, they would simply be picking up the threads of activities which they had been doing in a fairly haphazard way for years. Even the house-to-house photographer who had been involved for a period of over twenty years in sexual offences on young boys confirmed that after release he intended to continue his hazardous career calling at houses plying for trade as an animal photographer.

The three men who planned more specifically to arrange their own work in a sub-contracting capacity, in one case as a painter and in the other two as lorry drivers, were not reconvicted within one year of release. However, this does not mean that their original employment plans had necessarily worked out. We have definite information on only one of this group and, while he planned to buy a lorry to do sub-contract work, within two weeks of his release he was working as a driver for a firm on a local delivery and was still doing the same job six months later.

The remaining twelve men maintained that they were entering small businesses which were run by relatives or friends. Although they sometimes gave themselves the status of junior partners, this was usually a delusion of grandeur. Six were planning to work in the building trade, mostly as painters but in one case as a plasterer. Two others were looking out for old cars or scrap metal for a 'mate's business', another maintained that he was going to be an odd-job man for a friend who owned a caravan site, while yet another was the tic-tac man for a bookmaker. Two others planned to work in the catering industry – one was helping in his sister's cafe, while the other maintained that he was returning to a restaurant business in which he was a junior partner. The common denominator for all these men is that, while they are attracted to working in small businesses, they are really only involved in a peripheral capacity. Whatever the sentiments of these men about how they would set the business aright after their release, the friends and relatives involved were apparently coping perfectly well without their assistance. Sometimes, though, this apparent belief in their potential is justified, for in one case where the man went to work as a painter for a friend, they built the business up satisfactorily, so they were kept busy throughout the winter. In fact, the friend had never been so successful before. Another situation, on the other hand, was more disastrous. In prison a sparrow-like young man of 25 years of age maintained that he had been asked to return to work in a restaurant business because of the struggle that the owner (or, in his terms, his former partner) had in keeping the business going. The owner phoned Apex about six weeks after his release to say he had taken on a young man who had worked there before and he 'had been working satisfactorily up to last night. In the middle of last night, he stole £100 cash, my car and even bits and pieces belonging to the children – in fact, a clean sweep'. It appears that Apex figured in his tale to the restaurant owner on his reappointment as being some sort of insurance cover for ex-prisoners! The present disaster had all come as a total surprise to the owner, as this employee had been working so satisfactorily up to that point. It perhaps would not have come quite as a surprise to the probation officer who had written an earlier report:

> There appears to be an element in his character that renders him resistant to any form of lasting relationship. He is inclined to attribute his failures to lack of affection, security and the poor emotional background that undoubtedly existed during his earlier life. . . . It seems that prolonged responsible behaviour requires an effort which he is quite unable to sustain. He is quick to relapse into the type of company where he is able to impress, to be sure of acceptance by lowering his principles and standard of behaviour.

*D. Those who plan to seek employment in the open market*
There were 50 men who rejected the Apex service and were confident of finding their own work. In four cases, either relatives or friends were supposed to be actively engaged in finding work, but in the remaining cases they seemed to be relying largely on their own initiative. Although all this group was insistent at the prison interview that they would have no difficulty in finding work, it was strongly suspected that some did not intend to look very hard for work on release. To some extent this is reflected in the subsequent reconviction rates of this group, for of those from Wormwood Scrubs, 37·5 per cent were reconvicted, while 56·0 per cent of the Pentonville men were reconvicted.

Of the few men in this group of whom we heard something after their release, there was a tremendous contrast in how well they settled into work.

One cannot estimate the various proportions who succeeded or failed to settle in various ways, but one can perhaps begin to appreciate the range of possible outcomes for men who say they are confident of finding their own work. Some settle satisfactorily in conventional paid employment, some sense utter hopelessness in their situation, others find a solution, however temporary, in a self-employed situation, others who have been self-employed in the past try unsuccessfully to find a solution in paid employment, and there are probably a few men who have no intention whatsoever of making any attempt at finding employment in spite of their protestations to the contrary within the prison setting.

One man, for example, who had been discharged with ignominy from the Army as a result of his present offence maintained that he still wanted 'to serve under a flag somewhere, anywhere', but started work as a stevedore soon after release noting that 'the pay is good, otherwise I am not keen on this type of work. I hope to be leaving the country soon'. Nine months later he was still working as a stevedore and made no comment about leaving either the job or the country. He had said that he would have no problem on release and although he appears to have changed his plans his pre-release confidence seemed justified. On the other hand a young man who had appeared to be supremely confident of finding himself a job on release as an accounts clerk and maintained that he anticipated no trouble wrote about a month after leaving prison:

I thank you for your concern regards my employment since I left Prison. At the moment I am still unemployed and even if you get me a job, you will not solve my problem. So please concentrate on people who want your help, as I am sure there are hundreds who will be grateful for all the assistance you can give them.

The reason you or an ordinary job can't help me is because I am heavily in debt. I owe £50 fine; £118 to my previous employers; £21 to Montague Burton; £32 to John Temple (both tailers); £30 overdraft in Barclays Bank; £46.8.4. for my life policy; £50 to a car firm for my car which I could not carry on with payments when I went to prison. And the most important reason is I have to go to Court to try and get custody of my child. The only way I can win the case is if my mother stops working and stays at home looking after said child. I would therefore have to give my mother at least £12 a week. So you see, a job would not solve my problems. Again thank you for your concern, but (apart from) somebody lending me £1000 and I paid it back at £4 a month. If I had the money I would definitely get a regular job. There is nothing you or anybody can do. Best wishes in your job.

Although an attempt was made to induce him to seek the advice of a probation officer on these matters, events subsequently show that he felt that desperate measures would provide the only solution. Within a month of writing the above letter he had committed the offence for which he was ultimately to receive a six-year prison sentence. The offence was robbery while armed with the offensive weapon of a starting pistol. Whatever other comment one can add, this young man of 23 years of age seemed clear in his mind that a job in isolation would not solve the financial problems which his recent prison sentence had aggravated rather than resolved.

A similarity he shared with some others in this group who were soon reconvicted was his emphasis that he could easily find a job on release. Often this was an accurate assessment and their problem was settling into the work they had found. Tom had emphasized in prison that he soon found himself bored with a normal job but he thought he would probably have to settle down to provide a home for his girl-friend and the baby conceived when he had escaped from open prison. Tom was eventually found to be living with his parents on release and there was no further mention of his girl-friend. His parents' house was sandwiched between a railway line and an empty boarded-up house. In fact the whole street was due for demolition and already half the houses were gutted. Tom was very affable and led the way into what was described by his interviewer as a 'real old-fashioned front parlour – china dogs and all that'. He said that he had taken over a cafe from his mother. She had rather let the cafe deteriorate but he was having some fruit machines installed. He said he would have to pay her about £40 a month. He resisted the suggestion that it sounded like hard work – 'No, I am not doing any meals – not open till ten – and it's mainly for kids'. Tom looked like a man who was beginning to solve his work problems by 'graduating' to the field of self-employment. However, this further emphasizes the importance of a follow-up after release, for there was no indication that this would be the outcome at the time of the prison interview.

Roger, on the other hand, had in the past dabbled in scrap metal dealing but said that he recognized that this type of enterprise was a sure way of returning to prison. He maintained that he would easily be able to find his own work as a site carpenter. He found himself employment within a few days of his release, writing 'I do not like the work but it gets one a few bob'. Three months later at Christmas he wrote saying that he was not working because 'the weather has not permitted me to. I start as a coalman in January. I haven't had many opportunities [sic] of a good job yet'. Within those three months he had been fined for stealing property to the value of £150, so his attempts to settle down appear to have been short-lived. He did manage to keep out of prison in spite of a further offence of failing to stop for a police officer. Soon afterwards his philanthropy came to grief with a further fine for taking liquor into one of Her Majesty's Prisons! At the end of his first year after release, in spite of three separate court appearances, he had managed to avoid a prison sentence, but one could not imagine that he would be surviving much longer in conditions of freedom.

While Roger is an example of a person who probably did try to settle into normal employment, albeit for a short time, George, in contrast, probably exemplifies those who never had much intention of earning a living by legitimate activity. George maintained that immediately after release he was due to go into hospital for a tonsilitis operation, but he insisted that afterwards he would have no trouble in finding and settling into work. Some time after his release his common-law wife said that he had not worked at all since he had come out of prison the last time and, 'anyway, his friends at the caf' would laugh at him if he got a job'. This conversation took place while her 'husband' was serving a three months' sentence for living off her immoral earnings. She was rather a pathetic creature, maintaining that he had sent her out on the streets with a friend to get money for him to go to Malta for a holiday. She said that at present they all just live on 'National Assistance' and asked plaintively whether they could stop giving him it because as long as they do he 'won't never work'.

### E. Those with no stated employment plans

As one might perhaps expect, this group of 25 men is a fairly high risk category in terms of potential reconviction. A high proportion of those from Wormwood Scrubs were reconvicted – 54·5 per cent – and the proportion was slightly higher still for those from Pentonville – 64·3 per cent.

One suspects that the men with whom we had subsequent contact were a biased sample of this category in that they were making some attempt to make a legitimate living in one form or another. Men whose reconviction pattern suggests that they were actively engaged in criminal activities were rarely traced for a follow-up interview. The attraction of self-employment was the temporary (and, for some, perhaps the permanent) solution. John's mother phoned to ask if Apex could speak on John's behalf in court for 'something fairly trivial'; she knew that Apex wanted men to settle in work after release and she proudly related how John had settled into work by setting himself up with a partner 'manufacturing and selling children's dresses and were soon to extend the range to undies'. They had been working in the Petticoat Lane area for some months and she obviously felt that her trials and tribulations over the fate of her son were at an end.

A more surprising recruit to the ranks of the self-employed was a former company secretary:

> I have to thank you for your kind letter of enquiry as to my current circumstances and hasten to assure you that I am now satisfactorily settled. . . .
>
> As you will remember, I was a partial amnesiac when you last saw me, and my medical advisers can offer limited hope of this situation improving, if at all.
>
> On their advice and with the concurrence of my wife, we used our capital to purchase a small news-agent's business and are both settling in nicely.
>
> I do not envisage other than being able to live reasonably well, certainly not to our previous standards of accommodation or ease, but at least a sufficiency and seriously this is all that man really can ask of life. . . .

This is obviously one solution for the white-collar offenders, but others who wish to return to similar work on release can find the problem more difficult. A few weeks after his release Apex received an extremely neatly written letter from a young man who had been completely overwhelmed and preoccupied in prison by the sudden break-up of his marriage while he was serving his sentence:

> . . . Getting down to the matter in hand Sir. You told me that if I was to run into any trouble, in getting a job on being released from Prison, to contact you.
>
> Well, this is my reason for writing. The local Labour Exchange feel that I need to get some sort of labouring job, to enable me to put some stamps on my card. This, so they say, will give the background I need to get back into office work again.
>
> I have tried to get a labouring job but it seems that there are just no vacancies at present.
>
> I am writing to you Sir, in the event that you may have a possible suggestion to make, one that I have overlooked myself and could help me with my problem. . . .

Unfortunately, this proved to be an example of a man who could clearly state his employment problem but who failed to come to Apex as arranged, so losing contact before Apex could do anything at all. He was reconvicted seven months later for the 'possession of dangerous drugs'.

On the other hand, others for whom the prognosis for settling into work would seem dismal sometimes summon an unexpected resourcefulness. For example, Ernest was a sex offender who was particularly disturbed about the nature of his offence and his experience in prison seemed only a preliminary to a complete mental breakdown. He would have welcomed help from Apex but declined because Apex revealed something of the criminal background to the employer. Prior to his sentence he had been training to be a taxi-driver but was unable to return to this after release. He had no employment plans:

> When I left [prison] as you know it was the holiday weekend and I was fortunate to start work on the following Tuesday and it is the same kind of work as I was doing when I met you nearly every morning, cleaning drains and toilets so I was well able for the job when I got it.
>
> My employer does not know that I had just come out of prison, I told him that I had been self-employed for the last few months and I gave my last two previous employers before I got into that trouble . . . the job is not too bad, it entails a lot of overtime with it so it suits me fine.

This is the only clear-cut case to emerge of a man learning a new occupation while serving his sentence and being able to make a useful application of it after release.

SUMMARY

It is clear not only that men reject the Apex service for a variety of reasons but also that the variety of employment plans have a variety of outcomes. Those intending to start a course of some kind after release seem to stay out of trouble for the first year, but one should not jump to the conclusion that this is because of taking the course, for at least one man stayed only two days at the course arranged. Those hoping to be re-employed by their last employer had generally favourable outcomes although there were instances when matters had not been finally settled before release and the men had a very anxious phase immediately after release while a decision was still being reached. In the remaining categories of employment-plans, it is apparent that these are not rigidly followed. Some of the men who planned to be self-employed had on release settled for normal paid employment, while others who had given the impression that they would find an ordinary job on release had drifted into self-employment. In several cases, men who had rejected Apex but appeared to have no employment plans when they were interviewed in prison had settled down remarkably well, summoning an unexpected resourcefulness. Although it is likely that we heard from more of those in the rejection group who had settled than from those who were probably continuing to flounder, there is still enough evidence to indicate that one cannot generalize too freely about the whole of the rejection group.

## REFERENCE

1 Martin, J. P., *Offenders as Employees*, London, Macmillan (1962), pp. 32–4.

# Analysis of the Full Acceptance Group and Subsequent Outcome

## Introduction

In Part II we described the research design and procedure of offering the Apex service in the two prisons; we noted that the Apex service did not appear to have the overall effect of lowering the reconviction rate of the men who accepted the service; we then showed that the Wormwood Scrubs and Pentonville samples were not two distinct groups; further, we demonstrated that there were some significant differences between men who fully or partially accepted the Apex service and men who rejected the Apex service.

The purpose of Part III is to discuss in much greater detail the outcome for those who fully accepted the Apex service and to try to discover whether the Apex service seemed to benefit any particular group of men. We will examine the interviews arranged by Apex for men on their release, the proportion of men attending the interviews arranged, the proportion of men accepted for jobs by employers, the proportion starting the jobs as agreed, and the length of time spent in the first job arranged by Apex. There will then be an attempt to develop a measure to predict men who are most unlikely to be helped by the Apex service. We will then discuss the efforts involved in trying to find suitable interviews for the men who accepted the Apex offer. Finally, there is an attempt to consider what normally are the employment plans of men leaving prison who have not had the Apex offer; for this purpose, the plans of the Wormwood Scrubs control group are considered.

However, before discussing the outcome for the men who fully accepted the Apex service in detail, there is a preamble in order to introduce the method of Discriminatory Analysis which is used to derive three risk categories and subsequently to indicate those men most unlikely to be helped by the Apex service.

## CHAPTER 8

# Brief Description of Discriminatory Analysis and Division of Full Acceptance Group into Three Risk Categories

Throughout the present project there are a number of occasions when we compare two or more groups. For example, we compared the treatment and control groups on various dimensions, and the full acceptance, partial acceptance and rejection groups were all compared. Figure 1 further illustrates a number of possible comparisons when one examines the outcome of the efforts of Apex for those who fully accepted the Apex service. Those for whom interviews were arranged can be compared with those for whom interviews were not arranged and so on until, for instance, the 19 men who stayed three months or more can be compared with the 46 men who started the job arranged but stayed less than three months. Even this does not exhaust by any means the possibilities of comparison, for one could quite reasonably argue that it would be interesting to compare on various dimensions the 19 men who stayed three months with the remaining men who had originally accepted the Apex service and so try to distinguish the type of man who is likely to settle in work arranged by an employment-placing service. All these possible comparisons taking one dimension or variable at a time would produce an unmanageable number of tables and the practical value of such an operation is doubtful. However, with the men who accept the Apex service perhaps a more useful approach is to try to construct a measure which would enable the placing officer to estimate his chances of success in getting a man to settle into the work he has arranged or before this to select only the men who have been shown from past experience to benefit from the service. This would be the first step towards eliminating the large number of men for whom the value of the Apex service has proved at the best doubtful, and diverting the resources more profitably towards helping men who have at least a reasonable likelihood of starting the work arranged. If a considerably larger number of men were helped, at least *prima facie*, by the Apex service in terms of getting settled quickly into a work routine, it would then be appropriate once again to consider whether this type of employment service does help to lower the reconviction rate of such men compared with a similar group of

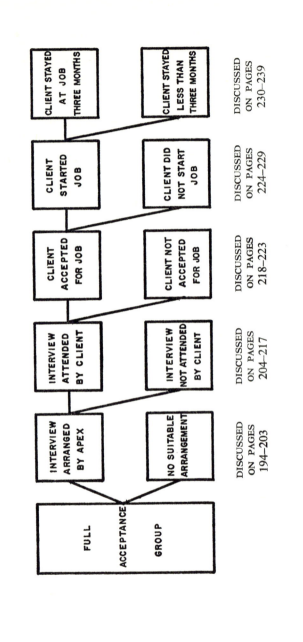

FULL ACCEPTANCE GROUP

INTERVIEW ARRANGED BY APEX

NO SUITABLE ARRANGEMENT

INTERVIEW ATTENDED BY CLIENT

INTERVIEW NOT ATTENDED BY CLIENT

CLIENT ACCEPTED FOR JOB

CLIENT NOT ACCEPTED FOR JOB

CLIENT STARTED JOB

CLIENT DID NOT START JOB

CLIENT STAYED AT JOB THREE MONTHS

CLIENT STAYED LESS THAN THREE MONTHS

DISCUSSED ON PAGES 194–203

DISCUSSED ON PAGES 204–217

DISCUSSED ON PAGES 218–223

DISCUSSED ON PAGES 224–229

DISCUSSED ON PAGES 230–239

men who are not helped in this way. What the present project has shown is that the Apex service has failed to lower the reconviction rate when offered to a random sample of 'star' and recidivist prisoners, but what will emerge in the following chapters as a corollary is that the service had only a marginal impact on the lives of the men involved. The present exercise is to produce an objective measure which will more clearly identify the men who really may benefit from an employment service for ex-prisoners.

It is not unusual to try to find a basis by which two or more groups can be distinguished, or, as the eminent statistician, R. A. Fisher, states more elegantly, 'When two or more populations have been measured in several characters, $x_1, \ldots, x_8$, special interest attaches to certain linear functions of the measurements by which the populations are best discriminated.'[1] Fisher notes the use made of this fact in craniometry by E. S. Martin who applied the principle to the sex differences in measurements of the mandible. Similarly, M. J. Moroney considers

the case of the archaeologist who wishes to determine the particular race of men to which a skull or portion of a skull probably belongs. It is well known that the skull configuration is broadly characteristic of race; but within each race any length or angle we measure will be a variable quantity, so that the individual skull, while conforming as a whole to its family shape, will have individual measurements such as are commonly observed in skulls of other families. Since it is not the individual measurements but the *set* which is the basis of discrimination, the problem of weighting and combining the individual measurements to get a single figure which will give the most sensitive diagnosis naturally arises.[2]

His other example from technology is perhaps a closer analogy to what we are attempting in the present study:

Rubber cements are easily recognizable in use as good, bad or indifferent. There is no defined unit for the measurement of adhesion, which is too complex a phenomenon to be forced into a simple definition. All we can say is that it is recognizable and that certain tests can be carried out whose results correlate with it.[3]

In a similar manner, we know for the Apex project what has happened at each juncture in terms of the number who attended interviews, started work, etc., but we cannot define simply the characteristics of each group. It is the purpose of the discriminant function to serve as an index for discrimination between the groups, and, as we shall see, this value may be useful in setting up a prediction study.

There are the usual statistical problems that occur when the information available contains a mixure of variables, such as age, and attributes, such as marital status. For the present discriminatory analysis we have largely avoided this problem by disregarding attributes and concentrating the analysis on variables. There are, however, possibilities of getting around the problem of dealing with attributes, as Hammond and Chayen demonstrated in their use of multiple regression in *Persistent Criminals*. They noted the number of items present or absent, and so 'the score totals . . . can be treated . . . as though they were variables in much the same way that psychological traits are often scored and treated as though they represented a unidimensional series'.[4] This was not attempted in the present study, for in the vast majority of cases either the attributes were not important discriminators or they correlated with variables which had already been included in the analysis. We will mention, though, in the text describing each discriminant function any further items we have noticed which could possibly help to improve the particular measure.

The nine variables which have been used throughout for the discriminatory analysis are as follows:

   A. Age at time of sentence
   B. Age at first conviction or finding of guilt
   C. Previous convictions as an adult
   D. Period in freedom since last custody
   E. Probation experience
   F. Proportion of working life spent in custody
   G. Longest period in any one job
   H. Time since longest job
    I. Time in job when committing present offence.

All the men in the full acceptance group* were coded for each of these variables on the scales shown as Appendix A.

---

\* Although 229 men fully accepted the concept of the Apex service, seven were not offered full facilities because they lived outside the Greater London area. One other man for whom an actual job was arranged as a ceiling fixer's labourer was discharged earlier than expected on a judge's instruction and so he was released before being informed that a job had been arranged for him on release: he has been disregarded in the subsequent analysis.

There are obviously many refinements possible which would improve the sophistication of the scales, but the limiting factor in the present study was either the accuracy or the amount of information available. Using these fairly broad categories in each case, it was possible to make a reasonable estimate in the very few cases where the exact information was not available.

For a fairly comprehensive discussion on discriminant functions and some of the questions connected with the precision of the processes employed, the reader is referred to R. A. Fisher's article 'The use of multiple measurements in taxonomic problems'.[5] The present example does not attempt to examine any of the theoretical implications but is simply designed to introduce a practical measure which will be used on several occasions in the text.

We have already indicated that the Wormwood Scrubs and Pentonville samples have a number of interesting similarities and a number of statistically significant differences. The greatest difference between the two samples is the number who have had a previous prison sentence, for while over 94 per cent of the Wormwood Scrubs sample have never been to prison before, almost 100 per cent of the Pentonville sample have served at least one previous prison sentence. As this fact is largely the basis of the distinction between 'stars' and 'ordinaries', this is hardly a surprising result. However, we have previously hinted that this may not be the best distinction in terms of estimating the possible risk of reconviction, for although in broad terms the typical man of Wormwood Scrubs is a better prospect than the typical man of Pentonville there is a tremendous degree of overlap between the two populations. In other words, the young man in Wormwood Scrubs who has already served a sentence in an approved school, a borstal and a detention centre (and perhaps a couple of periods on probation as well) may seem a less hopeful prospect than the recidivist who has served two prison sentences but has had no other criminal convictions.

We wish to compute a linear function of the nine variables measured on each individual in the two prison samples. This will serve the dual purpose of examining the extent of the discrimination between the two prison samples on the basis of these nine variables and also demonstrate the procedure of the discriminatory analysis. (On account of the limitation of the computer programme used, that the sample size must equal or be less than 300, this analysis has been restricted to the men who fully accepted the Apex service in both prisons.) This linear function can serve as an index for discrimination between the groups. It is determined 'from the criterion of "best" in that the difference between the mean indices for the two groups divided by a pooled standard deviation of the indices is maximized'.[6] One must emphasize that the most obvious discriminating factor in this case, namely the number of previous prison sentences, has been disregarded, as the main purpose of this exercise is to demonstrate the discriminant function on the nine variables used subsequently.

The typical value of the discriminant function in the present case is found as:

$$D = a\ \bar{A} + b\ \bar{B} + c\ \bar{C} + d\ \bar{D} + e\ \bar{E} + f\ \bar{F} + g\ \bar{G} + h\ \bar{H} + i\ \bar{I},$$ where $\bar{A}, \bar{B}, \bar{C}, \bar{D}, \bar{E}, \bar{F}, \bar{G}, \bar{H}, \bar{I},$ are the mean scores of the nine variables and a, b, c, d, e, f, g, h, i are discriminant function coefficients.

If we substitute the values obtained for the Wormwood Scrubs sample, the mean is 0·01796, and for the Pentonville sample the mean is −0·01108, the difference between the average values of the compound measurements being 0·02904. However, the individual measurements for the 221 members of the two groups range from 0·03846 to −0·03737. To calculate the value for an individual one uses the following formula:

$$V = (-0·00171)A + (0·00133)B + (-0·00288)C + (0·00381)D$$
$$+ (0·00481)E + (-0·00133)F + (-0·00145)G + (-0·00164)H$$
$$+ (-0·00007)I,$$ where A to I are the variables used (see

Appendix A) and V is the value for a particular man.

The characteristics of the men with the highest and lowest scores illustrate the extreme cases of the two samples. The man with the highest value was aged 23 and had been first convicted at the age of 13 but had only one previous adult conviction. He had never had any previous custody but had been on probation on two occasions. At present he was unemployed but had been employed at his longest job less than two years ago. On the other hand, the man with the lowest value was aged 50 and had been first convicted at the age of 17 but now had 27 previous adult convictions. On the last occasion he had been at liberty for less than one month and in fact had spent nearly half of his working life in prison. In spite of these numerous court appearances, he had never been on probation. He also was unemployed at the time of his present offence but it was about seven years since he had held his longest job (in fact he had done only casual work since that time). Incidentally, both these men started the work arranged by Apex but neither stayed longer than one month at the job, so although they were so widely different when the two prison samples were compared they were almost identical in their response to the Apex service!

When one plots the actual distributions of the compound measurements for each of the two samples, there is some quite considerable overlap of the distributions of the two samples. In other words, an infallible prediction of which prison an individual was a member of could not be based solely on the nine variables used in the present example.* However, the overlap area may well have its value, for this is a way to identify the members of the Wormwood Scrubs sample who had somewhat similar characteristics to some of the men in the Pentonville sample.

We have, of course, simply taken two samples – one from Wormwood Scrubs and one from Pentonville – and one wants some sort of estimation of whether these samples can be considered as really representative of the respective prisons. In other words, we want to know the degree of confidence which we can place in the average values of the two samples as an indication of the true values for the two populations. This is a very typical statistical question and one approach is to state the interval within which the true value we are estimating may be said to lie. One can, in fact, calculate various levels of confidence, but in this study we have used throughout the conventional estimate of a 95 per cent confidence interval (i.e. $x_i = \bar{x} \pm (t_{.05}) \frac{\sigma}{\sqrt{n}}$). We express our confidence by saying that in a long series of estimates of this type, we would expect to be correct in 95 out of every 100 predictions. In the present case, calculating the 95 per cent confidence limits for the mean of each group indicates the range within which we are confident the true value for each population lies, but this also happens to isolate conveniently all the overlap between the two distributions between the higher 95 per cent confidence value of the Pentonville sample and the lower 95 per cent confidence value of the Wormwood Scrubs sample. Hence, for practical purposes, this produces a very convenient division into three groups. Group A contains 66 men who were all from the Wormwood Scrubs sample, Group B (the overlap of the distributions of the two groups) contains 39 men from the Wormwood Scrubs sample and 51 from the Pentonville sample, and Group C contains the remaining 65 men from the Pentonville sample.

The next step is to examine whether this sort of division is reasonable in terms of their subsequent reconviction within one

*This, of course, is not surprising as the most appropriate measure, namely previous prison experience, has been omitted.

year after release. Table 14 shows that this procedure produces a more useful grouping of the men in the full acceptance group. Group A has a reconviction rate of 18·8 per cent; Group B (Wormwood Scrubs) and Group B (Pentonville) have almost identical proportions reconvicted, namely 43·6 per cent and 45·1 per cent respectively; Group C has a reconviction rate of 66·2 per cent. It is important to emphasize that the formula from which Table 14 is derived was calculated at least six months before any of the Pentonville reconviction figures were known and all nine variables concerned behaviour before release from their present sentence. If, on the other hand, one considers the reconviction rates of the full acceptance group solely in terms of the particular prison, 28·2 per cent of those from Wormwood Scrubs compared with 56·9 per cent of those from Pentonville were reconvicted within one year after release. One can see, therefore, that the present analysis has managed to capture in a meaningful manner the overlap between the two prison samples.

TABLE 14   *The reconviction rates of Groups A, B and C*

| Group | No. of men | No. of men reconvicted within one year | % reconvicted within one year |
| --- | --- | --- | --- |
| Group A (Wormwood Scrubs) | 66* | 12 | 18·8 |
| Group B (Wormwood Scrubs) | 39 | 17 | 43·6 |
| Group B (Pentonville) | 51 | 23 | 45·1 |
| Group C (Pentonville) | 65 | 43 | 66·2 |
| TOTAL | 221* | 95 | 43·4 |

* There was no reconviction information on two men, so the percentage reconvicted has been calculated on a reduced base.

It is interesting to add that not only were a lower proportion of men in Group A reconvicted within one year after release compared with the Wormwood Scrubs men in Group B, but also the men reconvicted in Group B were given more serious sentences than those men reconvicted in Group A. Five out of 12 men (or 41·7 per cent) of Group A received custodial sentences compared with 13 out of 17 (or 76·5 per cent) of Group B (Wormwood Scrubs). This latter fact may of course simply reflect their more serious criminal history.

On the basis of the evidence of Table 14, it is not unreasonable to call Group A 'low risk category', Group B 'medium risk category', and Group C 'high risk category'. In the following chapters we will examine the impact that Apex seems to make on these various risk categories.

In his introductory text on statistics, M. J. Moroney notes:

There seems to be very little application in industry of Discriminatory Analysis; yet one would imagine that it should prove extremely useful in many situations. Quite apart from possible technological applications, there seems to be a case for trying it in personnel selection for the pooling of selection test results.[7]

Perhaps the Apex project is the type of exercise which Moroney had in mind.

# REFERENCES

1 Fisher, R. A., 'The use of multiple measurements in taxonomic problems' in Fisher, R. A. (ed.), *Contributions to Mathematical Statistics*, New York, John Wiley & Sons (1950), paper 32, p. 179.

2 Moroney, M. J., *Facts from Figures*, Harmondsworth, Penguin (1962), p. 315–16.

3 Ibid., p. 316.

4 Hammond, W. H., and Chayen, E., *Persistent Criminals*, London, HMSO (1963), p. 153.

5 Fisher, R. A., op. cit.

6 'BMDO4M discriminant analysis for two groups' in Dixon, W. J. (ed.), *BMD Biomedical Computer Programs*, Berkeley and Los Angeles, University of California Press (1968), p. 185.

7 Moroney, M. J., op. cit., p. 319.

## CHAPTER 9

# The Job Interviews Arranged by Apex

As we have fully explained in Part II, the basic idea of the Apex project was to find a suitable job interview on release for all the men interviewed in prison who wished to participate. We are now concentrating on the 221 men who were thought to have fully accepted the Apex service in the sense that they wanted the director of Apex to find them work on release. Not unnaturally, there was a considerable range of types of employment required, but the level of employment tended to be in semi-skilled and unskilled occupations. There was not a problem of men suggesting occupations that were totally unrealistic in terms of their own experience, but rather the poverty of any alternative suggestions when their normal occupation was no longer possible for some reason. The arrangement was that, if their desired field of employment was not totally inappropriate, the director of Apex agreed to make 'a reasonable number of enquiries' and then either return to discuss the matter again at a further interview or pursue the second choice of field of employment which had been agreed. Even where finding the desired work would seem a fairly hopeless task, the policy of Apex was to make at least a few enquiries and then explain the response of the firms to the men rather than to dismiss a suggestion out of hand at the prison interview. This was sometimes the case when men requested work in shops or in commerce and selling where for instance their present offence almost certainly debarred consideration of employment with a reputable firm and, although the director tried to avoid raising hopes of success, he made fresh enquiries each time. (On occasions the director was surprised at the offers or suggestions made by firms when he was engaged in this apparently hopeless task!) This policy was not adopted, however, on the one or two occasions where any action towards fulfilling a dream was likely to produce unrealistic elation with the inevitable subsequent let-down. A 48-year-old recidivist with a serious drink problem and a long mental history who had always been a kitchen porter maintained that he would easily become a top-grade ballad singer if given the necessary audition; he was told by the director that Apex did not have any contacts in this field. Usually, though, such dreams emerged almost as an afterthought when a more mundane choice of employment had been agreed by the director and the man concerned. Unless closer questioning revealed talents that had some link with previous work experience (and, in these cases, some reassessment of suitable employment might have to be made), the policy was to suggest that this might well be quite a reasonable long-term goal but was probably not appropriate for the first job after release.

Table 15 indicates the fields of employment for the two prison samples in which the men would like work after release. More accurately, they represent the employment plans discussed with the director of Apex and the areas in which he had agreed to make at least some enquiries.

TABLE 15  *Employment plans after release – field of employment in which respondent is primarily interested*

| Field of employment in which subject desired work after release | Wormwood Scrubs (%) | Pentonville (%) |
|---|---|---|
| Professional groups and public bodies | 2·9 | — |
| Shops | 2·9 | 5·2 |
| Commerce and selling | 1·9 | 3·4 |
| Manufacturing and extraction firms | 22·9 | 21·6 |
| Catering industry | 5·7 | 14·7 |
| Transport undertakings | 14·3 | 5·2 |
| Service industries | 7·6 | 13·8 |
| Civil engineering and building | 23·8 | 26·7 |
| Clerical work (any field) | 4·8 | — |
| Unskilled work (any field) | 10·5 | 7·8 |
| Miscellaneous* | 2·9 | 1·7 |
| TOTAL | 100·0 | 100·0 |
| No. of prisoners | 105 | 116 |

* This category includes Armed Forces and Merchant Navy.

The table gives no indication of the level of occupation desired within a particular field – indeed, 'professional groups and public bodies' includes a first-class architect and a rather mediocre stoker for a public body. The question of skill and ability in a particular trade or profession is often difficult to assess with accuracy within a prison setting. Instead of settling finally with each man whether he regarded himself as a skilled or semi-skilled man in a particular trade, we attempted to ascertain the type of work he had done or the machines he had operated. Armed with this knowledge, the director was able to discuss with potential employers whether certain borderline cases had the type of experience which suggested a skilled or semi-skilled man (this type of discussion was often held with sympathetic employers who were not necessarily potential employers in the particular case discussed). The impression with so many of the men who accepted the Apex service was that they were in a 'no man's land' between semi-skilled and skilled tradesmen or between semi-skilled and unskilled workers and were difficult to categorize; even those who wanted simply unskilled manual work of some kind often had atrocious work records and/or physical or mental disabilities. In contrast, there is some evidence to suggest that the men who are genuine tradesmen or who had the physique and regarded themselves as heavy manual workers tended to reject the Apex service as unnecessary. Even so, one suspects that the tendency of Apex was to over-rate rather than under-rate the calibre of some of the men. In other words, if a man maintained that he was a skilled painter and gave some definite indication of experience in the trade, then the policy was to try to arrange a skilled painter vacancy although the director perhaps suspected his ability on an intuitive basis. This was one area where intuition was sometimes validated by subsequent events after release!

Although the original plan had been to supply each man who fully accepted the service with an appropriate interview to attend within a few days of release, there was some variation in the arrangements for the 221 men. In fact, 159 of the men were released from prison with the full knowledge of the details of the interview or interviews arranged. Of these, 140 men (60 from Wormwood Scrubs and 80 from Pentonville) had one definite interview to attend, a further 15 men (10 from Wormwood Scrubs and 5 from Pentonville) had the opportunity of attending two different job interviews, while four men (3 from Wormwood Scrubs and 1 from Pentonville) had already had the interviews as a result of either employment parole or their potential employers' coming into the prison to see them before release. On release all these men had an arrangement in hand similar to that originally envisaged when the Apex project was designed.

Of the remaining 62 men (32 men from Wormwood Scrubs and 30 men from Pentonville), 10 men (5 from each prison) changed their minds about accepting the Apex offer – 5 men maintained that they had made or would prefer to make their own employment arrangements after all, while a further 5 men turned down the offer of the interview arranged.

Of the men who subsequently decided to make their own arrangements, one's father found him a job as a lorry driver's mate, two others had decided to try to return to former employers but wanted to avoid any contact with the firms until after release as they wished to hide the fact of their criminal record. The other two men decided to return to being self-employed – in one case as a decorator and in the other as a carpenter. Both these men had over fifteen adult convictions and it is difficult to believe that either had earned any money within the last five years as a self-employed decorator or carpenter. The carpenter at the first interview said that he wanted Apex's help in getting employment on discharge and mentioned that he would like a living-in job as a kitchen porter. At the second interview he had completely changed his mind. He emphasized that on discharge he was going to limit his drinking to one small bottle of wine per day. All he wanted to do now was to get himself some carpentry tools and wander around doing odd jobs in carpentry. He was quite adamant on this occasion that he did not want Apex to find him work. The other five men turned down the offer of the interview arranged just prior to release. On two occasions it was clearly apparent that the interview arranged was not up to their expectations. In one case a young heroin addict stated at the first interview a preference for work as a storeman but would accept 'anything with a living wage'. Apex failed to secure an interview for a stores job and arranged an interview as a labourer as a temporary measure. He refused this on the grounds that he did not want outside work with the winter soon approaching. He maintained that a fellow inmate had offered him a job as a packer in his firm on release 'if I am stuck'. After release he was not able to work and was on sick benefit suffering from nervous debility, and six months later his probation officer noted that 'he does not consider looking for work, and indeed it would be unrealistic if he did, but he maintains a steady, though spasmodic, contact with me at the office'. A few months later he came over when he saw the research officer in the buffet at Waterloo station. He said that he was more addicted to heroin than he ever was and felt less and less inclined to want to get off drugs. He had continued to keep in touch with his probation officer but still continued to have the problems of loneliness. He mentioned that he had seen a job as a machinist the other day but had not had the courage to take the job, and 'anyway I couldn't hold a job down'. In spite of sincere and well-meaning attempts, it seemed that the only contribution Apex had made in this case was to add to his guilt about the way he had let people down and the fact that he was not a useful member of society by being totally unable to hold down a job.

The other man who was clearly disappointed at the interview arranged had stated at the initial interview a preference for a driving job but otherwise wanted any unskilled work apart from road sweeping. He turned down the job arranged as a storekeeper on the grounds that it was inside work. Some time after release he was found another interview as a van driver/warehouseman but apparently did not attend the interview. He started work about three months after release as a maintenance worker; he probably found this job himself and maintained that he liked the job after being there for over a month. Another man rejected the interview offer as he had not been accepted for an alcoholics' hostel as anticipated and was moving into a different area on release (Apex subsequently found another interview but he did not contact the employer as arranged). The responses of the remaining two men were somewhat more complex. It appeared as though they had accepted the Apex service in the belief that no offer would be forthcoming and this would reinforce their views of the hopelessness of after-care organizations. One young man from Wormwood Scrubs had an atrocious criminal record but did have some reasonable experience as a meat cutter. A large organization was willing to consider him for further training with a view to a career with the organization. He rejected the offer, putting forward the view that they could not possibly teach him anything further of the trade. He started a job which he presumably found on his own initiative as a bacon cutter soon after release. Four months later, in response to a postcard from the research officer, this 22-year-old bacon cutter replied saying that he had left the first job and now 'I have my own shop'. The remaining man in this group had little experience to offer an employer except in driving (for which he was disqualified) and turned down an interview with an engineering firm because it was too far to travel, fares would cost too much, travelling would take too long and it would be difficult with the winter coming on. This is all quite reasonable except that he had always maintained that he would get accommodation near his work as long as he was found work. He stated this again a few minutes after rejecting the interview offer, but then qualified this by saying that he had never thought of living in Enfield. This latter example is perhaps the type of tortuous reasoning which one suspects is more usual after release and leads to men not attending interviews.

A further 27 men released without full details of the interview arranged had only a minimal delay before this state of affairs was rectified – a telephone call to Apex or arrival home to find a letter from Apex waiting for them explaining all the details was usually all that was necessary. There were, however, the remaining 25 men who agreed with the director that they had more pressing problems on release than the simple provision of a job and it was arranged with them that they would contact Apex at a definite date and time after release when they would be given final details of an interview arranged or Apex would start looking for work for them after their initial contact. Most of this group not only had accommodation problems but did not have any definite idea of even the area of London where they intended to settle; it was usually this reason which made job placing before release an impossible task. Not surprisingly, this group included a high proportion of alcoholics and drug addicts who had usually been leading an extremely unsettled existence before this present sentence. In the event, only 7 of this group contacted Apex after release and only 4 remained in contact long enough for Apex to be confident that they had in fact received notification of the interview arranged.

To summarize, therefore, there were 190 men who were notified of an interview that they could attend within a few days after release, while 31 men of the full acceptance group were not similarly placed. The latter group consisted of men who had changed their minds about accepting Apex help and other men who either failed to contact Apex as arranged or for whom, in one case, Apex failed to find a suitable interview within a few days after release. This latter case was a negro who wanted work as a welder, and while he had not had first-class experience, even after sixty-five placing efforts no interview could be arranged. (All the other 23 negroes who fully accepted the Apex service had an interview arranged satisfactorily although, as we shall show later, there is some evidence that negroes were not accepted so readily by employers when they actually attended the interviews.)

Although 190 men could be said to have a bona fide job interview to attend within a few days of their release, it need not necessarily be in their first choice* of field of employment, and of the 191 men who made their first choice within the eight main fields of employment 65·4 per cent were found suitable interviews in fields of their first choice, a further 22·0 per cent were found interviews in other fields of employment, and there was no satisfactory conclusion in the remaining 12·6 per cent of men who made particular choices. One must emphasize that the change from one field of employment to another may not be as dramatic as it may sound. In fact one must not too readily assume that the alternative arranged is less suitable. For example, a prisoner who had hoped to return to his former employment as a porter with a public body was able to make a new start as a furniture removal porter with a firm of haulage contractors. He made good use of this opportunity and it is reasonable to suggest that this seems a much more promising outcome than if he had returned to employers who told Apex that they regarded him as a risk to 'all our mini-skirted typists'.

The evidence suggests that a request for employment within the field of 'civil engineering and building' is the easiest to satisfy but this is closely followed by five of the other major fields – professional groups and public bodies, manufacturing and extraction firms, catering industry, transport undertakings and service industries. The two most difficult fields appear to be 'shops' and 'commerce and selling'. This is perhaps not a surprising finding in view of the security aspect of some of these positions. However, while there were a multitude of reasons why men were not necessarily placed in the field of their first choice it was noted that men requesting positions in shops or in selling were particularly likely to be new entrants to this type of work, so apart from all the other problems some just did not have the experience required. In the few cases where the request for building work was not met, it was almost invariably because the request was made at a time of the year when the building trade was particularly slack. In other cases, there seemed to be no suitable employment of the kind they requested which was within the travelling distance or reached the wage packet they stipulated and so it was necessary to consider their other choices of employment.

---

* The few men who said from the outset that they were not willing to accept alternatives of work if their first choice of employment was not possible to satisfy were categorized as 'Partial Acceptance – Specific Request'. For example, one man wanted Apex only to enquire about possible work as a fireman, while another was interested only in becoming a deep-sea diver.

As we have noted, it is another question to consider the level of occupations within each field of employment. Non-manual occupations are under-represented in most prison samples compared with the general population, and the present sample probably has fewer men aspiring to white-collar occupations even than most prison samples. In fact, only four men had interviews arranged in non-manual occupations which were above the level of routine clerical work. Table 16 analyzes the fields of employment in which interviews were arranged in terms of the level of occupation within each field. It is important to emphasize that the level of occupation indicates the job for which an interview has been arranged rather than the proved calibre of the applicant. One should also add that the distinctions between skilled and semi-skilled and unskilled manual work are notoriously difficult to draw. In the present study, two raters estimated the levels of occupation. Where there was any discrepancy each individual case was discussed. Table 16 clearly

TABLE 16 *The level of occupation within the field of employment in which interviews were arranged*

| Field of employment of interview arranged | Non-manual (other than routine grades) | Skilled manual and routine grades of non-manual | Semi-skilled manual | Unskilled manual | TOTAL |
|---|---|---|---|---|---|
| Professional groups and public bodies | 1 | 2 | 3 | 3 | 9 |
| Shops | – | 3 | 1 | – | 4 |
| Commerce and selling | 2 | 2 | – | – | 4 |
| Manufacturing and extraction firms | 1 | 6 | 29 | 26 | 62 |
| Catering industry | – | – | 10 | 14 | 24 |
| Transport undertakings | – | – | 15 | 1 | 16 |
| Service industries | – | 8 | 9 | 3 | 20 |
| Civil engineering and building | – | 20 | 6 | 23 | 49 |
| TOTAL No. | 4 | 41 | 73 | 70 | 188* |
| TOTAL % | 2·1 | 21·8 | 38·8 | 37·2 | 100·0 |

* Two men were to discuss a suitable level of occupation with the employer.

G*

indicates that the majority of the men (76 per cent) had interviews arranged in semi-skilled or unskilled manual work.

While the vast majority (86 per cent) of men seemed to have an acceptable job interview arranged, it is worthwhile to consider briefly whether this was the case for each of the three risk categories. Table 17 clearly shows that the Apex service is not having an equal impact throughout the sample, for easily the greatest proportion of those for whom no interview was arranged for whatever reason came within the Pentonville 'high risk' category – just under a quarter of this category were in this position compared with approximately 10 per cent in the other two categories. While any reasonable man is unlikely to argue that the chances were more than slight of the 16 men of the high risk category taking up a job interview if it had been arranged before release (i.e. instead of waiting for them to contact Apex after they had arranged their own accommodation), one must still recognize that these men were not given exactly the same opportunity as the others.

TABLE 17  *Number and percentage of job interviews arranged in various risk categories together with reconviction rates*

| Risk category | Acceptable job interview arranged (%) | | No acceptable job interview arranged (%) | | % of acceptable job interviews arranged |
|---|---|---|---|---|---|
| | No. | reconvicted | No. | reconvicted | |
| Low risk – Wormwood Scrubs | 60 | 15·5* | 6 | 50·0 | 90·9 |
| Medium risk – 'Wormville'† | 81 | 43·2 | 9 | 55·6 | 90·0 |
| High risk – Pentonville | 49 | 67·3 | 16 | 62·5 | 75·4 |
| TOTAL | 190 | 41·0 | 31 | 58·1 | 86·0 |

* There was no reconviction information on two men in this category and this figure has been calculated on a reduced base.

† 'Wormville' is the category which contains 39 men from Wormwood Scrubs and 51 men from Pentonville.

What happens to all these men after release, for one could quite reasonably hypothesize that the 31 men for whom there was no satisfactory employment arrangement immediately on release would have a much higher reconviction rate than the rest of the full acceptance group? At first glance, it would appear that they certainly seem to perform more disastrously after release, for 58 per cent are reconvicted within the first year compared with 41 per cent of the rest of the full acceptance group. However, this direct comparison is misleading for we have already indicated that over half the former group were in the high risk categories and this weighting should be taken into account. Controlling for risk category, Table 17 indicates that for the low risk category those for whom no satisfactory arrangement was made had a higher reconviction rate (50·0 per cent) than was the case for those men for whom Apex had arranged an apparently acceptable interview (reconviction rate 15·5 per cent). This pattern is repeated to a certain degree for the medium risk group, but is clearly not the case for the high risk category. The latter result is perhaps surprising, for one of the reasons for not arranging an interview was that men had no accommodation arranged and were generally vague about their release plans; one would have thought that this would have a bearing on subsequent reconviction figures, but this does not seem to be the case. This is somewhat reminiscent of Hammond and Chayen's findings in their study of preventive detainees that when criminal history, mental characteristics and prison offences are taken into account, the value of considering the home background for compiling a prediction score is not really worthwhile:

> The small *negative* weight for home background is interesting; it shows that adverse home background is associated with the other factors and that once the effect of these associated factors has been allowed for, poor home background is no longer a factor which predisposes the offender towards reconviction.[1]

In conclusion there is some evidence that there was no satisfactory arrangement made for some of the more vulnerable members of the low (and perhaps also the medium) risk category. It is difficult to sustain the alternative explanation that the Apex service helped some of the other members of the low and medium risk categories to produce this differential reconviction rate, because there was no indication of any overall lowering of the reconviction rate compared with the control group.

## REFERENCE

1 Hammond, W. H., and Chayen, E., *Persistent Criminals*, London, HMSO (1963), p. 157.

## CHAPTER 10

# An Examination of Whether the Men Attended the Interviews Arranged

The key to whether we could test the hypothesis concerning the value of finding employment for men immediately on release largely rested on the ability of the director of Apex to find suitable jobs. On the other hand, the key to whether there was any truth in the hypothesis that the effort of Apex in finding employment would be rewarded by a lower reconviction rate largely rested with the men. In this chapter we begin to shift from examining the performance of the director of Apex to examining the performance of the men, for we are now concerned with whether or not the 190 men (97 Wormwood Scrubs, 93 Pentonville) of the full acceptance group who had been supplied with details of interviews actually attended the interviews which had been arranged for them.

For research purposes it would be desirable to record that similar details had been given to each man about the interview arranged, but in actual fact as the project progressed the director of Apex gave more and more specific details. Eventually not only were the more obvious instructions included, such as the time and date of the interview, the person to see and the address of the firm, but also fairly detailed suggestions on how to get to the organization by public transport. This was largely in an effort to try to avoid men's real or imagined excuse that they could not find the firm concerned. These full instructions are somewhat in contrast to the first part of the Wormwood Scrubs project when there were a few occasions when not even a specific time and date for an interview were given but the arrangement was simply that the man could see the personnel manager at the man's earliest opportunity after release. This is not a satisfactory procedure for it is open to a number of dangers. The prisoner may suspect that Apex has not even contacted the firm concerned (although in fact this was never the case in the present project) or the employer may not recognize the man sent by Apex as any different from the multitude of casual callers with whom he may have to deal or, alternatively, the prisoner may turn up many weeks after his release still expecting that the employer will be holding open the vacancy. Hence, for many reasons a specific time and date is much more appropriate and puts the arrangement on a more businesslike footing. On the other hand, it is vital to emphasize to the ex-prisoner that the interview can probably be re-arranged if he contacts either Apex or the employer before the scheduled time of the interview. There is no doubt that the timetable of the ex-prisoner can easily get disrupted by the queueing sometimes necessary to obtain social security benefits or the time-consuming trail of trying to find accommodation.

Seventy-nine men (35 Wormwood Scrubs, 44 Pentonville) apparently failed to attend the interview as arranged. In 73 of these cases (33 Wormwood Scrubs, 40 Pentonville) there appeared to be no unprompted contact by the men with either Apex or the employer at the time of their release to explain their behaviour. Of the remainder, in one case a Pentonville man asked after his release if Apex would cancel the interview. He phoned Apex a few days after he should have attended the interview but said that he had to go to hospital for an injection to cure a penicillin rash. The director of Apex asked if he wanted the interview to be re-arranged, but the director reports that 'this was obviously the wrong thing to say. He hedged for a moment and then said that he was going "down to the Corporation" for he had heard of some good jobs on the dustbins or something'. In another case there is evidence that an employer who had agreed to re-engage a former employee had written to the man in prison endorsing his offer and the prisoner had replied, unbeknown to Apex at the time, that he was probably not interested after all as he had made alternative plans! In the remaining four cases (1 Wormwood Scrubs, 3 Pentonville) the men contacted Apex when they knew that they would fail to arrive in time for the interview at the arranged time and date, but they also failed to attend the re-arranged interview and contact was broken.

Of the 111 men (62 Wormwood Scrubs, 49 Pentonville) who made at least some contact with the employer, 93 (56 Wormwood Scrubs, 37 Pentonville) attended the interview at the correct place at the correct time. The confusion in the remaining cases was varied, but in eight cases (2 Wormwood Scrubs, 6 Pentonville) it was the comparatively straightforward matter of failing to attend the original interview but satisfactorily attending a re-arranged interview. The fact that a higher proportion of Pentonville men attended re-arranged interviews probably reflects the more efficient 'retrieval' procedure as the project progressed rather than any real difference between the two samples. In the other ten cases (4 Wormwood Scrubs, 6 Pentonville) there was definite confusion but Apex was not directly involved in trying to resolve the situation. These were the cases when men eventually arrived for interviews but not at the agreed time (in contradistinction to men who phoned Apex in the hope of re-arranging the scheduled interview) or, as happened in one case, when the ex-prisoner arrived at the firm punctually but was interviewed for the wrong job by the wrong man – in fact he went for a job as a fitter's mate but was taken on as a labourer at the sewage works. This perhaps indicates the difficulty of being a reticent ex-prisoner and having the name Smith!

As we shall see when we discuss whether or not the men were accepted for the jobs, failure to attend an interview at the time arranged does inevitably have a poor effect on a man's chances of securing a position (even if the vacancy has not been filled by the time of his late arrival!). These men demonstrate the muddle with which a proportion seem to conduct their lives and one begins to have some insight into the number of jobs and opportunities which are lost not because of a criminal background but because of a lack of a sense of timing. Apex and sympathetic employers were able to retrieve situations and job opportunities which almost certainly would have been lost in the normal course of events.

However, one must avoid the impression that failure to attend an interview arranged by Apex inevitably means that the men are to be found queueing for social security benefits. There is perhaps an understandable tendency to assume that men who have wandered from a course so carefully planned by after-care workers must be heading for disaster. In fact, the impression gained from follow-up interviews is that one cannot generalize so glibly. As an example, Willy had been very happy that he had an interview to attend on release and was very profuse with his thanks. One suspected the worst when he had not attended the interview after release and had not contacted Apex. A follow-up indicated that he had been too sick to attend the interview arranged by Apex but had found him-self a job within a few days as a labourer doing conversion work. He liked the job because he was able to move about from area to area. At the second follow-up, five months later, he was still at the same job and the interviewer noted:

I found Willy alone. It was a hot evening but I found Willy stripped to the waist sitting watching telly with the windows tightly shut and a stove full on. He went on watching telly most of the time I was there only giving me about a quarter of his attention. All the same he was quite pleasant and forthcoming. He said he was still working for Blank and Blank where he had gone in preference to the firm where Apex had found him a job. His reason, he said, was simply that it was nearer and someone had suggested he tried there. He was very satisfied – plenty of overtime and he thought it would be permanent.

Although the matter was not relentlessly pursued at the interview, there was some evidence to suggest that he was not too sick to attend the Apex interview but had simply been exercising his own choice in considering the two possibilities. In another case, the young man took the unusual step of writing and thanking Apex for arranging an interview but went on to say that 'I did not attend the interview as my brother-in-law has arranged for me to be employed by his firm and this will be a better job'. Another phoned at a later date to say that he had been to his local employment exchange and had already been accepted for a job as a labourer (one suspects that this is a case where the pre-release procedure of the Department of Employment had worked particularly well).

It was not possible to locate the majority of the men who failed to attend an interview and it appears that a considerable proportion of these men were fairly mobile and that the area in which they thought they would settle sometimes had only a remote link with reality. One man who said that he wished to return to a former employer in Hampshire was soon after release seen in Hounslow, while another who was supposed to be living in Hounslow sent a postcard from Bristol asking if Apex could get him work!

Others who were contacted after release had obviously not settled in any work routine. Eddie was seen the day prior to his release. He had received the letter explaining the details of the job arranged as a plumber and was, as the director notes:

on top of the world because (*a*) he thought I wouldn't be able to get him a plumbing job (so did I) (*b*) my contact with Mr. C. had resulted in Eddie getting some work for Saturday (*c*) of my arrangements with the M.S.S. about his tools (*d*) he has had a pleasant letter from the Bank Manager in answer to a letter we suggested he wrote. He was most profuse in his thanks; invited us both to his house at any time and asked if he could keep in contact with us after release.

The next day an officer from the Ministry of Social Security phoned to say that Eddie had arrived at the MSS at 2.00 p.m. having not been home, said he was not going home, was not going to the job and wanted a ticket for a doss-house for the weekend. He had apparently spent all but 30s of the £4 from the prison discharge grant and the MSS was going to give him 30s for lodgings with instructions to report to its nearest office on Monday for more money. A short while later the manager of the MSS phoned to say that he had interviewed Eddie personally and after some time had got a story from him. This was to the effect that Eddie had had an affair with a girl prior to going into prison and he thought his wife had found out and he was frightened to go home. When he was a little more co-operative the manager asked him if he wanted to see his child again and after a long discussion Eddie eventually agreed that it would be best to go home. A month later an interviewer heard a somewhat different story:

I saw Eddie, his wife, who is very good-looking, and their eighteen-month-old son. Eddie reacted very strongly at the first mention of Apex. He started throwing his arms about and exploding like a rocket sayings things like, 'I don't want to have nothing to do with it', and 'I'm fine, I'm free, I don't like to have anything to do with anybody' and then a lot about how humiliated he'd been and then more about being free and not wanting to have anything to do with anything. After a bit he calmed down and I gathered that he felt guilt towards Apex but not hatred. The person he felt hatred for was the man at the Social Security where he felt he had been unforgivably humiliated. He went on a lot about how he'd been offered 30/-, 30/- – what could he do with that? The tools they'd offered weren't such as any self-respecting plumber would consider for a moment. He had been so humiliated that he'd felt he had to get away and so he'd gone off to St. Albans. He didn't say for how long.

He was evasive about what he was doing now. He recited a long list of things he was not doing – 'I'm not in a job; I'm not self employed; I'm not sub-contracting – but I'm free. . . .' My conclusion is that he is now doing occasional odd jobs. He is still terribly touchy and hasn't digested his prison experience – can't bear the idea of being asked why his cards are not stamped and isn't likely to try to get a regular job for this reason – kept on saying things like 'I don't want anyone knowing anything about me, see?'

It was a fairly familiar pattern for some of the men to drift into self-employment. Self-employment is not simply a way of avoiding the problem of confronting an employer, but has its own attraction in that one can organize one's own work routine. Reginald had been self-employed before the present sentence but insisted that he wanted to settle down in paid employment after release. He failed to attend the interview arranged in his chosen work as gardener. The interviewer recorded a visit to

> the small, stucco council house, run down and kicked about. I had a short talk with Reginald on the front step. He said he couldn't ask me in as he was in the act of putting in a new fireplace in the front room. He said he had started up a gardening business with one of his brothers . . . he said he was much better off now that he had borrowed some money. He has also bought a car.

It was not uncommon for pressing domestic chores to be the apparent reason for not starting work immediately on release. This was the case with Patrick who maintained that the place was in chaos as a result of his absence in prison although it is difficult to believe that the old warehouse that his large family occupy could ever be otherwise. He had written earlier to say that:

> I have been to see about a job myself which I am sure I shall get where no one will ever know anything about where I have been as I have payed for what I have done and I want to live with my Family in peace from now on. I am very Gratfull for what you have done for me but now I am home I shall be able to look after myself and my Family. I know that the jobs you got ware Good ones but as I had not got the letters with me I did not know the Addresses. . . .

A follow-up revealed that he had failed to get the job and had now decided that for the time being he would stay at home and make the place comfortable, which he seemed to do very well in the circumstances. His wife was entering hospital for an operation the next week and he obviously had plenty to do in coping with a household of six children ranging from 14 years to 13 months. This was not a dissimilar situation from Arthur who had not quite as large a family, but Arthur and his wife had decided to try to keep at home a severely subnormal child as well as coping with another child and a mother-in-law. The interviewer noted that:

> Arthur said that he couldn't find Blank Painters Ltd., where he had been supposed to go for an interview. He said he'd spent about eight shillings in fares. He didn't intend to try again. He was happily engaged in repainting the flat so that it would be nice for his wife after the baby is born. It is expected soon. He

was not going to think about another job until after Easter when he might go in with his father who is a painter. He assured me that he intended to keep in touch with Apex and was very grateful etc.

He telephoned Apex after Easter but failed to arrive for an interview. Over a year later after no further contact with Apex, an interviewer visited Arthur.

Arthur let me in and led me to the 'front' room. Newly painted but not yet furnished – just a red, plastic-covered three-piece suite and net curtains and linoleum on the floor. We stood in the centre of this room, which Arthur was obviously rather proud of, while we talked. Arthur seemed very much more confident and secure than when I last visited them a year ago. He was very forthcoming and confiding and obviously pleased with the way he has tackled his difficulties. He now has a steady – what he called a 'for life' job as maintenance man with Blank Hotels. He has been doing this for about six months. Before that he had a painting job which he kept for around seven months before he became redundant, but from this employer he got a 'very good' reference on the strength of which he got himself the hotel job. Getting it was a stroke of luck as he happened to walk in and ask when they were in need of a man. Arthur said that his time in the Scrubs had cured him of any desire for a life of crime. 'It either makes you or breaks you,' he said. 'I used to look down at the chaps in the exercise yard, walking round and round in a little circle and I used to say to myself, 'yes, you're the bright boys, you're the clever ones; no, I'd rather be safe.'

## THE DIRECTOR'S INTERVIEW ATTENDANCE PREDICTIONS

During the early part of the Wormwood Scrubs study, the first director of Apex had caused much discussion by insisting that if he were allowed to select the men on an intuitive basis there would be a dramatic rise in the number of men who started at the job arranged by Apex. This idea was disputed by the research officer who felt that when two men were matched for previous criminal record and job history there was no estimate above chance level of which one would attend the interview. There was no opportunity of adding a further study to test this belief and it was felt at this juncture that there was a danger that if it was incorporated into the main study it could degenerate into a self-fulfilling prophecy.

However, during the latter half of the main Pentonville study, it was clear that the then director of Apex would not regard any results as a threat to his own position and so he was asked to write a short report after seeing each member of the full acceptance group for the last time in prison when he had discussed what had been arranged regarding a job interview on release. His instructions were simply to record his impression as to whether or not each man for whom an interview had been arranged would attend that interview and further to record how he felt each man had reacted to the interview offer. He was encouraged to use his experience as a placing officer to make an 'interview attendance prediction', and to base his prediction on a subjective impression gained at the interview and not on previous criminal record and job history. In other words, this was some attempt to test the director's intuitive 'feel' of the situation as to whether or not a man would attend an interview.

These items were not pre-coded, for it was felt that the director would feel freer to record his subjective impressions if he was allowed to write a short open-ended report. Discounting one man who rejected the interview offer when seen by the director, there were 70 men on whom the director made some comment after the final prison interview. Open-ended questions are notoriously difficult to code, but regarding the 'interview attendance prediction' his comments seemed to polarize fairly readily between comments that the prisoner would attend or was likely to attend and comments suggesting that he would not attend or that there was a high element of doubt expressed about his possible attendance. (There were cases when the director added that, although he thought the man would attend the interview arranged he felt he would probably refuse the job offered, but these can obviously be regarded as predictions that he would attend the interview.) The director predicted that 39 men were likely to attend and 17 men were unlikely to attend, and he failed to make any suitable comment of prediction for the remaining 14. Table 18 indicates the outcome of the various predictions with regard to whether or not the men actually attended the interview arranged and also the numbers in each group who started the job (although there was no prediction on this latter behaviour):

It is clear from the table that the director is not able to predict on an intuitive basis whether a man is likely to attend the interview he has arranged, and, although the result is not significant at the 5 per cent level ($x^2 = 2 \cdot 86$; 1 d.f.; N.S.) the trend is in fact in the opposite direction, for whereas only 46 per cent of those whom he

TABLE 18  *The director's interview attendance predictions for the Pentonville sample and the various outcomes*

|  | Predictions No. | (%) | No. who attended | % who attended | No. who started | % who started |
|---|---|---|---|---|---|---|
| Prediction that he is likely to attend interview arranged | 39 | 56 | 18 | 46 | 6 | 15 |
| Prediction that he is not likely to attend interview arranged | 17 | 24 | 12 | 71 | 7 | 41 |
| No prediction made | 14 | 20 | 7 | 50 | 7 | 50 |
| TOTAL | 70 | 100 | 37 | 53 | 20 | 29 |

thought would attend did so, 71 per cent of the supposed bad risks did so! The difference is just as striking when one considers the percentage of the various groups who actually started the job, but one must emphasize that the director was not attempting to predict that particular outcome.

The director noted in addition how he considered each man had reacted to the offer of the interview. These reactions seemed to fall suitably into three types which are described as follows with some examples of the comments used by the director:

*Demonstrative pleasure* – e.g. extremely happy, very pleased, thrilled, very jolly.

*Contented but less demonstrative* – e.g. quite happy, quite pleased, interested.

*Cautiousness or hesitancy* – e.g. cautious, shaky, not too happy, cool reception, non-committal.

TABLE 19  *Reaction to interview offer noted by director and various outcomes*

|  | Reaction No. | (%) | No. who attended | % who attended | No. who started | % who started |
|---|---|---|---|---|---|---|
| Demonstrative pleasure | 27 | 40 | 17 | 63 | 12 | 44 |
| Contented but less demonstrative | 30 | 44 | 13 | 43 | 7 | 23 |
| Cautiousness or hesitancy | 11 | 16 | 5 | 45 | 1 | 9 |
| TOTAL | 68 | 100 | 35 | 51 | 20 | 29 |

All except two of the 70 men could be coded into one of these categories and these categories are compared in Table 19 in terms of attending the interview and starting the job.

The table tends to suggest that there may be some value in accepting a man's reaction at face value, particularly with regard to whether the man will eventually start at the job arranged. The present analysis, however, fails to control whether the men were simply responding to better job offers, and so cautiousness or hesitancy may reflect some inappropriateness of the interview offer. This factor could easily be controlled if a series of men wished to be, for example, building site labourers, for then the comparative measure for each man would be more nearly their reaction to a suitable job offer. On the other hand, a response of cautiousness or hesitancy does seem to indicate a very disorganized group of men, for even of the five who eventually attended the interview arranged only one arrived at the correct place at the correct time while the other four either arrived a day or so late or had to have their interviews re-arranged (this compares with only six out of thirty men in the other two categories who failed to arrive correctly first time).

Table 20 combines the director's prediction on attendance and his comments on the reaction to the offer. There were 54 out of a total of 70 for whom there was enough information for this particular analysis.

TABLE 20 *The director's interview attendance predictions combined with reaction to offer and various outcomes*

| | No. | (%) | No. who attended | % who attended | No. who started | % who started |
|---|---|---|---|---|---|---|
| *Prediction of attendance* | | | | | | |
| Demonstrative pleasure | 18 | 33 | 9 | 50 | 5 | 28 |
| Contented but less demonstrative | 16 | 30 | 6 | 38 | 1 | 6 |
| Cautiousness or hesitancy | 3 | 6 | 1 | 33 | — | — |
| *Prediction of no attendance* | | | | | | |
| Demonstrative pleasure | 4 | 7 | 4 | 100 | 3 | 75 |
| Contented but less demonstrative | 6 | 11 | 4 | 67 | 3 | 50 |
| Cautiousness or hesitancy | 7 | 13 | 4 | 57 | 1 | 14 |
| TOTAL | 54 | 100 | 28 | 52 | 13 | 24 |

Although the numbers in each group are extremely small, it is clear that a man's reaction to the interview offer is a better indication of whether he is likely to attend the interview than the director's own intuitive prediction. In actual fact, when one holds constant each reaction in turn, there is evidence that the director tends consistently to select the bad risks!

One must emphasize that this is simply a test of one person's intuitive sense and the first director could, of course, still maintain that he could have predicted with considerably more success. However, this short section indicates that such claims should be regarded with extreme caution and one suspects that intuition is not really a profitable source of improving the success rate of Apex.

PROPORTIONS IN EACH RISK CATEGORY TO ATTEND THE INTERVIEW ARRANGED

If one examines the three risk categories, there is not a dramatic difference in the proportions in each group who attend the interview arranged, although again the low risk and medium risk categories have a more favourable outcome than the high risk category. Whereas 65 per cent of the low risk and 59 per cent of the medium risk category attended the interview, only 49 per cent of the high risk category did likewise, as is shown in Table 21.

TABLE 21 *Number and percentage of interviews attended in various risk categories together with reconviction rates*

| Risk category | Attended interview (%) | | Did not attend interview (%) | | % attending interview |
|---|---|---|---|---|---|
| | No. | reconvicted | No. | reconvicted | |
| Low risk – Wormwood Scrubs | 39 | 16·2* | 21 | 14·3 | 65·0 |
| Medium risk – 'Wormville' | 48 | 39·6 | 33 | 48·5 | 59·3 |
| High risk – Pentonville | 24 | 62·5 | 25 | 72·0 | 49·0 |
| TOTAL | 111 | 36·7 | 79 | 46·8 | 58·4 |

* There was no reconviction information on two men in this category and this figure has been calculated on a reduced base.

In fact, there are two related possibilities as to why the difference between the high and low risks is not even greater. As the project progressed, the 'retrieval' procedure improved considerably so that interviews could be re-arranged if necessary, and this would benefit the Pentonville rather than the Wormwood Scrubs sample. The other related point is that there would be a much greater difference between the risk groups if only those men who attended the interview at the correct place and at the correct time and date were included.

In the same way that it would be remarkable if men for whom no interview had been arranged were shown to benefit from the Apex service, it would be equally remarkable if those who did not attend the interview arranged gained much from the Apex project. Within each risk category, Table 21 compares the reconviction rates of those who attended interviews arranged by Apex and those who did not attend interviews. This suggests that there is no difference in terms of subsequent reconviction for the low risk category whether or not the men attend the Apex interview, but there is a slight indication for the medium and high risk groups that failure to attend the Apex interview begins to highlight the vulnerable group within the risk category. Although the follow-up was extremely limited, there was some suggestion that when the men in the low risk group failed to attend an Apex interview they made their own employment arrangements (and sometimes these were more appropriate to their own situation), while the men in the higher risk groups who failed to attend seemed more rarely to have taken alternative employment action.

The risk categories are, of course, calculated largely on the basis of the men's previous criminality and their previous work history, so in considering whether or not a person is likely to attend a job interview it may well be worthwhile to examine certain attributes which may seem more relevant to the situation after release. Two such possibilities are obviously a man's marital status and his proposed domicile after release. Of the 94 men who maintained they were single, 52 (or 55·3 per cent) attended the interview arranged, while this was the case with 44 (or 62·9 per cent) of the 70 married men. Of the remaining 26 men (who said they were either separated, divorced, or widowed), 15 (or 57·7 per cent) attended the Apex interview. Of the 116 men who stated that they were returning to their family household (either birth or marriage), 70 (or 60·3 per cent) attended the interview, while the remaining 74 who were either making other arrangements or for whom there was no information on domicile plans after release 41 (or 55·4 per cent) attended the Apex interview. Neither of these attributes seems a particularly good discriminator – at least in the form in which they have been analyzed in the present project.

TABLE 22 *Number and percentage of men who attended interviews in terms of field of employment in which interviews were arranged*

| Field of employment in which interview was arranged | No. of men for whom interview was arranged | No. of men who attended interview | % attending interview arranged |
|---|---|---|---|
| Professional groups and public bodies | 9 | 8 | 88·9 |
| Shops | 4 | 2 | 50·0 |
| Commerce and selling | 4 | 3 | 75·0 |
| Manufacturing and extraction firms | 63 | 37 | 58·7 |
| Catering industry | 25 | 15 | 60·0 |
| Transport undertakings | 16 | 11 | 68·8 |
| Service industries | 20 | 8 | 40·0 |
| Civil engineering and building | 49 | 27 | 55·1 |
| TOTAL | 190 | 111 | 58·4 |

TABLE 23 *Number and percentage of men who attended interviews in terms of level of occupation at which interviews were arranged*

| Level of occupation at which interview was arranged | No. of men for whom interview was arranged | No. of men who attended interview | % attending interview arranged |
|---|---|---|---|
| Non-manual – higher grade | 4 | 3 | 75·0 |
| Skilled manual and routine grades of non-manual | 41 | 23 | 56·1 |
| Semi-skilled manual | 73 | 46 | 63·0 |
| Unskilled manual | 70 | 39 | 55·7 |
| TOTAL | 188* | 111 | 59·0 |

\* Two men who did not attend interviews were to discuss a suitable level of occupation with the employer.

Perhaps a more promising line of approach would be to consider that the field of employment and level of occupation in which
an interview is arranged is somewhat more pertinent to the question
of whether a man is likely to attend a job interview, as in Tables 22
and 23.

Table 22 indicates that there is a slight variation in terms of the
field of employment in which an interview was arranged. While the
two largest categories of manufacturing and civil engineering
approximate to the mean in each case with just under 60 per cent
of the men attending interviews, men with interviews with 'professional groups and public bodies' and in 'commerce and selling' have
a higher attendance rating, but this is largely explained by the fact
that it was in these two fields that most of the non-manual workers
were placed. As Table 23 shows, three out of the four non-manual
workers attended interviews arranged, while this was the case with
just under 60 per cent of the manual workers.

In conclusion, this chapter has indicated several interesting
features. In the first place, less than three in five of the men actually
attended job interviews which had been arranged in the belief
that the proposed jobs would answer their employment needs. If
one tries to predict which men are likely to attend the interviews
after release without considering their criminal record or previous
work history, there is some evidence that one is likely to be wrong
more often than right! When one does begin to take their past
behaviour into account, there is a tendency for the better risks to
be more likely to attend the interview arranged. Even so, for the
better risks who fail to attend, one should not get too despondent
about their future prospects, for not only do they not get reconvicted
to any greater extent but perhaps they simply arrange employment
more to their own liking. However, the prospects for the poorer
risks who fail to attend the interviews are less promising, for they
get reconvicted to a greater extent than the men who do attend.
When the poorer risks fail to attend, one suspects that in many
cases this is the end of their job-seeking activities on release. The
various fields of employment have somewhat similar proportions of
men who attend the interviews arranged, and where there is a higher
attendance rating it is in the fields in which most of the non-manual
workers were placed. There are similar proportions attending from
the various grades of manual work.

## CHAPTER 11

# An Examination of Whether the Men Were
# Accepted for the Jobs by the Employers

There were 111 men of the full acceptance group who attended at least one interview arranged by Apex within a few days of release, and we will consider the outcome of the most favourable interview* in terms of whether or not the employer offered employment. One must emphasize that when an employer agreed to see a prisoner after release this was not a definite promise of a job but he had given an indication to Apex that there was a suitable vacancy which the prisoner would almost certainly obtain if he conducted himself reasonably well at the interview. The present chapter heading gives the clue to the fact that certain men were interviewed by employers and not subsequently engaged.

Eighty-six men (51 Wormwood Scrubs, 35 Pentonville) were accepted for the job with no further complications in the sense that the employer offered employment on similar terms to those Apex had explained to the men before release.

As we shall note subsequently, eight of these men (6 Wormwood Scrubs, 2 Pentonville) refused the job offered at the interview while a further thirteen men (6 Wormwood Scrubs, 7 Pentonville) appeared to accept the job offered but failed to start the job on the day agreed with the employer. We are not at present concerned with these particular 21 men, for they can still be included among those offered a definite job and we shall deal with their reaction as a separate issue in another section. However, there were 25 men who were to all intents and purposes rejected for the job by employers although this was rarely a straightforward and outright rejection at the time of the interview. Table 24 indicates that, whatever the reasons for rejection, the 'high risk category' seems particularly vulnerable, for over one-third of the men in this category were not finally accepted for the job.

Men who fail to secure jobs after the elaborate procedure by which Apex attempts to 'soften the ground' would seem to be very likely candidates for getting into further trouble after release, for one assumes that they will fare even worse when finding work on

---

* The 'most favourable' outcome refers to those occasions where more than one interview was arranged within a few days of release.

TABLE 24 *Number and percentage of those accepted for jobs in various risk categories together with reconviction rates*

| Risk category | Accepted for job (%) | | Not accepted for job (%) | | % accepted for job |
|---|---|---|---|---|---|
| | No. | reconvicted | No. | reconvicted | |
| Low risk – Wormwood Scrubs | 32 | 20·0* | 7 | 0 | 82·1 |
| Medium risk – 'Wormville' | 39 | 35·9 | 9 | 55·6 | 81·3 |
| High risk – Pentonville | 15 | 66·7 | 9 | 55·6 | 62·5 |
| TOTAL | 86 | 35·7 | 25 | 40·0 | 77·5 |

* There was no reconviction information on two men in this category and this figure has been calculated on a reduced base.

their own initiative. However, it is probably unwise to pursue this too far, for this argument is not really supported by the evidence of the reconviction rates. Except for the medium risk category, where 55·6 per cent of those not accepted for the Apex job, compared with only 35·9 per cent of those who were accepted, are reconvicted within one year, there is nothing to support the contention that those not accepted will fare demonstrably worse than their counterparts. In fact, for the low risk category it would almost seem an advantage not to be accepted for the job arranged, for none of these men was reconvicted! Clearly this is a phenomenon which needs further examination, for up to now there has been no group in which none of the members has been reconvicted. It is remarkable how accurately employers seem to have skimmed off some of the better prospects and then rejected them!

First of all, though, it is worthwhile to consider why 25 men were not accepted for the job which had been originally discussed with Apex. In fact there was a whole range of reasons for this happening. At one extreme, there were cases where a reasonable man would suggest that the ex-prisoner was at fault, when the discharged prisoner did not appear for an interview until days and, on one occasion, weeks later (in this latter case, the prisoner appeared to be amazed that there was no longer a vacancy). At the other extreme, there are occasions when the employer seems somewhat tactless in the context of trying to help a man who has just left prison. In one case a coloured man attending an interview was told that he was accepted for the job in principle but the firm said that they had to fix the appropriate rate for his experience. After ten days of prompting by the prisoner and by Apex to ascertain the rate so that he could start the job, Apex was eventually told that the firm had decided that the rate was too low to offer him. It is impossible to speculate why this tortuous procedure of turning a man down was put into operation, but it is salutary to reflect that this was a large organization which had maintained that it was sympathetic to the problem of ex-prisoners settling into work. In most cases, though, it is the actions or attitudes of the ex-prisoner which cause some employers to reconsider their offer. If a man has been sleeping rough for a couple of nights before the interview, his general appearance has already deteriorated somewhat and this may prompt the somewhat revised statement that 'there is not a vacancy at present'. Similarly, if a man has exaggerated his qualifications and experience so that Apex arranges an interview beyond his capabilities, then he may well be rejected by a personnel manager with the knowledge to reveal these deficiencies; an ex-prisoner who persuaded Apex that he was a fully skilled and highly experienced motor mechanic was revealed as no more than an improver by a garage manager who gave all potential employees a test before offering a definite job. One suspects that many of the men who over-state their experience and skills in the prison interview do not get as far as even attending when Apex has arranged an interview for a job commensurate with their supposed ability. There was one particularly good example of this. Bert lasted less than a couple of days in freedom and the reason he did not attend the re-arranged interview was that he had been remanded in custody for assaulting a policeman. When Bert eventually arrived back in Pentonville, the prison decided to make use of his supposed ability as a baker and told him to prepare the dough. The Master Baker subsequently found him scrubbing the floor and on enquiring why he was doing this rather than the job he had been told to do discovered that Bert had no idea of bakery work at all and the story he had told Apex about his bakery experience was a complete fabrication.

In another case, the employer said that the original job offer was no longer available, but offered unskilled work as an alternative; it is difficult to estimate whether this was another 'kind' way of rejecting the applicant. In fact, although the present project was not able to investigate this further, one often suspected that the response of 'there is no longer a vacancy' or 'there is not a vacancy at present' can rarely be taken at face value. In the present situation where the employer had at least agreed to interview a man whom he knew was an ex-prisoner, failure to get the job probably indicates the complete failure of an ex-prisoner to project himself well at an interview. On some occasions where the matter is discussed with an employer subsequently, it would appear that some men seemed to put their worst face forward almost as a deliberate policy to lose the chance of a possible job! Some men are extremely unsure of themselves and interview badly (often appearing tremendously over-confident to the employer); this behaviour makes the employer uneasy and he either prevaricates or makes the excuse that there is no longer a suitable vacancy. Our most dramatic experience of this was when one employer interviewed a prisoner at the Apex offices and the whole process of damaging an interview situation was acted out in front of the director of Apex. The prisoner exaggerated his assets to such an extent that it was clear that the potential employer began to doubt the man's genuine abilities. One can be reasonably sure that, if this sort of problem occurs after all the preparation made by Apex, it happens extremely frequently when in normal circumstances neither the employer nor the ex-prisoner has the support of Apex. Apex has already overcome the greatest difficulty of explaining to the employer the gap of the last few months, so it is disturbing to consider how some ex-prisoners must conduct themselves at interviews when they are also trying to hide the fact that they have a criminal record. While the number of men failing to get a job at the first interview arranged by Apex may seem high, a closer examination of some of these case histories gives some indication of how the recidivist sometimes fails to secure a job by trying too hard – these men seem to tell employers either that they are worth twice the salary offered and make the employer uneasy by hiding their smallest shortcomings or they make a clean breast of everything and make the employer even more uneasy by showing what a complete and utter bum he is contemplating employing.

It is fairly evident that the men with the longer criminal records and poorer work records sometimes lost their job opportunities after totally failing to measure up to the employer's conception of a suitable employee. Sometimes it may be that they presented themselves after a night or two of 'sleeping rough', often declining to stay in a hostel, but more usually it seemed to be a case of talking themselves out of a job. More rarely, though, could this be the explanation for those in the low risk category who were not accepted for the job as arranged.

Tentatively one wonders whether one of the factors in this

instance may well be the ethnic origin. Although the fact that 19 out of 94 (or 20·2 per cent) men with white skin colour were not accepted compared with 6 out of 16 (or 37·5 per cent) negroes* is not a statistically significant difference, this misses the important point that four of the seven men not accepted in the low risk category were negroes. In other words, in a group where there was generally a high proportion of men accepted, the negroes were grossly over-represented among those not accepted by employers. While this is scanty evidence to substantiate colour prejudice on the part of these employers (and, of course, the men were rejected for reasons other than that of pigment!), this is some indication that the negro has a worse deal than comparable men with a lighter skin pigment from employers who are sympathetic by the definition that they are willing to consider employing ex-prisoners. If there is even a suggestion that this may happen with generally sympathetic employers, it is distressing to consider what happens when the negro ex-prisoner tries to obtain employment with employers who are even unsympathetic to the needs of ex-prisoners without the extra burden of being a negro ex-prisoner.

In considering whether any particular field of employment seems to have a particularly high non-acceptance rate, it is perhaps wise to limit the analysis to the four main fields in which ten or more men attended interviews. The evidence would suggest that, if the man manages to attend the interview, transport undertakings and civil engineering industries have the best record of putting their words of interest into action, for over 90 per cent of the men attending interviews in these two fields were offered a job in some capacity. In contrast, manufacturing firms and the catering industry offered jobs to just over 70 per cent of the men they interviewed. One must hasten to emphasize that there are many factors which may cause these differences in the acceptance rate. As examples, it may be that the director of Apex was somewhat more adept at assessing the abilities of those men wanting jobs in transport undertakings or civil engineering and sent them for more suitable vacancies; alternatively, the calibre of men seeking jobs in those fields may be somewhat higher. The possible explanations at this stage are almost endless.

As far as the level of occupation is concerned, there is an almost identical acceptance rate for all levels of manual work, and the slightly lower proportion for those seeking non-manual jobs is probably just a reflection of the small numbers involved.

* There is little evidence on this point for men of other ethnic origins. An Indian who attended the interview as arranged was accepted for the job.

What we have learned from this chapter is that the hazardous course has not been completed by the arrival of the ex-prisoner at the interview. He still has to negotiate this hurdle although he has sometimes made the hurdle more difficult by arriving there two or three days late! Three out of every four men interviewed are in fact offered work. Of those not accepted, there is some evidence that negroes seem to fare comparatively badly, while there is also a disproportionate number of men from the high risk categories. It is worth recalling how at each stage the high risk category has had a much poorer outcome compared with the other groups. In the first place, a higher proportion of these men were asked to come to Apex with the result that 25 per cent of the high risk category compared with 10 per cent of the others had no acceptable job interview arranged on release. Then 51 per cent of the high risk group failed to attend the interview compared with 38 per cent of the other two groups. Finally, this section has shown that 38 per cent of the high risk group are turned down by employers, while this is the case for only 18 per cent of the remainder of the men in the other categories. Before even considering whether any men in the high risk category started at a job arranged by Apex, the original number of 65 men has diminished to 15. This indicates to some extent the difficulty of helping those who probably need help the most.

## CHAPTER 12

# An Examination of Whether the Men Started the Job as Agreed with the Employer

We have already pointed out that 21 of the 86 men who were offered employment failed to start the work which was offered. In eight of these cases, the men refused the job at the interview so that the employer did at least know the position, but the remaining thirteen men agreed with the employer that they would start on a particular day but failed to make an appearance on that day (or any subsequent day, for that matter).

The reason given almost invariably for rejecting a job offer at the interview was the low pay offered. The most frequent situation was that a wage of £14–£16 per week was offered but the men maintained that they needed at least £20 per week. There is no reason at all to believe that employers were giving lower rates of pay because they were ex-prisoners and in fact the wage offered was the wage that Apex had suggested they could reasonably expect. The men felt, on the other hand, that this was simply the basic pay and that they could expect bonuses or overtime to make up the money. Only one of the men who turned down the job at the interview contacted Apex again to try to find another job interview and this one was undoubtedly as a result of a follow-up interview. Many of the others were not subsequently traced, although those that were are quite revealing. One intended to work for four days a week with an elder brother who sub-contracted demolition work. (The elder brother, Joe, happened to be there at the follow-up, and said that he had been working regularly at this for three years and emphasized that the money was good. Joe said he did not expect John to stick it even for one day, but 'he's all right' – John was soon afterwards sentenced to eighteen months for housebreaking.) Another was working as a plasterer's labourer for a man who sub-contracted, while another had found himself work as a hotel porter. One man whom we had expected to return to a previous employer who described him as 'a good and willing worker and would be only too pleased to take him on again on his release' turned down the job offered and went his own way. Answering an enquiry from Apex he wrote that he was on 'peace work (concrete lintols) [sic] I do not like the work. But am remaining until driving licence is returned this month then onto long distance driving'. Three months later he wrote further:

Many thanks for your inquiries as to my position in life and society. At present I am doing local deliveries for Blank Ltd. I have been told that there is a chance I may be able to go on distance work on an eight wheeler which should be in the next two or three weeks, if the job doesn't materialise I have told my employer that I shall change my job which I shall be reluctant to do as I am more than happy with this firm, the only beefs I have is the wages (which work out to £11 after deductions and the fact that my heart is set on distance work of which I am used to.

As to my home life I am doing very well as I have my parents full support behind me if I should need it (touch wood I'll never need it again) but once you've lived on your own I just can't wait to get back my own independance but will be unable to on my present wages, thus the need for changing my job if nothing comes of the other one.

Within six months of writing this letter he was reconvicted for store-breaking and larceny and sentenced to twelve months' imprisonment.

The other main category contains men who agreed with the employer that they would start but never appeared subsequently. Some men probably had no intention of starting the job while others seemed to have *prima facie* genuine reasons for failing to start. Robert was unable to start because he had 'flu but he also failed to start when he had recovered from 'flu. When a representative from Apex called on Robert, it was clear that

he is obviously disturbed that he is not in work, but a whole range of emotions come into play to explain why he is not. He certainly wishes to earn what he calls 'reasonable wages'. . . . One of the main problems is pride – he is anxious not to earn less than Betty, his wife, who is working as a copy typist. . . .

On this occasion the interviewer went beyond discovering information and suggested how Robert should set about finding himself work. Soon afterwards the wife phoned Apex to thank the visitor for his help and said that the pep talk had remarkable results. The next day Robert went out and got himself a job as a driver for a fashion house without revealing that he was an ex-prisoner. He lost the job a couple of months later after an argument with the checker of the firm.

H

Although almost a quarter of the men who were offered employment failed to start, it was fairly evident from conversations with the employers that this is not a practice peculiar to ex-prisoners, for in general employers were not unduly distressed or surprised by this turn of events. There were others, though, who emphasized that 'this sort of thing is what prejudices employers against taking on ex-prisoners'.

Although there is naturally some difference between refusing a job at an interview and failing to start after agreeing to do so, the link between these two types of behaviour is that all the men appeared to be rejecting jobs which were identical with, or at least very similar to, jobs they should have been expecting if they had understood what the director had arranged for them. On the other hand, the matter is not quite so simple as a misunderstanding by the prisoners. An impression is that with certain low-status jobs one almost inevitably overstates the advantages of the particular job one has arranged and one tends to forget that in reality work as a kitchen porter or as a factory labourer is not particularly congenial wherever it takes place. The prisoner in the prison setting is not only willing to believe something which seems likely to be to his advantage on release, but magnifies the discrepancy between fact and fiction. On his arrival at the interview he may well be confronted with the reality that the job arranged is neither better nor worse than similar jobs he has been doing on and off for years. Instead of accepting what is available, he is still in a post-prison euphoria of believing that this time everything is going to be different and perhaps feels that Apex has failed to provide a job which is substantially different from many others he may have held in the past. A follow-up a few weeks later may well show that he is working (if he is working at all) in a similar job to the one arranged by Apex, so in strictly rational terms the turn of events seems almost incomprehensible.

Support for this explanation comes to some extent from an examination of the fields of employment and levels of occupation where men have failed to start work as arranged. The highest failure rates occurred in those industries where the ex-prisoners perhaps felt they could get a similar job but with 'no questions asked' in the way described by Dr Martin in his book *Offenders as Employees*.[1] Over or around a quarter of the men who were accepted for jobs in manufacturing, catering and building industries failed to start jobs for which they had been accepted. Starting a job would seem to be a particular problem for the unskilled manual workers. While both those men accepted for non-manual (higher grade) work started as arranged and only 15 per cent of the skilled and semi-skilled manual workers failed to start, 13 out of 30 (or 43 per cent) of the unskilled workers failed to start as arranged.

Not only do the men who fail to start work tend to have had unskilled manual jobs arranged by Apex, but there is also an interesting age factor which to some extent distinguishes them from men who do start the work arranged. The group of 21 men who failed to start the work are all under 40 years of age and in fact the majority are under 25 years of age. In contrast, it is perhaps remarkable that all the 15 men of 40 years or over who were accepted for the Apex job did actually start the job; furthermore, seven of them were from the Pentonville sample and four of these were in the 'high risk' category.

We suggested in the previous section on whether a man was accepted for the job that his ethnic origin appeared to be relevant. Even in the present section where the question of starting the job seemed to rest on a decision by the man concerned a higher proportion of negroes (40 per cent) compared with other skin pigments (23 per cent) failed to start the work even after being accepted for the job. There is not a ready explanation for this phenomenon, although follow-up information suggested that they failed to start because they regarded the work as low-status (usually expressed as badly paid or dirty). This seems to support further the view that it is the low-status jobs which tend to produce the wrong expectations when they are discussed in prison rather than the stereotypical explanation that negroes 'don't want work when it is offered'. The slightly higher proportion of lower status jobs offered to negroes would explain why there is an apparent difference between whites and negroes on this dimension.*

When one considers the proportions who did not start in the various risk categories, Table 25 shows for the first time that this is not a useful indicator, for approximately one in four of the men in each category failed to start the work arranged after being accepted for the job. This is a quite remarkable result and could be interpreted as somewhat reassuring for after-care workers. After the previous evidence that those in the high risk category seemed to fare that much less well, this suggests that if one can manage

* There were only nine men who stayed one year or more in the first job arranged by Apex. Two of these were negroes and their occupations were carpenter and lorry driver. In other words, this suggests that if they are capable and are found skilled or semi-skilled jobs they stay as long as men of any other ethnic origin.

to get recidivists as far as being accepted for jobs by employers there is no indication at all that they fail to start the work to any greater extent than men with much less penal experience. Clearly, in this case, comparative youth and unskilled work are much more relevant than past criminal behaviour in assessing the likelihood of a man starting at the work arranged.

TABLE 25    *Number and percentage of men who started jobs in various risk categories together with reconviction rates*

| Risk category | Started job | | Did not start job | | % who started job |
|---|---|---|---|---|---|
| | No. | (%) reconvicted | No. | (%) reconvicted | |
| Low risk – Wormwood Scrubs | 24* | 17·3 | 8* | 28·6 | 75·0 |
| Medium risk – 'Wormville' | 30 | 30·0 | 9 | 55·6 | 76·9 |
| High risk – Pentonville | 11 | 63·6 | 4 | 75·0 | 73·3 |
| TOTAL | 65 | 31·3 | 21 | 50·0 | 75·6 |

* There was no reconviction information on one man in each of these categories and these figures have been calculated on a reduced base.

When we examined whether men were accepted for the jobs by employers, we suggested that those who were not accepted could perhaps be regarded as those who were vulnerable in terms of settling down after release. The subsequent reconviction rates, however, failed to support this view. One could pursue a similar argument in the present case, for men who fail to start the work arranged are more obviously rejecting a possible opportunity to settle down. On this occasion, in fact, Table 25 indicates that within each risk category a higher proportion of those who failed to start the job as agreed with the employer were in fact reconvicted within one year after release. It is interesting to note how there is a regular pattern, but as a similar proportion within each risk category started the job arranged it is also reasonable to compare the total reconviction rates of the two groups. While 20 (or 31 per cent) of the 64 men who started the job were reconvicted within one year after release, this is the case with as many as 10 (or 50 per cent) of the men who failed to start work as arranged. It is fascinating that, while previous history seems to have little or no predictive value in estimating whether a man is likely to start the job arranged, whether or not a man does actually start seems to have some possible predictive value in estimating subsequent re-conviction.

It is undoubtedly a complex issue why men who have been offered jobs should decide to flout the opportunity and decide not to start. However, the fact that it is the unskilled and the younger age group for whom this is a particular problem gives some indirect support to the view that it may be worthwhile trying to develop occupational skills in prison so that these younger men can compete in a different market situation. An employment agency can only maximize any skills offered by its clients and is limited in its success by the appropriateness of what abilities can be offered to employers. In contrast to the disappointing outcome of those who fail to start work, particularly in the unskilled field, one should acknowledge the remarkable success with those aged 40 and over. Despite some very low-calibre men involved, all those aged 40 and over accepted for the Apex jobs actually started work. While everyone is understandably enthusiastic to think of schemes to deviate the young man from a life of crime, this is useful evidence to indicate that we can usefully give an opportunity to men who are much older. Wordsworth has suggested that 'age might but take the things Youth needed not!'[2]

## REFERENCES

1 Martin, J. P., *Offenders as Employees*, London, Macmillan (1962), pp. 32–4.
2 W. Wordsworth, 'The Small Celandine: There is a Flower' in *The Oxford Dictionary of Quotations*, London, OUP (1962), p. 573.

## CHAPTER 13

# An Examination of Length of Time Spent in First Job Arranged by Apex

Of the men who fully accepted the Apex service, it appears that 65 men (39 Wormwood Scrubs, 26 Pentonville) started work as a direct result of the initial efforts of Apex in trying to find suitable work. In other words, one could argue that under 30 per cent of the men whom Apex had hoped to assist could really be expected to demonstrate any benefit from the project, for while one can propose elaborate suggestions as to how the fact of participation in the project may help in less tangible ways, this was far from the main purpose of the exercise.

Men who started work in the Apex job could perhaps benefit from the situation in several different ways. In some cases they might find the job suitable to the extent that they might settle in the work more or less permanently, while others might use this first job as a springboard to other job opportunities. As we shall describe, some seemed to find that it was possible to change jobs on their own initiative after holding the Apex job for even a short time and that it was also possible to conceal their previous criminal record in their new job.* On the other hand, if a man stayed three months or more at the job arranged by Apex, there was then a much better opportunity of moving on to other employment with comparatively little risk of the future employer discovering the criminal past. The suggestion that a 'safe' period is three months or more is made because national insurance cards are on a quarterly basis and some planning can ensure that there are no revealing blank periods on the card.

Not surprisingly, the men stay at the first job arranged by Apex for a variety of lengths of time. We have already indicated that 37 per cent of the Wormwood Scrubs full acceptance group compared with only 22 per cent of the Pentonville full acceptance group started the Apex job, and Table 26 goes on to indicate that the Wormwood Scrubs men tended to stay longer at the Apex jobs than Pentonville men.

---

* Many men, of course, do not reveal their criminal record when obtaining their *first* job on leaving prison, but this differed from the Apex policy of revealing the fact of a criminal record to potential employers.

TABLE 26  *Length of time spent in first job arranged by Apex*

| Length of time in first job arranged by Apex | Wormwood Scrubs sample who started Apex job | | Pentonville sample who started Apex job | |
|---|---|---|---|---|
| | No. | (%) | No. | (%) |
| Still working in Apex job after one year | 8 ⎫ | | 1 ⎫ | |
| Left Apex job after working for: | ⎬ 33·3 | | ⎬ 23·1 | |
| Three months but less than one year | 5 ⎭ | | 5 ⎭ | |
| Two months but less than three months | 9 ⎫ | 38·5 | 5 ⎫ | 26·9 |
| One month but less than two months | 6 ⎭ | | 2 ⎭ | |
| Two weeks but less than one month | 6* ⎫ | | 4 ⎫ | |
| One week but less than two weeks | 3* ⎬ 28·2 | | 5 ⎬ 50·0 | |
| Less than one week | 2 ⎭ | | 4 ⎭ | |
| TOTAL | 39 | 100·0 | 26 | 100·0 |

\* There were four men in the Wormwood Scrubs sample for whom there was no more definite information than that they stayed over a week but less than a month – two placed in each category marked\*.

The table shows that whereas one-third of the men in the Wormwood Scrubs sample who started the Apex job stayed at least three months or more, this is the case for less than a quarter of the Pentonville sample. In fact, exactly half the Pentonville group left after less than one month, compared with just over a quarter of those from Wormwood Scrubs.

As the numbers involved are comparatively small and it was not possible to trace all the men who left the Apex jobs to try to find out why in fact they decided to leave at that particular juncture, it is not worthwhile to say much about the apparent reasons why the men moved on. On the other hand, it is possible to demonstrate how a particular length of time at this first job may mask several different outcomes. For this purpose we will consider Peter and Pat, both of whom stayed at the job arranged by Apex for between two and three months. By chance the follow-up occurred a few days after Peter had left this first job and the notes are as follows.

Usual dreary terrace of this neighbourhood. Peter came to the door. We chatted for a few minutes and he told me that he'd left the fork lift job for Blank Ltd and had now started learning to be a milk roundsman. He said that he had been trying for this before he got into trouble. He said that the pay is better and he thinks with bonuses he'll average about £20. He's saving up to get married – next autumn – his girl has a good job earning £15. He didn't ask me in (perhaps his girl was there).

Soon afterwards the director of Apex phoned the group personnel manager of Blank Ltd to enquire how Peter was getting on in his job as a fork lift driver. The personnel manager said that Peter had left them recently to become a milkman and mentioned that he had a perfectly satisfactory record during his stay with them but left simply in order to earn more money as a milkman. Seven months later there was a further follow-up and it appeared that Peter was getting on very well with his milk round and thoroughly enjoying the work. (*Not reconvicted within one year.*)

In contrast, Pat, who had done remarkably well in keeping his job as breakfast chef for nearly three months – bearing in mind that his 21 previous convictions included sentences of 12 years' preventive detention, 6 years' preventive detention, 6 years' imprisonment, 2 years' imprisonment, etc. – had virtually collapsed by the time he left the first job and in spite of considerable effort the situation was not retrieved. The notes in his file indicate the point at which Apex had to try to assist him again.

Pat telephoned to say that he had been drinking a lot – he had started [i.e. drinking] about a month ago and had 'jacked the job in yesterday'. He said that Mrs. Smith was letting him stay on in his room until tomorrow (it was a living-in job) but he would then have to get out. He said that the reason for his leaving was that the fellow he was working with was lazy; he had got fed up and had gone to see the Chef and demanded his cards and money. He said that all the waitresses were on his side (etc. etc.). . . . (*Reconvicted eight months after release on various theft charges.*)

The period of two to three months in the first job after release is an interesting length of time, for potentially it can be used constructively as a springboard to another job. Often one of the key matters in making a profitable transition from one employer to another may be the extent to which the last employer can be used as a future reference. While there is only limited information on what happened to men after this first job, it is relevant to consider the reaction to the Apex follow-up enquiry of the various employers who gave these men their working opportunity. In addition to the above two cases, there were a further twelve cases where the length of time at the first job arranged by Apex was between two and three months. The comments of the employers as reported in the Apex files are summarized below.

*Case 0013 – machine moulder.* He had in fact handed in his notice this morning. Apparently his record had been satisfactory for the first month. In the course of his second month he began to deteriorate, taking time off, coming in late and being with his mates. Having teamed up with an experienced, reliable, but coloured chap, jealousies arose. At times [0013] claimed that the other fellow worked too fast, or that he worked too slow. Whatever the case, he was never willing to take the blame when he was clearly at fault. His reasons for wishing to leave were the fare expenses and that everyone had found out about his past history. He claims to have found work at a small factory (nearer his home). The news of his past record had been foolishly imparted by [0013] himself to a chap whom he thought he could trust not to pass it on. (*Not reconvicted within one year.*)

*Case 0645 – carpenter* . . . after going down to Bournemouth he somewhat abused the situation – getting drunk fairly often. . . . He said that [0645] was a reasonable craftsman but needed to control his drink. They asked a client whether they could take him on site but Mr. P. understands that soon they were not happy about the situation finding him drunk on site etc. (*Not reconvicted within one year.*)

*Case 0063 – despatch loader.* He left of his own accord for medical reasons. They had no complaints about his work and she had no knowledge of his subsequent whereabouts. (*Not reconvicted within one year.*)

*Case 0075 – painter.* The employer seemed to like him as a young man but as a painter he is really not good enough to stay on, but as a special concession they will keep him for a reasonable time while Apex tries to find him employment elsewhere. They suggest that he might be good as an assistant in a shop. (*Not reconvicted within one year.*)

*Case 0674 – lorry driver.* He had been all right while he was there. Then suddenly he had left without giving notice and they had to send on his cards to him. The employer says this sort

H*

of thing hardens one's attitude towards helping these men, but did emphasize that he was a perfectly satisfactory employee while he was there. (*Reconvicted ten months after release at Old Bailey for robbery with violence.*)

*Case 0092 – gardening labourer.* Extract from letter: 'He was dismissed from this service for the following reasons: Of the 11 weeks which he was in the employ of . . . ., only 4 were fully worked. He was frequently late reporting for duty, his excuses being that the buses were running late. This could not be accepted as other members of the staff using these buses were able to report for work at 7.30 a.m. With regard to his absenteeism, at no time was a doctor's medical certificate of sickness produced. . . .' (*Reconvicted four months after release for receiving.*)

*Case 0102 – messenger.* [The employer] had had to get rid of him because whichever department he allocated [0102] to, there were complaints. He didn't seem able to do the job, he was never where he should be and in spite of being given chances, never improved. . . . This has not soured him against the employment of ex-prisoners and he would be quite happy to see anyone I recommended. (*Not reconvicted within one year.*)

*Case 0113 – furniture removal porter.* On telephoning Mr. Smith [the employer] he said that about four weeks ago [0113] had gone in to see him and said that he had had the offer of a better job which he could get with Mr. Smith's backing. Mr. Smith said that as [0113] had been so good, although he didn't want to lose him, he was quite happy to give the backing. (*Not reconvicted within one year.*)

*Case 1240 – painter.* He said that he thought it was 'left of own accord' because there was no note of dismissal and it was before the date they had weeded out their staff for the winter. (*Reconvicted at this time, and he obviously 'left' to serve a sixteen-month sentence for various larceny and motoring offences.*)

*Case 1273 – building site labourer.* The timekeeper said that [1273] had been declared redundant. There was no trouble – it was just that the site was nearing completion. He added that [1273] had got another post 'right opposite' and as far as he knows is still there, for he sees him from time to time. (*Reconvicted six months after release for theft of purse and contents from unattended motor car.*)

*Case 1207 – driver.* I spoke to a clerk who was just dealing with [1207]'s tax form. She thinks that he left of his own accord but she is not absolutely sure of this – there was certainly no trouble anyway. (*Not reconvicted within one year.*)

*Case 1228 – metal window fixer – improver grade.* [The employer] said that [1228] had left of his own accord about a month ago saying that he had domestic troubles at home. He said that there was some trouble between his wife and children. During the time he had worked for them, Mr. D. [the employer] had been pleased with his progress. (*Reconvicted seven months after release for stealing property as servant, stealing driving licence and driving whilst disqualified.*)

The above pen portraits illustrate the wide range of outcomes of the first job arranged by Apex, discussed largely from the viewpoint of the employer. As a generalization, there were fewer favourable reports from employers when men remained in the job for less than two months and a larger number when the men remained three months or more. For reasons we have already mentioned, we decided to take the period of three months or more as a length of time which was likely to give an employee a useful base from which to make a sensible transition to another job if he wished and a length of time which was unlikely to make the employer feel that he had been used as some sort of makeshift arrangement; finally, if a man worked for at least three months at a job, this was some indication that the placing action by Apex was reasonably appropriate. Naturally, though, one must recognize that there is more than an element of arbitrariness in choosing the period of three months or more.

As Table 26 has shown, 13 men from the Wormwood Scrubs full acceptance group and 6 men from the Pentonville sample worked for this time at the first job arranged by Apex.

In view of the greater criminal and institutional experience of the Pentonville sample as a whole, one would probably expect that they would be less settled in jobs after release. Within that context, it is perhaps surprising that as many as 6 men from Pentonville stayed in the first job arranged by Apex for as long as three months, but this is largely clarified when one considers those who stayed for three months or more in terms of the various risk categories. Table 27 indicates that only 1 of the 11 in the high risk category who started work actually stayed for at least three months. On the other hand, a somewhat similar proportion of both the low and medium risk categories stayed three months or more and of the 9 men in the medium risk category who stayed that period of time 4 were from the Wormwood Scrubs sample and 5 were from the Pentonville sample.

TABLE 27 *Number and percentage of men who stayed at job three months or more in various risk categories together with reconviction rates*

| Risk category | Stayed for 3 months or more | | Stayed for less than 3 months | | Stayed for 3 months (%) |
|---|---|---|---|---|---|
| | No. | (%) reconvicted | No. | (%) reconvicted | |
| Low risk – Wormwood Scrubs | 9 | 0 | 15 | 28·6* | 37·5 |
| Medium risk – 'Wormville' | 9 | 22·2 | 21 | 33·3 | 30·0 |
| High risk – Pentonville | 1 | 100·0 | 10 | 60·0 | 9·1 |
| TOTAL | 19 | 15·8 | 46 | 37·8 | 29·2 |

* There was no reconviction information on one man in this category and this figure has been calculated on a reduced base.

The one 'success' in the high risk category demonstrates the unlikelihood of ever reaching complete accuracy with a prediction study in this field, for he seemed to grasp this work opportunity while breaking most prediction 'rules of thumb' in the process! In the rank order of 221 individuals calculated to produce the various risk categories (see Chapter 8) he was 220th and quite reasonably he would have been written off as hopeless by many social workers. Completely alone in the world and described at the reception interview as a 'completely institutionalised person' with a record of eleven previous prison sentences including a period of eight years of preventive detention, his employment demands had been realistic in regard to his work experience but his fears about life on the other side of the prison wall showed the effect of many years in prison. In spite of considerable efforts, he was still very concerned just before his release as to what he should tell the employer and how he would be able to survive until he received his first week's pay. Somehow or other he managed to get to the interview and find himself a furnished room near to the job. Over three months later, the employer mentioned that Charles was still with them painting machines and doing odd jobs around the place.

He added laughingly that Charles was a bit big-headed but was doing his job very well. The prison officer who wrote of his conduct in prison that he is 'quite happy to complete his daily chores and stay clear of trouble' may be as pleasantly surprised as Apex to know that Charles managed to do the same for a while on the other side of the wall. Unfortunately, within six months of his release, Charles had again appeared in court indicating that he had returned to his familiar activities of obtaining small amounts of cash by deception.

When one examines the question whether men who stayed for three months or more had a better reconviction rate within the first year than those who started the job but failed to stay for that period of time, there is some hint in Table 27 that those men who stayed three months or more in the low risk category did perform more favourably (and those in the medium risk category marginally more favourably as well). However, it is still a far cry from saying that this was the result of the beneficial effect of the Apex job, for one still has little idea what would have happened to this small group of men who stayed three months or more at the Apex job if Apex had not happened to arrive on the scene. Clearly a beneficial effect on this small group did not seem to have any influence in lowering the reconviction rate of the treatment group compared with the control group, but 19 men out of the total of over four hundred men in the treatment group is an extremely small proportion for such an effect to be demonstrated. Even so, the fact that only 15·8 per cent of those who stayed three months or more were reconvicted after one year remains an attractive *prima facie* argument for suggesting that the Apex service has some sort of beneficial effect or that one can identify a less vulnerable group by this procedure. Certainly there has been something of a trend in reconviction terms as the men gradually fulfil the aims of the Apex project in settling into work after release. Fifty-eight per cent of the men for whom no definite arrangement was made were reconvicted, as were 47 per cent of the men who did not attend the job interview after release, 40 per cent of those not accepted for the job, 50 per cent of those who failed to start, and 38 per cent of those who stayed less than three months. It is quite a dramatic drop to the 15·8 per cent reconvicted who stayed more than three months, but it is also salutary to recognize that only one in the high risk category managed to survive the course to this stage. (It is, of course, men in the high risk category who heavily weight the reconviction rates.)

It is probably not possible to decide, on the small numbers involved in the present project, whether Apex is having any effect on the reconviction pattern of those staying at least three months or more. A matching procedure on the basis of certain characteristics with individuals from the control group is not a promising solution, for the one item for which we are lacking information is which men would have accepted Apex if it had been offered to them. Even apart from these technical considerations, the number of men concerned is so small that any figures of comparison are likely to be highly inconclusive. Furthermore, if something similar happens to the experiment described by Berntsen and Christiansen where 'the effect of the treatment is particularly strong during the second and third year after release'[1] then the present period of one year for the reconviction check would be too short.

At some point, however, one should perhaps put aside the rather technical arguments about reconviction and remember that the Apex service is a job-placing service. Although events before the present sentence (by which the risk categories were calculated) are clearly relevant in assessing how long men will stay at the jobs, it is also important to consider the obvious point of the nature of the job arranged by Apex, for there is a tendency for there to be a higher mobility rate in certain unskilled occupations, such as the building and catering trades, in contrast to skilled work and non-manual occupations. When one examines those men who stayed three months or more, 8 out of 18 (or 44·4 per cent) men of the non-manual and skilled manual level stayed three months or more, whereas only 11 men out of 47 (or 23·4 per cent) of the semi-skilled and unskilled manual level stayed a similar period in the Apex job. If the level of occupation at which the interview was arranged is held constant, the difference between the various risk categories is much less startling. Why there is such a high preponderance of semi-skilled and unskilled workers in the high risk category is, of course, another matter, but it is not worthwhile to speculate about this on the present evidence.

Almost exactly a quarter of the men who started jobs in three of the four main fields of employment (namely, manufacturing, transport and civil engineering) stayed three months or more, but none of the eight men who started a job in the catering industry stayed this length of time. Over half the men who started in other fields of employment (the miscellaneous category) stayed three months or longer, but this is largely explained by the level of occupation of these men. Of the seven men in this category who stayed three months or more, five were non-manual or skilled manual and two were semi-skilled manual.

Taking the point further that Apex is after all a job-placing service, one can argue that within that context men who start the work arranged and certainly those who stay three months or more at the Apex job would seem to justify to some extent the resources spent in finding that job even if there is no definite evidence that this job-finding operation lowers the reconviction rates (this latter point should certainly be regarded as 'not proven'). However, in the present project there were 221 men who fully accepted the Apex service but only 19 men (or 8·6 per cent) who managed to stay at the job for three months or more. Clearly it is a wasteful and expensive procedure if Apex is to continue to try to give a high-quality placing service to everybody who opts for the service. To make it less expensive there are two possibilities – either to lower the quality of the service (i.e. in terms of placing effort undertaken for each man) or to be more highly selective so that Apex tries to help men who are likely to be able to use the opportunity. With the first possibility there is the danger of losing the baby with the bath-water, for, as we shall point out when we discuss placing effort in detail (see Chapter 15), many of the men who stayed three months or more were placed initially as a result of quite considerable effort (e.g. five out of the six men in the Pentonville sample who stayed at least three months needed more than ten contacts to be placed initially). The second possibility is more promising in theory – but the danger is that on the one hand, one selects safe bets in the sense that they would probably settle down satisfactorily without the help of Apex (this applies almost certainly to many in the 'low risk' category) or, alternatively, one's basis of selection is unsuitable (earlier we demonstrated that intuition seemed a totally unreliable source in deciding which men were likely to attend interviews). The next chapter, however, tries to develop a selection procedure which is objective, reasonably easy to calculate, and will include a wide variety of men who may be helped by the Apex service.

## REFERENCE

1 Berntsen, K., and Christiansen, K. O., 'A Resocialization Experiment with Short-Term Offenders' in Christiansen, K. O. (ed.), *Scandinavian Studies in Criminology*, Vol. 1, London, Tavistock (1965), p. 53.

## CHAPTER 14

# Development of a Measure to Predict Men Unlikely to be Helped by the Apex Service

We have proposed that the men who are most likely to benefit from the Apex service are those who stay at the job arranged by Apex for three months or more. There are others who start the job and make a sensible transition to another job after less than three months, but identification of this group involves making value judgements about what is a 'sensible transition' compared with others who leave for other reasons. To avoid this type of issue, we have concentrated solely on those who have stayed long enough to have had insurance stamps for one quarter of a year as a result of holding a bona fide job arranged by Apex. Apart from other advantages in holding a job for this period of time, at least the oft-quoted stigma of the blank insurance card has largely been removed. While holding a job for three months will naturally not solve all the problems of the ex-prisoner, it will go some way towards avoiding some of the difficulties in finding another job. This is particularly the case with manual workers who comprise the vast majority of the present sample, but for white-collar workers, particularly those in the higher grades, there is a probability that they have not put their prison sentence finally in the past, as they generally have to give a much more thorough account of their previous work history. Even so, whatever grade or level of occupation, three months' work is undeniably a good start to achieving a settled work pattern.

There were 19 men out of 221 men in the full acceptance group who stayed three months or more at the first job arranged by Apex, and Table 28 shows the proportions of men on various dimensions who stayed this length of time.

Several of the items recorded show quite a distinct relation to staying at the Apex job for three months or more. For instance, 21·1 per cent of the men aged 40 and over are successful by this standard compared with only 6·0 per cent of those aged under 40. A reasonable argument could be made for using the age at time of sentence as the 'qualification' for being helped by Apex, but the counter argument would be that it would either exclude too many successes (i.e. '40 or over' only would exclude 11 successes) or

TABLE 28 *Possible factors related to staying at least three months in Apex job*

| A. Basic items and social circumstances | Number in group | Men who stayed three months or more No. | (%) |
|---|---|---|---|
| Age at time of sentence: | | | |
| Under 25 | 89 | 5 | 5·6 |
| 25–39 | 94 | 6 | 6·4 |
| 40+ | 38 | 8 | 21·1 |
| Ethnic origin: | | | |
| White | 193 | 17 | 8·8 |
| Coloured | 24 | 2 | 8·3 |
| Other (e.g. Levantine/Asiatic) | 4 | 0 | 0 |
| Marital status: | | | |
| Single | 111 | 9 | 8·1 |
| Married | 78 | 9 | 11·5 |
| Other (e.g. separated/divorced/widower) | 32 | 1 | 3·1 |
| Domicile on release: | | | |
| Family household (by birth or marriage) | 128 | 14 | 10·9 |
| Not family household | 88 | 4 | 4·5 |
| No information | 5 | 1 | 20·0 |

B. *Previous criminal record*

| | Number in group | No. | (%) |
|---|---|---|---|
| Age at first conviction: | | | |
| Under 21 | 149 | 9 | 6·0 |
| Over 21 | 71 | 10 | 14·1 |
| No definite information | 1 | 0 | 0 |
| Previous adult convictions: | | | |
| Two or less | 65 | 10 | 15·4 |
| Three to five | 65 | 4 | 6·2 |
| Six + | 91 | 5 | 5·5 |
| Period in freedom since last custody: | | | |
| Less than one year | 82 | 2 | 2·4 |
| One year or more | 77 | 7 | 9·1 |
| No custody | 62 | 10 | 16·1 |
| Experience of probation: | | | |
| Nil | 82 | 12 | 14·6 |
| Once | 60 | 6 | 10·0 |
| More than once | 79 | 1 | 1·3 |
| Proportion of working life spent in custody: | | | |
| Nil | 62 | 10 | 16·1 |
| Less than 25% | 100 | 7 | 7·0 |
| 25% or more | 59 | 2 | 3·4 |

*C. Employment record*

| | | | |
|---|---|---|---|
| Job at time of offence – how long held: | | | |
| Unemployed | 121 | 8 | 6·6 |
| 3 months or less | 44 | 3 | 6·8 |
| Over 3 months | 55 | 8 | 14·5 |
| No definite information | 1 | 0 | 0 |
| Longest period in any job: | | | |
| One year or less | 58 | 1 | 1·7 |
| Two years or less | 65 | 4 | 6·2 |
| Over two years | 96 | 14 | 14·6 |
| No information | 2 | 0 | 0 |
| Longest period – level of occupation: | | | |
| Non-manual higher grade | 8 | 2 | 25·0 |
| Skilled manual and routine grades of non-manual | 31 | 5 | 16·1 |
| Semi-skilled manual | 69 | 7 | 10·1 |
| Unskilled manual | 81 | 1 | 1·2 |
| No information/Not applicable | 32 | 4 | 12·5 |
| Time since longest job: | | | |
| Less than two years | 52 | 9 | 17·3 |
| Less than six years | 73 | 4 | 5·5 |
| Six years or more | 80 | 5 | 6·3 |
| No definite information | 16 | 1 | 6·3 |

include too much wastage if the age-level was lowered to include more successes (i.e. '25 and over' only would include 118 or 89 per cent failures). In other words, the measure is too crude to be useful. The danger of combining factors in a crude fashion – i.e. those over 40, married, family household, first convicted over 21, two or less convictions, no custody, etc. – will produce the same problem, namely either too few 'successes' or too much wastage. The important ingredient which is missing is the way in which these factors interrelate, for it is probably not important to be over 40 *per se* but in subtle combinations with other factors. Similarly, if you are under 25, married and with a good work record, this may be the secret of how to overcome the apparent age liability of being young.

We have performed a similar exercise in an earlier chapter, for the use of the three risk categories which were calculated for the purpose of distinguishing between the typical Wormwood Scrubs inmate and the typical Pentonville inmate illustrates that for men in the high risk category (membership of which would be attained by varying combinations of the nine variables used) it is almost invariably a waste of effort if the aim is for men to stay in Apex jobs for at least three months. Only one out of 65 men managed to accomplish this, but, as we have seen, it is not by any means necessarily the fault of the men in the high risk category – for example, employers appear not to accept men from the high risk category as readily as men from the low risk category. Whatever the reason for the failure of this group, there is a good case for excluding the high risk category from the Apex service, and it is quite reasonable to suspect that this group needs much greater help than can be provided by employment in isolation. On the other hand, if one concentrates, say, on the low risk category, as a much higher proportion of this group stay at the Apex job for three months or more, one is immediately concentrating on a group which is entirely from Wormwood Scrubs and one wonders whether they need the help to any great extent anyway.

What one needs to do is to re-analyze the data in an attempt to obtain a new, and hopefully an even better, discrimination between those who stayed three months or more compared with the rest of the full acceptance group than can be obtained by considering the matter in terms of risk categories. A discriminatory analysis for the two groups was carried out using the same nine variables (see Appendix A) as were used for calculating the risk categories. The new formula to emerge as an index between the group who stayed three months or more and the rest of the full acceptance group is as follows:

$$V = (0.00255)A + (-0.00125)B + (-0.00150)C + (0.00076)D + (-0.00171)E + (0.00130)F + (0.00118)G + (-0.00071)H + (0.00044)I,$$ where A to I are the standard variables used and V is the value for a particular individual.

Using this formula and taking the 95 per cent confidence limits as a convenient division into three groups, Table 29 shows that this method produces an interesting result, for it enables the 'success' percentage for each group to be quite distinct, namely, 22·6 per cent, 11·4 per cent and 1·6 per cent, while the average for the whole sample is 8·6 per cent.

Table 29 therefore suggests that if Apex continued with the same policy described in earlier chapters and took a similarly random sample from the two London prisons, one could reasonably begin to expect that men with a score of a value of +0·00608 and above would have the best chance of staying three months or more at the job arranged by Apex, and on the present evidence one would reckon that between one-quarter and one-fifth of the men would stay in the first job arranged for that period. If one decides to

TABLE 29 *Number and percentage of men who stay at job three months or more in each 'chance' category*

| | Stayed for 3 months or more | | Others in Full Acceptance group | | Total | |
|---|---|---|---|---|---|---|
| | No. | (%) | No. | (%) | No. | (%) |
| High chance of staying 3 months or more* | 12 | 22·6 | 41 | 77·4 | 53 | 100·0 |
| Medium chance of staying 3 months or more† | 5 | 11·4 | 39 | 88·6 | 44 | 100·0 |
| Low chance of staying 3 months or more‡ | 2 | 1·6 | 122 | 98·4 | 124 | 100·0 |
| TOTAL | 19 | 8·6 | 202 | 91·4 | 221 | 100·0 |

\* Values of $+0.00608$ and above.
† Values of between $+0.00607$ and $0.00174$.
‡ Values of $+0.00173$ and below.

'draw the line' at a higher value than $+0.00608$, one would believe that the remaining men would have a greater proportional chance of staying at the job. For example, if one decides to take values of $+0.00804$ and above ($+0.00804$ being the mean value of the group who stayed three months or more), then 11 out of the 28 men with such scores stayed three months or more. Although this gives a 'success-percentage' of nearly 40 per cent, the problem is that it becomes increasingly difficult to 'qualify' for consideration (in the present sample, only 28, or 13 per cent, out of 221 men would qualify by attaining this score) and one would be offering the Apex service to a very small minority of the prison population. By taking the 95 per cent confidence limits (although this again is on a fairly arbitrary basis), 53 out of 221 men (or 24 per cent) of the present sample would have qualified for consideration.

Rather than suggesting that this method is particularly useful in predicting men likely to be helped by the Apex service, it is perhaps more realistic to propose that one can begin to estimate fairly accurately a high proportion of those with a particularly *low* chance of staying three months or more. Table 29 shows that in the 'low chance' group only 1·6 per cent of the men stayed three months or more. Although this percentage of 1·6 is similar to the proportion in the high risk group where only one man out of 65 (or

1·5 per cent) stayed three months at the Apex job, the important point is that the low chance group is considerably larger (containing 124 instead of 65 men) and also includes men from Wormwood Scrubs rather than just the poor risks from Pentonville.

We must emphasize, though, that this sort of calculation cannot justifiably be termed a *prediction*, for it was produced with the benefit of hindsight and has not been validated on a further sample. As Mannheim has so correctly suggested, 'it is generally agreed that no prediction table can be accepted as useful for practical purposes without validation by testing it on a group of cases different from the original one'.[1]

In the present study, we have had to forego the topic of validation apart from the small section at the end of this chapter where we examine the use of a simplified formula on men in the two pilot studies who had fully accepted the Apex service. Rather than underestimating the importance of a validation study, it is pleasant to record that the preparation of this report has enabled Apex to obtain the resources to organize a validation study of the measure and also further investigation of the topic of whether staying in the job for three months or more does in fact help to lower the reconviction rates of these men. It will be possible to report further on these topics in three years' time.

Even if one avoids the validation issue in any depth at this juncture, one still cannot avoid the practical criticism that the formula is unwieldy and difficult to calculate. In fact, practical men involved in the placing of ex-prisoners may well argue that it is more difficult to calculate the formula than to find an ex-prisoner an interview for a job! The next section attempts to simplify the formula for practical use.

A PRACTICAL TOOL FOR SELECTING MEN FOR THE APEX SERVICE

The nine variables used for the discriminatory analysis were chosen partly because each one seemed to relate to the outcome of the Apex job in some way and partly because the information was adaptable to a suitable form for discriminatory analysis. There is no suggestion that these are the best items possible, for there may well be others which have not even been considered, but the one claim which is made is that they are objective items – six of which can be taken from a careful examination of the criminal record while the remaining three items require fairly innocuous questions about previous job history (even the latter three questions could be obtained on some occasions from a detailed police or probation report).

It is the use of *nine* variables which helps to make the formula unwieldy but it is quite likely that one can use fewer variables without losing the potential effect of the measure. This is because many of the items correlate quite highly with one another (see Appendix A for an intercorrelational matrix of variables), so that when the last few variables are added it is possible that their information is largely redundant. For example, the various values given for the number of previous convictions may correlate closely with the values given for the various proportions of time spent in custody, so that one of these variables may be more or less redundant (which one to eliminate also depends, of course, on how they inter-relate with the remaining variables).

In discovering which variables are the least useful in producing the measure, one can proceed either by a systematic method of eliminating all the variables one at a time, then two at a time, etc., or by the method more nearly approximating to trial and error. In the present case, there was a compromise. First of all we examined the effect of disregarding one variable in turn, and there is very little effect when only eight instead of nine variables are used except in the two cases of omitting A (age at time of sentence) and C (previous convictions as an adult). In fact, even just taking these two variables, which seem to be important, one can construct a crude measure of whether an individual is likely to stay three months or more at the Apex job. Using the 95 per cent confidence limit as the criterion, there would be quite a good discrimination between the groups. However, the deficiency of using these two items alone as a screening device would be that it would exclude the offer of the Apex service from all men aged below 25 and would include those aged between 25 and 34 only if they had two or less previous adult convictions.

What we need for practical purposes is a compromise between the complicated formula using all nine variables (some of which are virtually redundant) and the simple procedure using only two variables which is a very crude and unsophisticated measure. The compromise of using five particular variables was decided on for two main reasons. In the first place, five suitable variables seemed to produce a result very similar to what one achieved with nine variables. Secondly, concentrating on variables which could be obtained from an inspection of the criminal record would mean that men could be selected as suitable Apex material without the necessity of a preliminary interview. With these criteria in mind, the following five variables were chosen, namely, age at time of sentence (A), age at first conviction (B), previous adult convictions (C), period in freedom (D) and present job time (I). With the exception of present job time, they can all be obtained from the criminal record; a question on present job time could easily be added to the reception interview as a standard procedure for prisons participating in a validation study.

Using these five variables, the formula to emerge as an index for discrimination between the groups as a result of a discriminatory analysis is as follows:

$$V = (0.00296)A + (-0.00098)B + (-0.00193)C + (0.00067)D +$$
(0.00076)I, where A, B, C, D, I are the variables and V is the value for a particular man.

Taking the 95 per cent confidence limit as a convenient division, Table 30 shows that this formula is a useful way of classifying the men and compares favourably with the results when nine variables are used. For comparison, the values given earlier in Table 29 are placed in brackets. This indicates the slight difference by using five instead of nine variables.

TABLE 30 *Number and percentage of men who stay at job three months or more in each 'chance' category (calculated on basis of five variables)*

|  | Stayed for 3 months or more No. | (%) | Others in full acceptance group No. | (%) |
|---|---|---|---|---|
| High chance of staying 3 months or more* | 12 (12) | 23·1 (22·6) | 40 (41) | 76·9 (77·4) |
| Medium chance of staying 3 months or more† | 4 ( 5) | 8·7 (11·4) | 42 (39) | 91·3 (88·6) |
| Low chance of staying 3 months or more‡ | 3 ( 2) | 2·4 ( 1·6) | 120 (122) | 97·6 (98·4) |
| TOTAL | 19 | 8·6 | 202 | 91·4 |

* Values of +0.00602 and above.
† Values between +0.00601 and +0.00263.
‡ Values of +0.00262 and below.
N.B. The numbers and percentages in brackets refer to the values from Table 29. These were calculated using nine variables.

TABLE 31 Simplified table using five variables to calculate the likelihood of an individual staying at the job arranged by Apex

| Age at time of sentence | | Age at first conviction | | Previous adult convictions | | Period in freedom | | Present job time | |
|---|---|---|---|---|---|---|---|---|---|
| 20–24 | 0 | 10–14 | 0 | 0–2 | 0 | Less than 1 year | 0 | Unemployed | 0 |
| 25–29 | 296 | 15–19 | −98 | 3–5 | −193 | 2 years | 67 | Up to 6 mths | 76 |
| 30–34 | 592 | 20–24 | −196 | 6–8 | −386 | 3 years | 134 | 1 year | 152 |
| 35–39 | 888 | 25–29 | −294 | 9–11 | −579 | 4 years | 201 | 18 mths | 228 |
| 40–44 | 1184 | 30–34 | −392 | 12–14 | −772 | 5 years | 268 | 24 mths | 304 |
| 45–49 | 1480 | 35–39 | −490 | 15–17 | −965 | 6 years | 335 | 30 mths | 380 |
| 50–54 | 1776 | 40–44 | −588 | 18–20 | −1158 | 7 years | 402 | 36 mths | 456 |
| 55–59 | 2072 | 45–49 | −686 | 21–23 | −1351 | 7 years or more | 469 | 42 mths | 532 |
| | | 50–54 | −784 | 24+ | −1544 | No custody | 536 | 48 mths | 608 |
| | | 55–59 | −882 | | | | | | |

The formula using five variables looks only marginally less complicated than that using nine variables, but if, for practical purposes, one disregards the decimal points and calculates the possible values, it is only necessary to add or subtract the five appropriate scores, as in Table 31.

As we have tried to emphasize, it is rather a policy decision concerning which value one uses as a suitable dividing line. If one uses the value used to obtain the high chance group, namely 602 and above, then one would exclude over three-quarters of those who are likely to accept Apex (assuming for a moment that the present sample was representative of the prison population as a whole). Alternatively, if one wished to include the high *and* medium chance groups, that is, taking a value of 263 and above, then one would still exclude well over half the men who are likely to accept (usefully exclude, one could argue, for only just over 2 per cent of the remainder are likely to stay at the job for three months or more).

Even if one takes the higher value (602 and above), the men need not be approaching sainthood to be included, for of the 52 men who attained that score in the present sample, 11 men were from Pentonville (of whom 3 stayed three months or longer) and 41 men were from Wormwood Scrubs (of whom 9 stayed three months or longer). Furthermore, when one considers that a man aged 50–54 (score $+1776$) who was first convicted between 15 and 19 years of age (score $-98$), who had between 12 and 14 previous adult convictions (score $-772$), who had been in freedom for less than a year (score 0), and who had been at the job at the time of committing the offence for less than six months (score $+76$) easily qualifies for consideration with a total score of $+982$, one cannot justifiably be criticized for dealing only with 'safe bets'.

On the other hand, it may be more appropriate to consider the procedure as a way of eliminating men who are most unlikely to be helped by the Apex service, for with only one in forty of the men in the low chance category staying three months or more at the Apex job there is some evidence that one is able to identify this group. In other words, one seems able to identify the 'certain' failures much more satisfactorily than the 'certain' successes, for even in the high chance group (see Table 30) there is less than a one in four chance of an individual staying three months or more.

One must recognize that to produce a more effective measure of probable 'success', many more variables would have to be introduced, and what must be realized equally is that if it is to be a tool which is easily applied by workers in the field it is unlikely that many more variables can be introduced without making the calculation unwieldy. Another approach is to regard those with a score of 602 and above (calculated from Table 31) as indicating potential candidates for the Apex procedure. If they accept the Apex service but fail to settle in the job arranged by Apex this may justify a more thorough investigation of whether anything more serious is amiss which did not emerge at the prison interview when they accepted the Apex service. A follow-up of some of the men in the present sample (who were later shown by discriminatory analysis to have had a high chance of staying three months or more) revealed that they were battling under appalling odds – one was suffering from cancer while another had all his time occupied in trying to cope with six children in atrocious accommodation. It could be argued that the latter case should have been discovered before release, but this type of argument indicates a failure to grasp and understand the pressures under which the after-care service is operating at present and will continue to operate in the foreseeable future. If one recognizes that some alternative provision must perhaps be made for those for whom a job in isolation is almost certainly a waste of time, then we must use such behavioural indicators as failure to settle into work that has been arranged as the red light that something may be amiss for those who could reasonably be expected to settle into work after release. If one appreciates that the red light warning will be revealed within the first few days after release if the Apex procedure is carried out for those with a high or at least medium chance of staying at the job for a reasonable length of time, then the opportunity for remedial action may not be passed. In the case of the man with six children we knew from the prison record that he had this number of children, but this was no basis for refusing to find him work on release! He was desperately anxious for Apex to find him a job and it was only in the aftermath of a follow-up when he failed to attend the interview that discussion with him on his particular problem of coping with six children became meaningful. One should perhaps emphasize that there was at least one other man in the full acceptance group with this number of children and he started the Apex job perfectly satisfactorily.

## A SMALL VALIDATION STUDY

In both Wormwood Scrubs and Pentonville prisons, a small pilot study was undertaken before starting the main project. The purpose of these pilot studies was to ensure that the proposed procedure worked satisfactorily and to give an indication of possible problems

which had not been anticipated when the research design was conceived. The Wormwood Scrubs pilot study consisted of interviewing
14 men of whom 7 fully accepted the Apex service, and the Pentonville pilot study consisted of 10 men of whom only 3 made this
response to the offer of the Apex service. One should emphasize
that the men in neither pilot study were selected at random but
chosen so that various age groups, offences, etc. were represented
(later it was realized that certain favourable groups had been over-
represented, and this helps to explain the higher success rate of the
Wormwood Scrubs pilot study). Furthermore, the procedure for
the Wormwood Scrubs pilot study was somewhat different, for 5
of the men were met at the prison gates on the morning of their
release and in some cases taken to the employment interview
arranged by Apex. This policy was discontinued before the com-
mencement of the main study, not because of any evidence dis-
puting its value but rather because there was not the staff available
for this to become a standard procedure. Partly because of meeting
some of the men on the day of release and perhaps partly as a
result of the initial enthusiasm to make Apex a success, a much
higher proportion of the men in the pilot study kept in contact with
the staff of Apex than happened subsequently. After the pilot study
an assessment was made of what it was possible to offer the whole
sample, and this resulted in the standard procedure which has
already been described (see Chapter 4).

Using the values obtained from the 'ready reckoner' of Table 31,
Table 32 indicates the individual values for the ten men in the two
pilot studies who fully accepted the Apex service.

The table shows that 3 men come in the high chance category
by scoring at least +602, while another 3 men come in the
medium chance category by scoring between +263 and +601,
while 4 men come in the low chance category by scoring +262
or below.

The comments on the outcome of the first interview arranged by
Apex on release indicate that there is not a clear-cut difference
between the three groups although the trend is as one would
expect. (In actual fact, a clear-cut difference with such small
numbers in each group would be very surprising, as the formula
on the original data only manages to achieve proportional differences between fairly large groups.) Of the 3 men in the high
chance group, one man who was found work as a painter stayed
over six months at the job, another stayed between one and two
months in a job before returning to work with the GPO (if the
GPO had been able to come to a decision with more speed, there

TABLE 32  *Calculation of individual scores for men in the pilot studies who fully accepted the Apex service, their expected chance of staying three months or more and the outcome of the first interview arranged by Apex on release*

| Case numbers | Age at time of sentence | Age at first conviction | Previous adult convictions | Period in freedom | Present job time | Total score | Expected chance of staying three months or more | Outcome of first interview arranged by Apex on release |
|---|---|---|---|---|---|---|---|---|
| *Wormwood Scrubs pilot study* | | | | | | | | |
| 2001 | +1184 | −588 | 0 | +536 | +152 | +1284 | High | Stayed between 6 months and 1 year |
| 2002 | 0 | −98 | −193 | +536 | +76 | +321 | Medium | Accepted for job but failed to start work |
| 2003 | 0 | −98 | 0 | 0 | +76 | −22 | Low | Stayed for over a year |
| 2004 | +888 | −490 | 0 | +536 | +608 | +1542 | High | Stayed between one and two months |
| 2007 | +296 | −294 | 0 | +536 | 0 | +538 | Medium | Stayed between three and six months |
| 2008 | 0 | −98 | −193 | +268 | 0 | −23 | Low | Not accepted for the job |
| 2010 | 0 | −98 | 0 | +469 | +76 | +447 | Medium | No interview arranged |
| *Pentonville pilot study* | | | | | | | | |
| 3001 | +1184 | 0 | −386 | +134 | 0 | +664 | High | Rejected interview before release |
| 3005 | +296 | 0 | −193 | +67 | +76 | +246 | Low | Did not attend Apex interview |
| 3007 | +592 | −98 | −386 | +67 | +76 | +251 | Low | Stayed between one and two weeks |

would naturally have been no need for Apex to have arranged the interim job and he would have been judged a success by the length of time he has subsequently stayed in the GPO job) and, finally, the remaining man in this group rejected the Apex interview offer before release as he maintained that he had made his own employment arrangements. Of the 3 men in the medium chance group, one stayed over three months in work arranged as a coach driver, another failed to start work although he had been accepted for work as a fitter's mate, while Apex failed to arrange an interview for the remaining candidate. Two of the 4 men in the low chance category were either not accepted for the job or did not attend the interview, while a third started the job but stayed less than two weeks. The fourth man in the low chance category is the exception that breaks every rule, for he stayed in the job as a routine clerk in a factory for over a year. On the other hand, it is perhaps fair to point out that he had quite considerable support from Apex in other matters such as a financial loan to obtain accommodation, and he phoned an Apex staff member seventy-six times during the course of a year and met him five times (this was in addition to being on statutory after-care as a young prisoner). This suggests what is sometimes possible if one is able to provide additional support rather than indicating the failure of the prediction formula. One strongly suspects that without this extra support he would have followed the pattern of the low chance group.

While the results are by no means conclusive, they do suggest that men with a high score are more likely to be helped by the finding of employment in isolation (which appears to have been the case in 2 out of 3 men in the high chance group) while men with lower scores are less likely to be helped by finding employment or, if they are, that it is not simply a case of finding employment in isolation from other types of after-care assistance. The present study indicates the potential value of this particular measure and of this type of approach, but there is no real evidence yet of whether that potential is fulfilled.

## REFERENCE

1 Mannheim H., *Comparative Criminology*, Vol. 1, London, Routledge and Kegan Paul (1955), p. 149.

## CHAPTER 15

# The Efforts Involved in Arranging a Suitable Job Interview for Men in the Full Acceptance Group

We have emphasized that the aim of the Apex service was to find a suitable job interview on release for all the men who fully accepted the Apex service, and we have described in some detail the outcome where Apex managed to make some arrangement for a man on release. However, we have not attempted to examine the effort involved in arranging interviews for prisoners to attend immediately on release. Such an analysis has a much more serious purpose than simply evoking a polite round of applause for the enormous trouble that the director took on occasions in trying to find suitable interviews and so fulfilling the object of the enquiry, but rather to indicate the disproportionate amount of time (and, therefore, money) which was spent on some men and to try to assess whether this expenditure can be justified.

From the outset it is important to point out that a straightforward justification would be the belief that every man leaving prison should be given the opportunity to attend an interview for a job which is reasonably commensurate with his ability and experience. If this belief is held, then the present section can simply be read as an indication of the cost of carrying out such a policy and the only real discussion is whether Apex tackled the matter in the most economical and effective way. However, while many would agree that such a policy for ex-prisoners would be admirable in theory, the vast cost of introducing the Apex service on a national scale could hardly be justified on humanitarian grounds alone and there would have to be some evidence that the cost would partly be met by a saving in other directions. Two obvious examples would be that if such a policy could be shown to reduce criminal activity after release and hence produce a saving in terms of detection, sentencing and containment, or if the policy of getting men into work quickly permitted a saving in terms of the social security benefits that would otherwise be paid, then the Apex procedure would be more happily placed for widespread approval and development.

The present report does not attempt to examine the issues that this type of cost-benefit analysis involves, but simply examines some of the more obvious outcomes to see whether there is any *prima facie* evidence to suggest that the extra effort involved is worthwhile on other than humanitarian grounds. However, as possible fodder for any enthusiastic economist who wishes to cost the procedure more accurately, perhaps one preliminary point should be made. It is unsatisfactory to divide the total cost of the agency by the number of men in the full acceptance group placed during the year to obtain an average cost per placement, for this exercise was not the sole operation of the agency. The director was involved in many other aspects of running a small organization apart from his placing work, and even more relevant is the fact that the placing work of the project was not his complete work-load of placing, for when the progress of the project allowed he interviewed and placed men who had been referred by other agencies. Furthermore, there were certain efforts to find suitable work for some of the men in the partial acceptance group, but as there was not the same commitment on the part of Apex to find a definite interview on release these have been disregarded in the present section.

In any enterprise in which one is attempting to obtain complete coverage, the cost per unit goes up and up as one tries to reach saturation of one hundred per cent. It would be a relatively cheap operation and certainly easy to cost if every man could be placed within three telephone calls, but in fact there was a tremendous range of contacts necessary to obtain a suitable interview for each man. Some men are placed by one appropriate telephone call while many telephone calls and letters are needed for others. There are reasons why this wide range of effort is needed, but inevitably it leads on to the further question whether this extra effort is worthwhile. This is examined in terms of whether the men for whom greater effort was necessary to find a suitable interview did start the job and then stay at the job for a reasonable length of time.

Contact by Apex while the man was still in prison normally consisted for those in the full acceptance group of at least three interviews and a letter. The first interview was always carried out by the research officer to introduce the Apex service and, on occasions, the research officer conducted a second interview if there was some doubt about the response of the man to the offer of the Apex service or if the research officer wanted some more information before involving the director. The director then interviewed those men who accepted the service to discuss with them their employment requirements and later saw them again to discuss the arranged interview. In addition, a letter was normally sent to each man before the last interview in prison and this contained full details of the employment arranged so that the man would have time to consider the offer prior to being asked at this final interview whether the arrangement was suitable and that he understood the various details.

However, the amount of work involved for each man between discovering his employment requirements and sending a letter with details of the interview arranged varied enormously. Not unnaturally, the basic factor was often the employment request from the man and how this related to the market situation. The market situation varies by area, and in the time of the present study, for instance, East London had greater unemployment problems than West London; by types of employment required, for example, one tends to believe that skilled men are in general much easier to place than unskilled or semi-skilled men (although Table 34 will tend to suggest otherwise); and in certain occupations, such as in the construction industry, the market situation varies fairly consistently with the time of the year. However, even where the employment request is similar and where men are to be released into similar market conditions, there can be wide differences in the amount of work involved in finding a suitable interview because of the characteristics of the men themselves. Two men, for example, who wish to be skilled painters can be totally different placing propositions; age, previous industrial experience and even criminal record can have an important bearing on how quickly a man is found a suitable interview. A further variable is the skill and experience of the director or placing officer, for he must not only be able to assess accurately the man's abilities (and agree with him the job, its area, wage, etc.) but must also be able to convey this information in a suitable manner to personnel officers. Over a period of time, it is reasonable to argue, the skill of the director will increase and hence he will tend to know which firms are the most likely to have a vacancy. However, there was a general policy at Apex not to turn too readily to firms who are known from previous experience to be sympathetic, but rather to attempt to consider each man on his own merits and then to approach appropriate firms from an industrial standpoint of suitability. The final factor which always plays an enormous part in how quickly a man is found a suitable interview is luck. With only one of possibly several hundred employers having a suitable vacancy the number of telephone calls needed to reach this suitable vacancy must depend to a great extent on luck. While knowledge of the market situation can often establish the likely range of the number of contacts necessary and the skill of the director can often reduce the number of appropriate contacts, in the final analysis it is usually luck which decides the actual number of contacts.

As placing work is conducted almost entirely on the telephone for men other than white-collar workers, the only way to obtain an accurate picture of the work involved is for the director to note conscientiously each telephone call as it is made. This calls for some discipline and the request seems to engender the same type of anxieties which often beset the requests of men engaged in more pernicious work-study activities. It was not until the arrival of the director who carried out the last part of the Wormwood Scrubs study and all the Pentonville study that the recording of contacts made was established on a fully satisfactory basis. Although the form which recorded the date of the telephone call, the firm approached and the response obtained had been introduced before his arrival, the last director maintained the procedure in a way which must be the dream of all research workers. A typical entry would be as follows: '5.3.69 Rang Charing Cross Hospital (836 7788) NV'. 'NV' indicates that the hospital stated that there were no appropriate vancancies.

There is thus information on the effort involved in finding a suitable interview for 34 men in the Wormwood Scrubs sample and all the men in the Pentonville sample who fully accepted the Apex service* who were found an interview before their release or within fifteen days after their release. There were some men who were asked to contact Apex after release before we started to look for work and others where the original placing work continued after release. For consistency, therefore, we have defined the *first* placing action as any work done by the director from the time he saw the man in prison to fifteen days after release.

However, even using the extremely well-kept work record by the director, there is an almost inevitable distortion of the work involved in placing men. Only anyone who has had to make a long series of phone calls can fully appreciate the number of calls that are either wrongly dialled or 'lost' in the telephone system. Similarly, there is also the difficulty of changed and new telephone numbers and finally the difficulty of speaking to the correct person at the firm. Often when one ascertains the correct person to talk

---

* In actual fact, the director recorded this information for every man he tried to help, but this section is concerned only with the men who fully accepted the Apex service, as we are anxious to show the effort involved in helping those for whom the Apex project was designed.

I

to, then he can be 'out of the office' either genuinely or as a result of instructions to his secretary. While all these can be extremely time-consuming operations, it was felt that to pay any regard to them would be seriously misleading when one attempts to assess the types of interview that seem more difficult to arrange. For example, it would probably be misleading to count four wrong numbers and six attempts to talk to a particular staff manager as ten contacts. Equally, though, it seems somewhat unrealistic to regard it as one telephone call. In the event we decided that we were interested in realistic contacts to place a man and that telephone calls were simply one of these measures. A contact was regarded as where there was an opportunity to explain the particular case to someone who appeared to be involved in the recruitment of workers for the firm. In other words, if the director was never able to get past the telephonist, this would not be regarded as a contact. Furthermore, where a telephone call was made and it was necessary to phone back because, for example, the appropriate person was out of the office or engaged, this is counted as *one* contact even if it was necessary to phone back many times. On the other hand, if one department of a company suggested that a telephone call to another part of the organization (which was usually separate physically) might be useful, then this is counted as *two* contacts if the further call was made. The criterion in the final analysis whether to count as one or two contacts is whether or not a different telephone number was dialled to establish a further contact.

We have already mentioned that every attempt was made to keep the man himself informed of developments, but, as there was a fairly constant number of letters for each man to do this, this aspect has been disregarded in the following analysis. Similarly, letters sent to employers apologizing for the non-attendance of the men at an interview have been disregarded as these are not related to efforts in finding the job interview which is the issue we are at present examining. However, on the occasions where it was felt necessary to send out letters to employers on a man's behalf in order to try to obtain a suitable interview, then this is clearly a more elaborate exercise than a telephone call – however difficult a telephone call sometimes turns out to be. The use of letters was almost entirely restricted to when men wanted white-collar employment or when a former employer was being contacted for possible re-engagement. However, when one does start correspondence with employers, there is undoubtedly the possibility that it will multiply with the inevitable acknowledgement of letters received, so it is rather unrealistic to regard one letter as being equivalent to one telephone call. Furthermore, arranging interviews for white-collar employment has many more ramifications than the more usual manual jobs. Taking one example of placing a professional man into work, it needed, apart from two long letters applying for the job, further letters to enable him to re-join two professional associations, further letters to contact possible referees, and so on. In his file there are fourteen letters regarding this one interview appointment, but in the present analysis this is still regarded as one contact! Rather than attempt any weighting to cover this anomaly, however, all contacts which include letters to employers have been marked in Table 33 with an asterisk (*).

Table 33 is an attempt to demonstrate the effort involved in arranging an interview for all the men who fully accepted the Apex service. It does not, however, include those men who were asked to come to Apex before any attempt would be made on their behalf but who failed to arrive within fifteen days after release, and only the final one-third of the Wormwood Scrubs sample is included. As it is not a normal distribution, it is probably misleading to calculate the mean number of contacts needed to arrange a suitable interview, but the median for the Wormwood Scrubs sample is six contacts and for the Pentonville sample eight or nine contacts. For the total available, the (weighted) median is seven contacts. Table 33 does in fact include a man for whom no interview was arranged and a few others where contact was lost before they could be told the interview arrangements, but they are still included to indicate the amount of work involved. However, even with these limitations in mind, Table 33 shows that, whereas for the Wormwood Scrubs sample just under 80 per cent needed up to ten contacts for a suitable interview, only just over two-thirds of the Pentonville sample were placed at this juncture of placing effort.

Table 33 perhaps exemplifies more than anything else the concept behind the Apex service, for it was an attempt to go to quite extreme lengths so that everyone would have the opportunity of an interview to attend after release. Many agencies would perhaps make up to half a dozen telephone calls on behalf of a man in whom they may be interested, by which time, *ceteris paribus*, the man would have just under half a chance of being placed. The point of interest is to examine the outcome of the extra investment of time and effort that Apex was willing to undertake if necessary to find a suitable interview for each man.

For the purposes of analysis, the number of contacts made before release and within fifteen days after release have been divided into five groups: 1–3 contacts, 4–10 contacts, 11–25 contacts, 26

TABLE 33 *Number of contacts with employers needed to arrange a suitable job interview for each man*

| No. of contacts* | Wormwood Scrubs No. of men | Wormwood Scrubs Cumulative percentage | Pentonville No. of men | Pentonville Cumulative percentage | Total (weighted)† No. of men | Total (weighted)† Cumulative percentage |
|---|---|---|---|---|---|---|
| 1 | 7*** | 20·6 | 12** | 12·0 | 33 | 16·3 |
| 2 | 3 | 29·4 | 7 | 19·0 | 16 | 24·3 |
| 3 | 1 | 32·4 | 3 | 22·0 | 6 | 27·2 |
| 4 | 3* | 41·2 | 5 | 27·0 | 14 | 34·2 |
| 5 | 2* | 47·1 | 3 | 30·0 | 9 | 38·6 |
| 6 | 3 | 55·9 | 7 | 37·0 | 16 | 46·5 |
| 7 | 3 | 64·7 | 10 | 47·0 | 19 | 55·9 |
| 8 | 1 | 67·6 | 3* | 50·0 | 6 | 58·9 |
| 9 | 1 | 70·6 | 4 | 54·0 | 7 | 62·4 |
| 10 | 3* | 79·4 | 2 | 56·0 | 11 | 67·8 |
| 11 | 1 | 82·4 | 4* | 60·0 | 7 | 71·3 |
| 12 | — | 82·4 | — | 60·0 | — | 71·3 |
| 13 | 2 | 88·2 | 3 | 63·0 | 9 | 75·7 |
| 14 | — | 88·2 | 4 | 67·0 | 4 | 77·7 |
| 15 | — | 88·2 | 1 | 68·0 | 1 | 78·2 |
| 16 | — | 88·2 | 4 | 72·0 | 4 | 80·2 |
| 17 | — | 88·2 | 1 | 73·0 | 1 | 80·7 |
| 18 | — | 88·2 | 3 | 76·0 | 3 | 82·2 |
| 19 | — | 88·2 | 3 | 79·0 | 3 | 83·7 |
| 20 | — | 88·2 | — | 79·0 | — | 83·7 |
| 21 | — | 88·2 | 3 | 82·0 | 3 | 85·1 |
| 22 | — | 88·2 | 2 | 84·0 | 2 | 86·1 |
| 23 | 1 | 91·2 | — | 84·0 | 3 | 87·6 |
| 24 | — | 91·2 | 3 | 87·0 | 3 | 89·1 |
| 25 | — | 91·2 | — | 87·0 | — | 89·1 |
| 26 | — | 91·2 | 2 | 89·0 | 2 | 90·1 |
| 29 | — | 91·2 | 1 | 90·0 | 1 | 90·6 |
| 30 | — | 91·2 | 1 | 91·0 | 1 | 91·1 |
| 31 | — | 91·2 | 2* | 93·0 | 2 | 92·1 |
| 33 | 1 | 94·1 | 1 | 94·0 | 4 | 94·1 |
| 38 | — | 94·1 | 1 | 95·0 | 1 | 94·6 |
| 39 | — | 94·1 | 1 | 96·0 | 1 | 95·0 |
| 42 | 1 | 97·1 | 1 | 97·0 | 4 | 97·0 |
| 51 | — | 97·1 | 1 | 98·0 | 1 | 97·5 |
| 58 | 1 | 100·0 | — | 98·0 | 3 | 99·0 |
| 65 | — | | 1 | 99·0 | 1 | 99·5 |
| 71 | — | | 1 | 100·0 | 1 | 100·0 |
| TOTAL | 34 | 100·0 | 100 | 100·0 | 202 | 100·0 |

* Either one telephone call or one letter is regarded as one contact. Where letters have been sent out to employers, each man is noted by an asterisk (*). In only one case, for the position of sales manager, was a stencilled letter sent out and on this occasion 29 letters were sent out.

† The Wormwood Scrubs numbers have been multiplied by three so that there is an equal number in the two samples. It is not weighted on the basis of the number of stars and ordinaries in the prison population.

After 25 contacts, only relevant numbers are included, e.g. there were no men for whom 27 contacts were made.

or more contacts and, finally, contacts involving letters (this has been made a separate group for it almost invariably involves either white-collar workers or men returning to their former employment). The analysis has been restricted to those for whom a bona fide interview was arranged and where we are absolutely certain that the man was informed of all the details. This explains the apparent discrepancy between Table 33 and the subsequent tables in this chapter.

While the category of only 1–3 contacts before arranging a suitable interview reflected to some extent the skill and expertise of the director of Apex, this is the sort of number of contacts that other workers in the field not directly connected with placing work might be encouraged to try. The category of 4–10 contacts was the sort of number that was still fairly economic to operate in terms of the number of men that could be helped with this amount of effort. The category of 11–25 contacts began to indicate where a specialized employment agency may be needed for it is beginning to be unreasonable to expect social workers to make this number of calls in addition to their other duties. Finally, the category of over 26 contacts contains men who are expensive for any organization to place in suitable work, and unless one feels that it is reasonable to pay any price for a man on release from prison to have a suitable interview to attend, then it may be necessary to consider the matter in terms of the outcome of spending all this money.

Tables 34 and 35 attempt to show the contacts needed to arrange interviews at various levels of occupation and in various fields of employment. The four placings in non-manual occupations above routine clerical work have not been included – the architect, sales manager and sales representative were found interviews by a combination of approaches to employers by letters and phone calls, while it needed 33 phone contacts to find an interview for the technical clerk. In addition, 7 men in other grades of occupation on whose behalf letters were written have been excluded because the letters were almost invariably to former employers rather than attempts to establish fresh contacts.

There is some evidence from Table 34 that it may be slightly more difficult to place ex-prisoners in skilled manual or routine grades of non-manual occupations, for only 11 per cent of these men were placed within three telephone contacts, while this is the case with around a quarter of men placed in semi-skilled and unskilled manual occupations. Table 35, on the other hand, which illustrates the number of contacts needed to place an ex-prisoner in a particular field of employment, suggests that there is very

TABLE 34 *Number of contacts needed to place a man at a particular level of occupation\**

| Level of occupation at which interview was arranged | | No. of telephone contacts | | | | |
|---|---|---|---|---|---|---|
| | | *1–3* | *4–10* | *11–25* | *26+* | TOTAL |
| Skilled manual and routine grades of non-manual | No. | 2 | 7 | 6 | 3 | 18 |
| | % | 11·1 | 38·9 | 33·3 | 16·7 | 100·0 |
| Semi-skilled manual | No. | 15 | 17 | 13 | 4 | 49 |
| | % | 30·6 | 34·7 | 26·5 | 8·2 | 100·0 |
| Unskilled manual | No. | 11 | 16 | 13 | 4 | 44 |
| | % | 25·0 | 36·4 | 29·5 | 9·1 | 100·0 |
| TOTAL | No. | 28 | 40 | 32 | 11 | 111 |
| | % | 25·2 | 36·0 | 28·8 | 9·9 | 100·0 |

\* All levels of *non*-manual occupation except routine grades have been excluded from this table.

TABLE 35 *Number of contacts needed to place a man in a particular field of employment\**

| Field of employment in which interview was arranged | | No. of telephone contacts | | | | |
|---|---|---|---|---|---|---|
| | | *1–3* | *4–10* | *11–25* | *26+* | TOTAL |
| Manufacturing and extraction firms | No. | 9 | 14 | 11 | 4 | 38 |
| | % | 23·7 | 36·8 | 28·9 | 10·5 | 100·0 |
| Catering industry and distribution of food and drink when not in shops | No. | 6 | 6 | 3 | 3 | 18 |
| | % | 33·3 | 33·3 | 16·7 | 16·7 | 100·0 |
| Civil engineering and building | No. | 6 | 10 | 10 | 3 | 29 |
| | % | 20·7 | 34·5 | 34·5 | 10·3 | 100·0 |
| All others | No. | 7 | 10 | 8 | 1 | 26 |
| | % | 26·9 | 38·5 | 30·8 | 3·8 | 100·0 |
| TOTAL | No. | 28 | 40 | 32 | 11 | 111 |
| | % | 25·2 | 36·0 | 28·8 | 9·9 | 100·0 |

\* All levels of *non*-manual occupation except routine grades have been excluded from this table.

little difference between the three major fields of employment and the 'all others' category. The only interesting feature is that placing a man in the catering industry can be either one of the easiest or one of the most difficult tasks, for this category has the highest proportion at both ends of the scale. The explanation of this is probably that, while the working force in the catering industry is a fairly mobile population, each potential employer (or contact) controls a comparatively small labour force – of course, though, there are many exceptions; in contrast, the labour officer for a construction company may be dealing with the labour requirements of many sites. In other words, all telephone contacts are not by any means exactly equivalent in potential value and any difference in the number of contacts between fields of employment may be simply reflecting the size of each unit in the total industry.

Table 33 has already indicated that it is slightly more difficult to place men from Pentonville than from Wormwood Scrubs. If one develops this to some extent by considering this in terms of the three risk categories,* Table 36 endorses the finding that it does become progressively more difficult to place men with poorer records. Whereas only a quarter of the low risk category need eleven or more contacts, this is the case for 37 per cent of the medium risk category and 44 per cent of the high risk category. This is a further illustration of the point that if there is an equivalent amount of effort made for each man, men in the higher risk categories have the worse deal. In other words it indicates that one must put more effort into work with more deteriorated offenders, just to give them the same opportunity as others, even before one makes any allowance for the fact that their needs are probably greater.

Whatever other justification for spending a disproportionate amount of time on certain men may be possible, the most immediately interesting consideration is how the men for whom varying amounts of placing effort were made compare when the outcome of the interview arranged is examined. One could argue that men for whom great trouble was taken to arrange an interview are the ones who normally find work difficult to find and hence are more likely to take advantage of the Apex service. However, it may be pertinent to point out that Apex did not indicate to each man in a forceful manner how long it took to arrange his particular interview, so many may not have realized the tremendous effort which was sometimes involved.

* A record of the amount of placing effort was started only when the Wormwood Scrubs study had been over two-thirds completed, so explaining why there are few numbers in the low risk category.

TABLE 36 *Number of contacts needed to place a man in terms of the three risk categories*

| Risk category | | No. of telephone contacts | | | | |
| --- | --- | --- | --- | --- | --- | --- |
| | | *1–3* | *4–10* | *11–25* | *26+* | TOTAL |
| Low | No. | 4** | 8* | 3 | 1 | 16 |
| | % | 25·0 | 50·0 | 18·8 | 6·3 | 100·0 |
| Medium | No. | 14 | 16** | 14*** | 4 | 48 |
| | % | 29·2 | 33·3 | 29·2 | 8·3 | 100·0 |
| High | No. | 10 | 16 | 15 | 6* | 47 |
| | % | 21·3 | 34·0 | 31·9 | 12·8 | 100·0 |
| TOTAL | No. | 28 | 40 | 32 | 11 | 111 |
| | % | 25·2 | 36·0 | 28·8 | 9·9 | 100·0 |

The four placings in non-manual occupations above routine clerical work and the seven other placings in the other grades where letters were written have been disregarded in this analysis.

An asterisk indicates that one man from this 'cell' stayed in the job arranged for at least three months or more. Two asterisks indicate two men, etc.

After the recording of placing effort started, twelve men stayed at the Apex job for three months or more. The number of telephone contacts needed for nine of these men is shown in Table 36, each man being represented by an asterisk (*). Visually, the impression is that, as the risk categories rise, the returns from the larger number of telephone calls also increase, but the numbers are too small to pursue this conclusively. Certainly the fact that three men stayed three months or more out of fourteen in the medium risk group for whom 11–25 contacts were needed is the beginning of an indication that there may be a role for a specialized employment agency, for one suspects that there was considerably more time and effort involved in placing these men in work than agencies specifically concerned with other aspects of after-care are likely to undertake. The remaining three men who stayed three months or more were placed primarily after contacts by letters to employers; these were an architect, a sales manager and a bill poster – a letter in the last case was sent to an employer where he had formerly worked explaining in some detail what had happened since he had left the organization.

While we have repeatedly indicated that the intensive placing service of Apex does not seem overall to have a dramatic effect in lowering the reconviction rate, it is interesting to consider whether men who took longer to place seemed to be a more vulnerable group in terms of subsequent reconvictions. Assuming that there is a relationship between the difficulty Apex had in placing a man and the difficulty a man would have in finding work by his own efforts, one could perhaps hypothesize that the higher number of telephone contacts needed would identify a potentially more vulnerable group. Table 37, however, gives no support to this argument, for of those needing 1–3 telephone contacts 50 per cent were reconvicted within one year, of those needing 4–10 telephone contacts 57·5 per cent were reconvicted and of those needing 11+ contacts 48·8 per cent were reconvicted. Table 37 shows clearly that, if the factor of risk group is controlled, there is virtually no difference at all. It is, however, interesting that the two groups which did marginally better were the low risk (1–3 contacts) and the medium risk (11–25 contacts) and both these groups had the highest proportion of men who stayed at the Apex job for three months or more (see Table 36). Naturally, with such small numbers one must first of all acknowledge that this may well be a chance fluctuation, but one is tempted to speculate. In the low risk category (1–3 contacts) there were two men who stayed at the Apex job for over a year and it is not unreasonable to suggest that the placing action may have prevented at least one reconviction (only one is needed to bring up the average to 25·0 per cent and so in line with the others). Similarly, the medium risk category (11+ contacts) contains the one man from Pentonville who stayed over a year at the first job arranged by Apex. As he was one-armed, wanting an unskilled job in the building trade, many would have regarded him as virtually unemployable. It may be a sentimental rather than a scientific assessment to suggest that we helped him to avoid reconviction, but the evidence begins to be appealing.

For completeness, one should point out that the men in the higher grade non-manual occupations and men for whom letters were written to employers are not included in Table 37. Of these eleven men, six were in the low risk category. Only one of these eleven men (and he was from the high risk category) was reconvicted within one year – fewer than one might perhaps expect. On the other hand, three from this group stayed at the Apex job for three months or more (two, in fact, for more than a year), and although for other reasons one would suspect that this is a less vulnerable group, a review of the case histories might suggest that an early reconviction disaster was avoided in at least one and perhaps two of these cases.

I*

TABLE 37  *The reconviction rates of men who needed various amounts of placing effort*

| Risk category | | No. of telephone contacts | | | |
| | | 1–3 | 4–10 | 11+ | Total |
| --- | --- | --- | --- | --- | --- |
| Low | % | 0 | 25·0 | 25·0 | 18·8 |
| Medium | % | 50·0 | 56·3 | 33·3 | 45·8 |
| High | % | 70·0 | 75·0 | 66·7 | 70·2 |
| TOTAL | % | 50·0 | 57·5 | 48·8 | 52·3 |

The percentage figures indicate the proportions reconvicted within one year in each cell—i.e. in the medium risk category needing 1–3 telephone contacts, 7 out of 14 men were reconvicted, so the reconviction rate is 50 per cent. The base figures for each cell can be obtained from Table 36. The '11–25' and '26+' categories have been combined to give larger base numbers on which to calculate reconviction rates.

In summary, therefore, it is probably fair to say that one can tentatively put an addendum to the almost categorical assertion of Chapter 5 that the Apex service fails to lower the reconviction rate for a random group of prisoners. In this chapter perhaps there are some shreds of evidence that the Apex service may have helped four or five men in terms of avoiding a reconviction within a year. One must add, though, that there is a higher proportion of hope than science involved in coming to this conclusion. If it were true, one could argue that the numbers are so small that there is no appreciable effect on the overall reconviction totals discussed in Chapter 5. Whatever the truth of the matter, it is still perhaps salutary to realize that after interviewing about 450 men there are perhaps less than half a dozen men for whom one can put forward much of an argument that one has prevented a reconviction within the first year after release.

CHAPTER 16

'Sans Apex' (Employment Plans of the Wormwood
Scrubs Control Group) and Further Discussion on
Those With no Employment Arrangements
on Release

We have spent considerable time and space considering the various
outcomes of those men who fully accepted the Apex service. In the
last chapter we described the sometimes considerable efforts which
Apex made in arranging suitable job interviews for these men. The
fascinating question to ask is what all these who accepted the Apex
service would normally have done. Obviously any hypothetical
questioning of the men interviewed for the Apex project would be
unlikely to be reliable and it is important to ask men who had not
been influenced by the advent of the Apex project. The control
group is ideal for this purpose for they were not 'contaminated'
by being interviewed by the research officer and, in theory at least,
these men could illustrate what would normally happen to a typical
group of men released from prison. In the present case, though, we
were anxious to keep the control group distinct and uninfluenced
and this meant that we were unable to organize any full-scale
interviewing or follow-up, so for this group our information is
limited to the employment plans which were mentioned to the
prison welfare department and the reconviction data. We have
already indicated that there was virtually nothing to suggest that
there was any difference after one year in the subsequent reconviction rates of the control group or those interviewed by Apex.
This gives the clue to suggest that, whatever the control group
did do without the influence of the Apex project, subsequent
criminal activity at least seemed to settle into a somewhat similar
pattern.

The control group was interviewed as a matter of normal course
by the prison welfare department before their release from prison,
but there was deliberately no attempt to change their normal
procedure by asking the welfare officers to ask any specific questions
for the purposes of research, for it was felt that this again might
destroy the very value of the 'uncontaminated' control group. However, at the conclusion of the Wormwood Scrubs study, the Probation and After-Care Department of the Home Office allowed the

research officer to examine the records in the prison welfare department. Although by this time the individual case records of all the men had been despatched to the appropriate after-care area, there was a card index file in which a short summary was recorded for each man giving his stated employment plans on release. Unfortunately there was no similar record kept at Pentonville prison.

The Department of Employment was also co-operative in this matter and we have already indicated that 29·3 per cent of the Wormwood Scrubs control group were given a pre-release interview by one of their placing officers in contrast to the 20·8 per cent of the men interviewed by Apex who chose also to have a pre-release interview by the Department of Employment. Although there appears to be a tendency for the introduction of Apex to lower the percentage of men who wished to see the Department's official before release, this is not statistically significant and certainly suggests that the majority of the men made other arrangements than simply relying on the statutory agency.

The card index file in the Wormwood Scrubs prison welfare department had information on 134 men in the control group, and these responses were categorized in a similar manner to the men interviewed who had rejected the Apex service. There was no information on the employment plans of the remaining 21 men. While it is not possible to decide whether these men were not interviewed by a welfare officer or simply that the outcome of the interview was not recorded, it is relevant to note that they were certainly not a random group in terms of subsequent reconviction. Nine (or 42·9 per cent) of the 'no information' men were reconvicted compared with only 23·1 per cent of the rest of the Wormwood Scrubs control group.

Table 38 itemizes the employment plans after release for the Wormwood Scrubs control group as recorded in the file of the prison welfare department. The figures in fact underestimate the number of this group who were seen by the Department of Employment before release, but the explanation is that a person may be seen by the D.E. and also have other plans, such as 'plans to work with relatives and friends'. It is important to realize that the D.E. category in Table 38 contains only those men for whom the sole comment on their employment plans is that they are relying on the efforts of the D.E.

Table 38 suggests that there is a similar relationship for the control group between stated employment plans and subsequent reconviction, as we have already demonstrated for the rejection

TABLE 38  *Employment plans after release of the Wormwood Scrubs control group*

| Group | Employment plans after release | No. | Control group (%) | % reconvicted |
|-------|-------------------------------|-----|-------------------|---------------|
| A | Intends to start with GTC or other course | 6 | 3·9 | 16·7 |
| B | Believes that he will be re-employed by former employer | 20 | 12·9 | 10·0 |
| C | Plans to work in relation's or friend's business | 7 | 4·5 | 6·3 |
| | Intends to be self employed | 7 | 4·5 | |
| | Plans to arrange own work in sub-contracting field | 2 | 1·3 | |
| | Relatives/friends arranging to find work | 5 | 3·2 | |
| D | Plans to get specific job (skilled or semi-skilled type of work) | 29 | 18·7 | 24·4 |
| | Confident of finding own employment (unskilled or type of work not stated) | 19 | 12·3 | |
| | Intends to rely on D.E. | 29 | 18·7 | |
| E | Reluctant to discuss employment plans/No plans | 10 | 6·5 | 70·0 |
| F | No information | 21 | 13·5 | 42·9 |
| | TOTAL | 155 | 100·0 | 25·8 |

group. Again categories A, B and C have substantially lower re-conviction rates than categories D, E and F. It endorses the earlier indication that those intending to be self-employed on release are not necessarily heading for immediate disaster (in fact, none of the 7 men in the Wormwood Scrubs control group who intended to be self-employed was reconvicted within one year). It is interesting to consider the one person who was reconvicted of those intending to start some sort of course. Re-examining the note in the welfare file raises the question of whether he was correctly categorized, for it states that 'he will temporarily be working with a friend as a painter/decorator but hopes to go to University in the autumn to study maths'. His family situation suggests that this may have been a vaguer notion than the impression this note gives and it is unlikely that he secured a place at a university before his release in May: anyway, a subsequent conviction for indecent exposure within one year and a similar conviction after thirteen months show that all his problems had not been completely resolved since his stay in prison.

Although the numbers in each category are comparatively small, it is still possible to consider them in relation to the information on the employment plans of men who were interviewed by Apex. In fact it could reasonably be argued that a consistent pattern is emerging. Table 38 shows that 13 per cent of the control group believed that they would be re-engaged by their last employer, whereas Table 12 (page 161) has already shown that 21 men in the Wormwood Scrubs rejection group thought they would be reinstated by their former employers on release. In addition one must take into account the rest of the men interviewed, for among these were men who hoped to return to their former employer, although as a safeguard they had also accepted the Apex service. In fact, for 10 of these men Apex arranged an interview with their last employer (this disregards the placements by Apex with earlier employers than the last one, for this was almost invariably on the initiative of Apex rather than as a result of a suggestion by the man). This suggests that at least 31 men out of a total of 227 men interviewed in Wormwood Scrubs would probably have maintained that they hoped to return to their former employment. This percentage of 13·7 is not very dissimilar to the 12·9 per cent of the control group.

Similarly, assuming that those who planned to be self-employed, to arrange their own sub-contracting work or to work in a relative's or friend's business were not likely to be attracted to the Apex service and hence are all in the rejection group, then the proportion of 11·9 per cent (27 out of 227 men interviewed) is directly comparable with the 10·3 per cent of the control group who planned one of these activities. A similar argument could be used for those men who intended to start a government training course or another full-time course, for such plans are fairly unlikely to be altered as a result of the arrival of Apex on the scene.

In the Wormwood Scrubs sample, therefore, there seem to be between a quarter and a third of the men who were fairly committed to a course of employment action after release. These comprise (in approximate terms) 13 per cent who hoped to return to their former employment, a further 11 per cent who saw themselves as involved in a small business enterprise and up to a further 5 per cent who intended to start or continue a training course of some kind. It is the remaining two-thirds or so who are likely to be interested in the introduction of an employment service for discharged prisoners.

If one relates this reasoning more closely to the responses of the men interviewed at Wormwood Scrubs, one can demonstrate that the acceptance rate for Apex was remarkably high from the two-thirds of the men who had not decided what they intended to do after release. Of the 227 men interviewed, 63 men could perhaps reasonably be regarded as non-starters for normal placing work – 21 men in the rejection group and 10 men in the acceptance group were hoping to return to their last employment, a further 27 men were involved in a small business enterprise, another 3 men intended to start a course and 2 others were too disturbed to be offered a straightforward placing service. Of the remaining total of 164 men, 102 (or 62·2 per cent) fully accepted the Apex service (discounting the 10 men who in fact may well have returned to their former employer without the help of Apex), 26 men (or 15·8 per cent) partially accepted the Apex service, while only 36 men (or 22·0 per cent) rejected the Apex service outright. In other words, less than a quarter of the men who appeared to have their employment options still open to them had no use whatsoever for this employment-placing service. Obviously these are the men for whom it would be fascinating to know their real reasons for rejecting the Apex service rather than those men in the rejection group who had largely settled their thoughts on employment before being interviewed by Apex.

A similar analysis of the men interviewed at Pentonville could proceed in the following way. There are 8 men in the rejection group and 3 men in the acceptance group who hoped to return to their last employment, another 11 men who had plans to become involved in a small business enterprise and a further 2 men who intended to start a course after their release. Disregarding the men in the miscellaneous group who were not offered the Apex service, this leaves a total of 190 men who seemed to have no definite plans on release, and only 46 (or 24·2 per cent) of these men rejected the Apex offer completely. This proportion of just under a quarter is very similar to the Wormwood Scrubs figure of 22 per cent of men who rejected Apex despite no definite alternative plans.

It is almost impossible to interpret from the present evidence why the majority of these 82 men from both prisons rejected the Apex service in spite of having nothing definite arranged. Seven of them (2 Wormwood Scrubs, 5 Pentonville) did state clearly that they were rejecting the Apex service because it was the policy of Apex to reveal to their future employer that they had a criminal record. This may have been why others rejected the Apex service, but they did not make this explicit.

To sum up, it would appear that out of the 439 men interviewed in the two prison samples, there was evidence that 354 men (or over 80 per cent) still apparently had their employment options open to them in so far as they had no stated plans. Of these 354 men, 272 (or 77 per cent) made some sort of acceptance of the Apex service while 82 (or 23 per cent) rejected outright the Apex offer of employment service.

We shall never know the number of men in the rejection group without any definite employment plans who did in fact intend to seek work on release, or in fact the proportion who successfully found employment on release. Many may have already decided to continue a criminal career rather than to settle into normal employment. If one compares these 82 men of the rejection group with the men in the two prison samples who made some sort of acceptance (either full of partial), the two groups have a remarkably similar distribution in terms of the proportion of their working life in custody, as is shown in Table 39.

Assuming that all men who have spent a similar proportion of their life in custody have similar chances of being reconvicted, it is possible to compare the two groups to see whether those who had opted for the Apex service seemed to fare more successfully than those who had chosen to reject the service.

The conclusion of this chapter tends to reflect what we have learned generally from the Apex project. There are a proportion of men who have already considered their employment plans on release and, not surprisingly, they tend to reject the offer of an employment-placing service. In terms of the reconviction follow-up

TABLE 39  *Comparison of those who accept the Apex service and those who reject Apex but have no stated employment arrangements on release*

| Proportion of working life spent in custody | Acceptance of Apex service* | | | Rejected Apex but no known employment arrangements | | |
|---|---|---|---|---|---|---|
| | No. | (%) | (%) reconvicted | No. | (%) | (%) reconvicted |
| Nil | 78 | 28·7 | 19·7† | 24 | 30·0 | 34·8† |
| Some but less than 10% | 70 | 25·7 | 50·0 | 20 | 25·0 | 40·0 |
| 10% but less than 25% | 53 | 19·5 | 39·6 | 15 | 18·8 | 66·7 |
| 25% or more | 71 | 26·1 | 63·4 | 21 | 26·3 | 76·2 |
| TOTAL | 272 | 100·0 | 42·6 | 80‡ | 100·0 | 52·5 |

* Includes all who accepted Apex service in some form except the 13 men whom Apex helped to return to their last employer, for it is suggested that these men are a somewhat distinct group. (Only two of these men were reconvicted.)
† Where there is no reconviction information, the reconviction rate is calculated on a reduced base.
‡ The information on two men is too incomplete for it to be possible to estimate the proportion of their working life spent in custody – both were in fact reconvicted within one year of release.

of one year, these men seem to do comparatively well. Of the remaining men who have no apparent plans on release, Apex makes an impact inasmuch as a high proportion (nearly 4 out of every 5 men) accept the offer of placing help, even if for a few it is limited to placing advice. Generally the men who accept the Apex service do somewhat better in reconviction terms than those men who reject the Apex service but who have no known employment plans. However, as there is no lowering of the overall reconviction rate compared with the control group one is reluctantly forced to conclude that there is no evidence that it is the Apex service which causes this difference. It must be something on the lines that those who accept the Apex service would have performed more satisfactorily in reconviction terms than the rejection group, even if Apex had not arrived on the scene. On the other hand, when the outcome of the Apex service was examined in detail, it is obvious that it really made an impact only on a minority of the men who fully accepted it. On the evidence available, one cannot make a final judgement as to whether the Apex service made an effective contribution towards this minority's settling down. Certainly one suspects that one needs a much longer period than one year after release to indicate the final outcome. What this project has indicated is that, with one particular set of market conditions at least, there is little to suggest that the Apex approach is likely to have an appreciably beneficial effect on the majority of men leaving prison, and any work in the future should usefully be directed towards identifying more closely the small minority who may in fact be helped in this way. This is indeed the purpose of the validation study of the prediction formulae which Apex is at present carrying out.

It is perhaps pertinent at this juncture to consider briefly an experiment reported in the literature which is similar in many respects to the design of the Apex project. In this Danish study the authors maintain that 'socio-psychologically oriented supporting therapy combined with relatively comprehensive welfare measures creates conditions which lead to significantly lower recidivism than does the traditional treatment of Danish short-term prisoners'.[1] Clearly, this result is an interesting contrast to the less optimistic findings of the Apex project. Disregarding the two possibilities either that Apex failed to lower the reconviction rate because its placing work was in some way less effective than one could reasonably expect or that the findings of Berntsen and Christiansen were due to a chance fluctuation, it is worthwhile to consider the differences in the two procedures, particularly as the two projects seemed to be concerned with rather similar criminal populations. The Danish project was a much more comprehensive operation from the time of assessing the prisoner to the range of assistance which could be offered. The prisoners were interviewed by social workers and psychologists and 'a detailed report was prepared for each prisoner: it contained a plan for his treatment while in prison and for appropriate welfare measures'.[2] The report emphasizes that 'no sharp line divides the investigation and the work of resocialization'[3] and in consequence the treatment began at a fairly early stage of the prison sentence. There was a wide range of practical help offered to the 126 participants.

> The social work consisted in finding work (54 cases) . . . in finding accommodation (24 cases), clothing (30 cases), and in helping the prisoner with trade union and health insurance membership formalities (47 cases). Sometimes very modest financial help was given on the prisoner's release (31 cases), and sometimes it was necessary to help the prisoners in negotiations with tax authorities (15), with Public Assistance offices (22), and other public authorities and institutions as well as private creditors (60). Often assistance was needed to straighten out difficulties with wives or husbands, parents or other relatives (58). Twelve prisoners began an anti-alcoholic treatment. . . . Through talks with particularly unbalanced prisoners the psychologist tried to cure depressions and to ward off conflicts.[4]

After a follow-up when all the prisoners had had an opportunity of being in freedom for at least six years, 41 per cent of the experimental group had had further experience of some form of penal incarceration compared with 58 per cent of the control group. Although this excellent short paper raises many questions, there are apparently no major methodological flaws in the research design and it seems possible to accept the major finding at its face value. Berntsen and Christiansen themselves consider what it was in the treatment that was valuable. 'Was it certain factors of the treatment which can be isolated and described fairly easily? And again, if so, which factors? Or was it the treatment as a whole which produced the right effect? Or was it certain recurring features of the treatment which may be identified by a detailed analysis of the existing data?'[5]

Although the Apex project was designed without the knowledge of the work of Berntsen and Christiansen, the Apex project undoubtedly provides some evidence to indicate that one of the factors of the Danish treatment 'which can be isolated and described fairly easily', namely the aspect of finding employment on release, is unlikely to be *per se* the philosopher's stone.

## REFERENCES

1 Berntsen, K., and Christiansen, K. O., 'A Resocialization Experiment with Short-Term Offenders' in Christiansen, K. O. (ed.), *Scandinavian Studies in Criminology*, Vol. 1, London, Tavistock (1965), p. 35.
2 Ibid., p. 37.
3 Ibid., p. 42.
4 Ibid., p. 43.
5 Ibid., p. 53.

## CHAPTER 17

# Amount of Contact After Release and Further Placing Efforts

After all the detailed discussion on the outcome of the *first* job arranged by Apex for the men who had fully accepted the Apex service, we must remember that simply arranging one job on release was never intended to be the full extent of the Apex service. It was in fact mentioned in the stencilled letter handed out to all the men interviewed in both Wormwood Scrubs and Pentonville that the director of Apex was aware that the first job might not work out satisfactorily and hoped that the men would contact Apex if they had any employment difficulties. Moreover, all men in the partial acceptance and rejection groups who were not wanting jobs found for them by Apex immediately on release were told individually that they were welcome to contact Apex if their employment plans did not work out as well as expected. After the emphasis on the pre-release aspect, it is perhaps of interest to examine the amount of contact from the various groups after release and to discuss briefly the outcome of this contact.

The amount of contact with an employment-placing service is obviously a function of many factors of which only one is the actual need for the service. On the one hand, men whom one would assess as needing such a service fail to arrive, while on the other hand, it would be naïve to believe that all the men who did arrive at the Apex offices actually wanted employment found for them. However, if a man from the sample arrived stating that he wanted Apex to find him work, there was no attempt to browbeat a man to try to discover whether he 'really wanted to settle into employment'. Any request for employment was taken at its face value, but ironically this straightforward approach sometimes resulted in a sudden change of request from the client when it was realized that the director of Apex was not a social worker who was trying to probe motivations and so enable the client subtly to change his demands.

The former point about the number of potential clients in the sample with a genuine need failing to arrive is a matter which will always remain obscure unless a full-scale follow-up is arranged. In the present case, all one can do is to outline the procedure and suggest the possible deterrents. All the men interviewed were handed the stencilled letter which contained the address of Apex, but men needing an employment-placing service after release may have either misunderstood or forgotten the existence of Apex. Even more simply, potential clients may have mislaid the letter and not known how to make the necessary contact. Even if they did remember or locate the address, they might have felt that the offices were well outside their 'manor' and so have failed to contact Apex whereas they might have done so if the organization had been situated within walking distance of their address. One can, of course, pursue this type of speculation, but the fact is that with a perfectly straightforward entry in the London telephone directory and offices less than half a mile from the centre of Soho, it is perhaps difficult to believe that Apex compared unfavourably with other organizations in this matter and that anyone could reasonably be expected to contact Apex if he felt strongly disposed to do so. If anyone interviewed in prison phoned or wrote to Apex, it was mentioned as a standard procedure that Apex would refund travelling expenses to and from the Apex offices, so equally this could not be regarded as the reason why any man failed to follow up any preliminary contact to see someone at Apex.

There was some fear at the outset that Apex would be inundated by men faced with the harsh reality of the employment situation after release and that they would all rush to Apex for assistance to find them work. Within a short time one soon realized that this was a totally unrealistic fear, for the proportion of men who contacted Apex on their own initiative after release was comparatively small.

Before discussing the numbers who contacted Apex and the outcome of this contact, one must point out that there were attempts to follow up some of the men after release for research purposes. This was particularly the case with the Wormwood Scrubs sample. There is little doubt that a contact either in person or by letter could influence a man's decision to ask for the assistance of Apex in finding work. However, one can probably assume that any such contact is likely to encourage rather than discourage subsequent requests for help. To avoid an artificially high level of contact being recorded which would simply reflect the activity of the research follow-up, certain conventions will be followed in this section. A contact is disregarded if the person has simply been interviewed in his home environment or makes a straightforward response to a follow-up letter, for in these cases there is certainly no *prima facie* request for help. However, if the contact continues with Apex beyond the interview, or if the letter is replied to for any reason other than for job-finding, this is noted as 'social contact with Apex'. Although in some cases there does simply seem to be the desire to keep in touch with the organization on a friendly basis, there is sometimes a more obvious area of advice or help sought.

Not surprisingly, most men contacted Apex in the hope that Apex would find them work. At least this was the stated reason for their contact. One felt that some men expected that a suitable job would be offered to them while they were still on the phone and that they were not interested any longer when they discovered that there was not this type of immediate service available. All the men who contacted Apex after release were almost invariably difficult placing propositions and there was the additional hazard that in cases where interviews were arranged it was not unusual for the men to have changed their address within a few days of seeing the director of Apex but failing to notify Apex of this change and subsequently never being heard of again.

The men who at least *prima facie* stated that they wanted Apex to find them work have been divided into two major groups – those resulting in 'unsuccessful placing action' and those resulting in 'successful placing action'. 'Unsuccessful placing action' means that the client failed to start work in spite of the efforts of Apex. It can cover a multitude of situations from the men who contacted Apex but failed to arrive at Apex to discuss their employment requirements to men who had actually accepted a job arranged by Apex but failed to start work. Hence one can see that it is a fairly stringent test before a case can be considered as 'successful placing action', for he must actually start the job arranged by Apex.

A further proviso before discussing the figures is that any contact by the full acceptance group within fifteen days after release is disregarded, for this has been considered elsewhere as part of the first placing action. This avoids duplication, but obviously these cases should be considered if one wants an estimate of the total numbers who contacted Apex for any reason after release.

Table 40 shows the numbers or men who contacted Apex after release and the outcome from the total number interviewed in the two prisons. The table indicates that approximately 80 per cent of the men interviewed did not contact Apex for any reason after release, while 13·4 per cent of the men contacted Apex after release with a view to further placing. Of the latter category, 22·0 per cent of the cases resulted in successful placing action while 78·0 per cent were categorized as unsuccessful placing action.

TABLE 40    *Amount of contact after release (disregarding first placing action up to fifteen days after release)*

| Contact and outcome | Wormwood Scrubs No. | (%) | Pentonville No. | (%) |
|---|---|---|---|---|
| Successful placing action | 8 | 3·6 | 5 | 2·3 |
| Unsuccessful placing action | 27 | 12·0 | 19 | 8·9 |
| Social contact with Apex | 11 | 4·9 | 14 | 6·5 |
| No contact with Apex* | 179 | 79·6 | 176 | 82· 2 |
| TOTAL† | 225 | 100·0 | 214 | 100·0 |

\* This disregards contact for research purposes.
† The eleven men in the miscellaneous group have been disregarded in the above analysis as they were not offered the Apex service. In fact, none contacted Apex after release.

For completeness it is worth noting that four members of the control group who were, of course, not offered the Apex service in prison contacted Apex in the normal course of its work as an ex-prisoner's employment agency. The outcome of one man from the Wormwood Scrubs control group could be regarded as a very successful placing action, for he was placed as a contracts executive, which was a job worth over £3,000 p.a. The wife of one of the men in the Wormwood Scrubs full acceptance group whom Apex had successfully placed contacted Apex on behalf of her brother-in-law who had been released from prison nearly four weeks earlier. She said that her mother-in-law was worried about her son, for she felt that 'Arthur is bitter about being put in prison and seems to have no interest in finding work . . . and reckons there is no work around'. Although Arthur was in the control group, the director of Apex agreed to see him, but he never arrived for the interview. (Neither the contracts executive nor Arthur was in fact reconvicted by the one-year check.) Of the two men in the Pentonville control group who contacted Apex neither was placed successfully; in one case it seemed he simply wanted a 'hand-out' while in the other case he failed to attend the job interview which was arranged for him. Both of these Pentonville men were reconvicted within the year.

The men interviewed in prison made various responses to the offer of the Apex service and it is interesting to consider which group tended to provide clients after release. One would expect that it would be men either from the full acceptance group or from the partial acceptance group, as these men had more contacts with the Apex organization before release. Table 41, combining the two prison samples, supports this suggestion, for it shows that a significantly high proportion of the acceptance groups contact Apex after release compared with members of the rejection group. In spite of the differences between the groups, it is interesting that the rate of successful and unsuccessful placing actions is virtually identical for each group.

TABLE 41  *Amount of contact after release in terms of Apex groups*

| Contact and outcome | Full acceptance | | Partial acceptance | | Rejection | |
|---|---|---|---|---|---|---|
| | No. | (%) | No. | (%) | No. | (%) |
| Successful placing action | 8 | 3·5 | 3 | 5·4 | 2 | 1·3 |
| Unsuccessful placing action | 29 | 12·7 | 10 | 17·9 | 7 | 4·5 |
| Social contact with Apex | 18 | 7·9 | 2 | 3·6 | 5 | 3·2 |
| No contact with Apex | 174 | 76·0 | 41 | 73·2 | 140 | 90·9 |
| TOTAL | 229 | 100·0 | 56 | 100·0 | 154 | 100·0 |

*Some contact with Apex v. No contact with Apex*
FA v. R : $x^2 = 13·17$; 1 d.f.; $p < 0·01$
FA v. PA : $x^2 = 0·24$; 1 d.f.; N.S.
PA v. R : $x^2 = 10·92$; 1 d.f.; $p < 0·01$

If one compares all the men who made some contact with Apex with all those who made no contact, a few interesting features emerge. Age seems an important factor, for whereas 21 (or 28·8 per cent) of the 73 men aged 40 or over contacted Apex after release, this was the case with only 63 (or 17·2 per cent) of the 366 men aged below 40 ($x^2 = 5·20$; 1 d.f.; $p < 0·05$).

If one considers this further, the difference is almost totally explained by the fact that a higher proportion of older men simply seemed to make some form of 'social contact'. If one disregards the 'social contact' group, then 13·7 per cent of the under-40s and

13·4 per cent of the older age group contacted Apex. The fact that the older age group tended to demand some form of 'social contact' – a type of service which Apex was not designed to offer and was reluctant to develop – may be an indirect indication that a higher proportion of the older age group may respond favourably to the type of after-care support offered by the Probation and After-Care Department.

Fourteen (or 40·0 per cent) of the thirty-five men born in the West Indies contacted Apex after release whereas this was the case with only 17·3 per cent of the men born elsewhere ($x^2 = 10·68$; 1 d.f.; $p < 0·01$). As only one of the contacts by West Indians was categorized as a social contact, whereas for the men born elsewhere over one-third of the contacts were regarded as social contacts, this tends to suggest that West Indian prisoners were having particular employment difficulties after release. In fact, of the thirteen successful placing actions, five concerned West Indians – although only 8 per cent of the men interviewed in the two prison samples were born in the West Indies.

Although the amount of previous penal institutional experience seemed to have little relationship with whether men contacted Apex after release, there was a greater likelihood that the contact of those with no previous institutional experience (before the present sentence) would result in a successful placing outcome. Perhaps a more surprising feature is that those who had had a criminal career of seven years and under fifteen years seemed to be assisted more frequently after release by the Apex service than those who had had a criminal career of less than seven years (excluding those with no previous convictions). Of the former group of 152 men, 6 of the 25 men contacting Apex for any reason had successful placing outcomes, whereas of the latter group of the 146 men who had had a shorter criminal career only 1 of the 23 men contacting Apex was successfully placed. Although the numbers are very small, this is further tentative evidence that men with a criminal career of seven years or more may be particularly ready to respond to after-care assistance. We have already shown that men with criminal careers spanning seven years but under ten years have a significant tendency to accept the Apex service, and perhaps contrary to expectation they seem to respond more favourably than those with a criminal career of less than seven years.

If one considers the present offence, the most unlikely to contact Apex after release are those who have committed a driving offence (e.g. driving while disqualified, taking and driving away, etc.), for only 3 of the 53 men in this category made any subsequent contact.

In contrast, 14 of the 39 in the 'fraud, false pretences, embezzlement' category contacted Apex, although only half of these contacts seemed to be requests for placing action. (In fact, there was only one successful placing outcome.) The highest proportion of successful placing actions was for sexual offenders where 10 out of the 62 men contacted Apex, of whom 4 were placed (in addition, the successful placing in the control group was for a sexual offender).

Finally, it is interesting to consider whether men who had employment difficulties before the present sentence tended to use the Apex service after release more frequently. A rough measure of employment difficulty is whether men were employed at the time of the offence. There is a slight indication that men who were previously unemployed tend to contact Apex to a greater extent, for 22·2 per cent of these men did so compared with 16·5 per cent of the men who were employed, but the difference is not statistically significant. However, just over one-third of the contacts of the previously unemployed group were assessed as 'social contacts with Apex' with no apparent interest in work, whereas this was the case with just over a quarter of the contacts for the previously employed group. In other words, the percentage of genuine placing requests for the two groups was somewhat similar, but there was a difference when the placing outcomes were considered. Whereas only 4 out of 30 resulted in successful placing actions for the previously unemployed group, this was the case with 9 out of 28 for the previously employed – a further indication that it is most difficult to help those who probably need help the most.

Making the simple dichotomy of successful and unsuccessful placing action conceals the wide range of activity within each group. In some cases the men seemed to expect that they would be referred to a suitable job when they made their initial contact by telephone and sometimes broke contact when they realized that Apex did not have a store of unfilled and well-paid vacancies immediately to hand. In other instances, Apex still had not managed to place men after a contact lasting several months, but even the harshest critics could hardly criticize the effort involved in most of these cases. In one case, there were 104 telephone calls to different firms to try to secure a job as a messenger and then the applicant failed to attend the interview arranged because he said that there was no complete guarantee that he would get the job. In another case, several interviews were obtained for a young man well qualified as an industrial designer; he always attended the interviews and usually was pleased with his performance; it remained virtually inexplicable why he just failed to secure jobs even after the director of Apex had subsequent conversations with potential employers. There were at least 42 carefully chosen job applications which were individually typed and further batches of stencilled letters sent to firms on a more speculative basis. Although he kept in approximately weekly contact by phone, the fact that there were a further 34 letters written to his home address from Apex illustrates the effort involved in arranging interviews for white-collar employment and the attempt to keep a man informed of developments so as to maintain his interest.

In the 46 cases which resulted in unsuccessful placing actions the length of contact gives some indication of the amount of activity involved. In 19 cases the contact with the client lasted one week or less; in a further 18 cases the contact lasted more than one week but less than three months, while the contact with the remaining 9 men lasted at least three months or more. Although 'contact with client' is calculated from the time of the first contact by the client until the last action by Apex or the last contact by the client whichever is the later, men do vary their regularity in maintaining contact, so the length of contact in a couple of cases is artificially high because of the rather haphazard nature of their contact.

For the 13 cases where there was a successful placing action, the length of contact was measured from the date the client first contacted Apex to the date of actually starting work in the job arranged by Apex. As most men were asked to come to Apex to discuss their employment requirements before any placing action occurred, and then it usually took time to find a job to satisfy their various requirements, one suspects that the procedure goes beyond the time-scale which most men can sustain. Two men were in fact placed within a week of contacting Apex – a job as chauffeur needed six telephone calls to different employers while the bakery factory labourer was placed after only one telephone call. In six cases, men were successfully placed within a month – the jobs of factory labourer, van salesman, messenger, spray painter and hospital porter needed one, two, eight, thirty and thirty phone calls respectively to different employers (the effort involved in placing the hospital porter was not recorded). The delay in time in the case of one of the factory labourers was because he contacted Apex while serving a prison sentence subsequent to the one he was serving when originally interviewed by Apex and he obviously had to wait for his date of release before taking up the job. This also happened in one of the remaining five cases where the contact lasted over one month before the man started work. In three cases the delay in starting work was largely because the client failed to come to Apex as arranged, so placing action could not get quickly under way, rather than the problem being one of finding suitable work. These men were placed as a brewery labourer, warehouseman, machine operator and kitchen porter. Finally, the remaining client can only marginally be regarded as a placement, for he required part-time work. However, it may indicate that an important feature of effective after-care is the appropriateness of the help rather than the amount of help. He was a young coloured first offender who had shown the initiative to enrol at a technical college on a full-time basis to study for 'A' levels as the first stage towards fulfilling his aim of becoming a teacher. When a voluntary worker visited his home about two months after release, he had started his course but was worried about being a financial burden on his father. He indicated a large pile of new books which had cost more than ten pounds. He wanted temporary or part-time work and had already considered working at the Post Office during the Christmas vacation but could not face completing an application form in which he knew that he would have to admit his conviction once again. Suitable part-time work was eventually found and his several letters of appreciation suggest that he may not have been able to overcome this hurdle himself – 'I can assure you this job will help me considerably financially. Your service only demonstrates the humane job you do. . . .'

If there is a common denominator among those who were successfully placed, it is that most of them had found that their original employment plans had gone astray – the most obvious of these was the docker who had expected to be reinstated by the National Dock Labour Board and the bus conductor who thought that London Transport would re-consider their decision. On the other hand, Apex made no real impact on the men who seemed to have only vague plans when interviewed in prison and probably contacted Apex after release as a final act of desperation. There will be exceptions to every rule of this kind, but finding employment is unlikely to be the panacea. Even so, what is evident is that in this type of case one must act very much quicker than Apex was usually able to act. If this point was remedied, one still suspects that the value of an employment-placing service is likely to be extremely limited.

It may be relevant to consider when the initial contact with Apex was made, for one could hypothesize that some men may leave the decision to contact Apex until it is too late and the situation has already deteriorated too drastically. The contracts executive who was in the control group but rather fortuitously contacted Apex wrote just under two months after release. His notes in the welfare department file suggest that he was confident that he would find his own work easily enough, but he wrote to Apex saying 'I have had the misfortune recently of serving a short sentence in one of H.M. Prisons and since release am experiencing acute difficulty in obtaining employment'. This experience was sufficient to ensure that he closely co-operated with the director of Apex in an ultimately successful attempt to find appropriate employment.

The men in the rejection group are perhaps the most interesting to consider in this discussion, for there was fairly minimal contact with all of them before release. On the other hand, one suspects that subsequent contact with Apex by the full and partial acceptance groups is more closely a function of the quality of the initial contact in prison. It is interesting that the two successful placing actions for men in the rejection group were on both occasions when the man had made the contact between one and two months after release. In contrast, of the seven unsuccessful placing actions for men in the rejection group, three contacted Apex within one week of release, one within two weeks, one within three weeks, one between two and three months of discharge and the remaining one between three and six months of discharge. Although the numbers are very small indeed, it does seem that a contact between one and two months after release is the optimum time for a greater likelihood of a successful placing action. It is possible that for some this length of time in freedom may have a salutary effect in that they can realize some of the problems confronting them but are still able to respond to appropriate action.

We have not discussed in detail the requests of the 6 per cent of the men interviewed who subsequently contacted Apex about matters other than work. Although we had tried to emphasize the specific service which Apex was operating, there was a group of men with whom Apex had established some sort of friendly contact while they were in prison and they seemed to wish to renew this after release. As Table 41 has already shown, 20 out of the 25 men who had 'social contact' with Apex were from an acceptance group. Contrary to expectation, there was only the smallest trickle of men who came to Apex in the hope of direct financial assistance or 'hand-out'. The specific policy of the Apex service and a consistent procedure in dealing with clients was probably the reason why Apex was not continually confronted with inappropriate requests. On the other hand, in common with the experience of most other after-care agencies, only a minority contacted Apex after release on their own initiative. The stencilled letter handed to each man interviewed in prison stated:

> The Apex Trust is not just trying to find you one job and then forgetting about you. If there are problems regarding the job we find you, let us know; we may be able to solve the problem; or if the first job we find you is not suitable, we will then have to try again. We want to keep you in permanent employment, so we hope you will keep working while we are looking for other work on your behalf.

The conclusion must be that most men forgot about Apex after release; that there was very little feedback about any problems arising from the first job arranged; that almost all the men who contacted Apex after release were not in fact working at the time. In one case where a transition from one job to another was possible, it was in fact the employer who warned Apex that he would have to dismiss the painter placed by Apex as his work was falling below standard, but he was willing to employ him for a time while Apex found alternative work.

If one recognizes the almost inevitable failure of the ex-prisoner to contact Apex at an appropriate time, it is worthwhile to consider briefly whether there should be more contact with employers so that one could begin to forestall an approaching breakdown in the work situation. From our experience, one cannot make a general rule on this point, for there is no such animal as a 'typical employer'. On the one hand, there are employers who would not consider, or be somewhat deterred from, employing an ex-prisoner if there was even a hint that the ex-prisoner might have problems which could mean that he might not settle down as well as the next man. As a career developer wrote in a report on the Manhattan Court Employment Project, 'what firms seem to be looking for are: 1) hard-core unemployed who behave like middle-class employed, or 2) hard-core unemployed who behave like middle-class employed after several Pat O'Brien lectures by a supervisor'.[1] The advantage of this type of employer or staff manager is usually the fact that, if the ex-prisoner does succeed in settling down, he gets a good deal by not being spotlighted as being any different from the rest. When we did the three-month follow-up for the full acceptance group, it was somehow reassuring when the personnel manager said words to the effect that 'I assume that he is still with us', for even if the man had in fact left it seemed to suggest that he was not being watched as a marked man. When an employer or personnel manager did contact Apex, on most occasions there was little in fact that could be done to help the situation constructively. If an employer phoned to say that 'that chap you sent has failed to turn up today' there was little that could be done, for almost inevitably he had changed his address since contacting Apex. On the other hand, there was evidence that some personnel managers or employers can make a most competent assessment of a situation – in the same way that good probation officers can recognize the signs of danger – without intruding and accelerating the deteriorating situation. This is a rare asset and seemed to be found among employers who had been giving employment to ex-prisoners for years. There is a certain type of employer who seems to be enriched rather than shattered by his experiences over the years.

As far as subsequent contact with employers is concerned, therefore, very few contacted Apex on their own initiative. A general impression is that the contact rarely seemed to help the ex-prisoner concerned, only because the contact was usually a post-mortem rather than a diagnosis. On the other hand, the contact with Apex was probably very useful for the employer who felt that he had been seriously let down by a particular ex-prisoner. Discussion with Apex possibly meant that he was able to put this one experience into a much wider context. Instead of making the decision not to take an ex-prisoner again, a conversation sometimes might result in the employer continuing to recognize the importance of giving ex-prisoners the opportunity of employment. One must emphasize that the 'educational' aspect of the work of Apex has neither been measured nor perhaps sufficiently recognized in this report.

## REFERENCE

1 *The Manhattan Court Employment Project, Summary Report on Phase One: November 1, 1967, to October 3, 1969*, Vera Institute of Justice (1970), p. 41.

# PART IV

# After-thoughts

## Introduction

A research project as a learning experience often goes far beyond simply discovering whether a specific hypothesis is supported or falsified. In the present case, the research worker began to become aware in the course of carrying out this research project that some of the assumptions which were perhaps rather glibly accepted in planning the Apex scheme should be considered somewhat more closely. One example will perhaps emphasize this point. At the outset there was a tendency to assume that the provision of a specialized employment agency for discharged prisoners would solve the employment needs of ex-prisoners, but it was never seriously considered whether these needs were special and unique to the ex-prisoner. Further, the sociological literature which tends to emphasize some of the dangers in continuing to label men as ex-prisoners made little or no impact at the time of planning the Apex procedure, so the possible negative cost of providing an employment agency for discharged prisoners was not really recognized. It is perhaps one of the benefits of the discussion following the publication of the Seebohm Report[1] that everyone is now a little more aware of the importance of being convinced that there is a specialist need before setting up a specialist service.

A harsh critic will perhaps regard it as thoroughly reprehensible that some of the points raised in Part IV were not considered earlier in setting up the project. This is of course a perfectly acceptable point of view, for in truth some of the comments would have been particularly appropriate in a first chapter introducing a rather more sophisticated research programme. On the other hand, a more sympathetic critic would understand that it is only by carrying out a fairly limited piece of work that one can sometimes begin to appreciate the relevance of wider issues. Part IV appears in the correct chronological order as 'after-thoughts'.

# REFERENCE

1 *Report of the Committee on Local Authority and Allied Personal Social Services*, London, HMSO, Cmd. 3703 (1968).

## CHAPTER 18

# Some Implications of the Apex Project

The Apex project was conceived about a year after the publication of the ACTO Report in 1963 and the fieldwork of the project began in 1966 when many of the main recommendations of the ACTO Report were taking effect. While the timing of the Apex project was largely fortuitous, it is still interesting to place the study within this historical context.

There is no doubt that most of those actively involved in after-care felt that the 1963 report would alter the philosophy and structure of the after-care movement more fundamentally than all the attempts of the previous hundred years since Parliament had recognized the existence of the discharged prisoners' aid societies in the Act of 1862. We may come more and more to acknowledge the truth of Martin's comments, writing soon after the publication of the report, that it was 'unfortunate that future changes have not been based on more systematic analysis of the needs of the system. To talk of changes in administration without analysis of the fundamental needs of ex-prisoners may be to tinker with machinery without asking the relevant questions'.[1] But there were few who failed to grasp the fact that we were suddenly very far from the viewpoint of the 1935 committee that 'the primary object of after-care should be the reinstatement of the ex-prisoner in employment',[2] and that now the prevailing ethic would be: 'after-care is essentially a form of social casework'.[3]

One should of course recognize that even accepting the viewpoint that we were entering a new area in the philosophy of after-care (with perhaps the period between 1935 and 1963 as rather an interregnum period) one could still question whether the new backcloth would make one iota of difference to the average man discharged from local prisons. Nevertheless, whatever one's view about the nature and effectiveness of the 'post-ACTO' changes, there was no doubt at the time that one of the areas in which there would be little or no interest would be in an active policy of finding employment for discharged prisoners. Ironically, therefore, the Apex project can perhaps be regarded as giving a trial to a policy which had already received the death penalty as far as many authorities were concerned.

It is fair to emphasize that the main concern in planning the Apex project was to try to ensure that the procedure for finding employment for ex-prisoners was given a fair trial rather than to give much thought to the possible theoretical implications of such a policy. However, as the project progressed, it became evident that the clear-cut procedure of the Apex scheme highlighted some of the assumptions that we often fail to recognize in the field of after-care. At the simplest level, it has produced comments ranging from the view that such an activist policy will be the panacea for practically all ex-prisoners to the suggestion that this type of approach is likely to be harmful either because Apex unwittingly perpetuates the stigma of being an ex-prisoner, or, more simply, because Apex erodes still further the opportunity for the prisoner to learn to stand on his own feet. There is no evidence from the preceding chapters that either of these extreme views is substantiated, but before reaching any conclusion on these or related matters one should make at least two provisos.

One obvious question is whether Apex carried out efficiently the task which it had set itself of finding employment for ex-prisoners. To a large extent one can make one's own assessment from the evidence contained in Chapter 15, but an impression is that this was perhaps the most sustained attempt to find interviews for a random sample of ex-prisoners to attend on release which has probably ever been attempted. On the other hand, Chapter 17 has indicated that only a comparatively small proportion contacted Apex again after release although it was a declared interest to try to maintain the men in continuous employment after release. The fact that only a minority were helped by Apex in this way can either be considered as the failure of Apex *per se* or be accepted as fairly comparable with the experience of other 'defining agencies' who hope that the prisoner will keep in contact on a voluntary basis.

The more pertinent proviso is whether the measure used in the Apex project is the most appropriate one to measure the type of change which may occur as a result of an exercise of finding employment for ex-prisoners. One immediately suspects that the crude reconviction measure used in this study is unlikely to come anywhere near meeting the criterion. However, even if one simplifies the matter quite drastically and assumes for a moment that only those men who were assisted by Apex found employment on release and that only those men who were reconvicted committed criminal acts after release, one can appreciate that it is rather hazardous trying to trace a causal chain between employment on release and a reconviction pattern. Clearly employment on release is neither a necessary nor sufficient condition for no subsequent criminality to occur. In other words, if there is employment on release, this certainly does not mean that there will be no subsequent reconviction – the high proportion of men who are employed at the time of committing their offence empirically answers that suggestion; similarly, if there is no criminality after release, one cannot reasonably suggest that these men would inevitably be in employment after release. On the other hand, one suspects that this latter viewpoint of employment after release being a necessary condition of rehabilitation comes much nearer to what many regard as the role of employment in after-care.

At this juncture one should perhaps consider briefly to what extent the Apex technique of finding employment for discharged prisoners is within any theoretical framework for the rehabilitation of criminals. Cressey has suggested that 'there are two general and popular, but contradictory, principles for the rehabilitation of criminals. These two principles – the "group-relations principle" and the "clinical principle" – are, in effect, theories of rehabilitation'.[4] He indicates that the 'group-relations principle' is based on a personality theory in which 'the person is viewed as a product of the kinds of social relationships and values in which he participates',[5] and a criminological theory that 'maintains, in essence, that criminality is behaviour which the person in question has appropriated from the social relationships in which he has been participating'.[6] Operating within this framework, it is clear that if one wishes to modify an individual's behaviour there must be some modification of the groups to which he belongs. Although Cressey suggests that 'even imprisonment may be viewed as a system for attempting to force criminals to become members of organizations which do not own criminality, but instead, own anti-criminal behaviour',[7] the most impressive discussion is when Volkman and Cressey apply a derivation of this type of model in examining the rehabilitation of drug addicts at Synanon House.[8]

The Apex technique of finding employment on release could be regarded as consistent with the group-relations principle to the extent that the operation is directed toward changing the offender's post-institutional group relationships. This possibly happens in some cases placed by Apex, but almost certainly by accident rather than by design. The fact that Apex was sometimes willing to facilitate the return of men to their previous employment indicates that there was little consideration given to the possible effect of the pre-institutional work group, for there was naturally no evidence that the work group's behaviour had been modified while their work-mate was serving his prison sentence. The crucial issue, though, in terms of the 'group-relations principle' is that the Apex technique has a very low likelihood of helping the ex-prisoner to integrate into groups in which criminality as a way of life is not acceptable. Even if there was evidence that Apex managed to alter a person's work pattern (and it is questionable whether placing a man in employment is likely to do this), this still may not affect the sets of social relationships in which he has been participating. Cressey makes a similar point about educational courses in prison:

> A popular but apparently fallacious assumption is that taking an educational course, such as eighth-grade arithmetic, should make bad citizens (prisoners) good ones, because passing through such courses is a characteristic of good citizens. But perhaps such courses are rehabilitative only to the degree that they may change inmates' postrelease associations.[9]

Perhaps even more readily one makes a similar assumption about the importance of the ex-prisoner being employed.

In contrast to the 'group-relations principle' where crime is rather regarded as 'the property of groups, not of individuals',[10] the 'clinical principle' at its extreme regards criminality as an individual disorder. The emphasis is on the view that the individual is essentially autonomous and that 'criminality is a personal trait or characteristic of the person exhibiting the behaviour'.[11] Within this framework, criminality should be corrected or treated clinically. In many ways, the Apex technique is somewhat analogous to the 'clinical principle', for it assumes that finding employment for a man somehow eradicates his criminality without any reference to the conditions under which it was acquired. Unlike the clinician, though, Apex does not attempt in any way to 'correct' any individual disorders. Instead of teaching an individual how to overcome or at least confront the problem of finding employment as an ex-prisoner, Apex simply attempts to remove this barrier.

Becker has emphasized as one of the particularly striking factors which shape deviant careers 'the experience of being caught and publicly labelled as a deviant'.[12] It is paradoxical that Apex, which in the long term is hoping to de-label the prisoner, in fact chooses in the short term to perpetuate the label of ex-prisoner in placing the men in employment after release. It may be that one can justify this type of action on occasions by following Becker's own analysis. Although criminal statuses and roles constitute only one of the many statuses and roles of an individual, one should perhaps consider whether criminality has in fact become what Becker has termed a 'master status' so that the separate social roles occupied by the offender become submerged by his involvement in criminalistic role behaviour. This is why it may be necessary to recognize that the prisoner identity he has acquired sometimes makes the task of obtaining a job exceedingly difficult. Schwartz and Skolnick conducted an experiment to try to demonstrate the effects of a criminal court record on the employment opportunities of unskilled workers, and showed that of twenty-five employers shown a 'no record' folder, nine gave positive responses, while of the twenty-five employers approached with the 'convict' folder, only one expressed interest in the applicant. While they use this finding to make the unexceptionable point that 'a record of conviction produces a durable if not permanent loss of status'[13] and go on to indicate a straightforward opportunity structure viewpoint of 'if the ex-prisoner finds difficulty in securing menial kinds of legitimate work, further crime may become an increasingly attractive alternative',[14] one should not too readily assume that the amount of effort required by an agency in placing a particular ex-prisoner correlates very closely with the effort needed to find work by the same prisoner relying on his own initiative. If an ex-prisoner wishes to rid himself of deviant status, role and identity, it is unlikely that he would do this most effectively by announcing himself as an ex-prisoner but rather by entering a field of employment where there is the practice of deliberately asking no questions about a man's past. (Of the 97 firms involved in Martin's enquiry, 51 had some sections where no questions were asked.)[15] Naturally, it is not so easy for an ex-prisoner to enter a level of occupation where there is more considerable probing by an employer, for this will almost inevitably reveal his ex-prisoner identity even when he decides not to reveal it himself from the outset. The point still remains, though, that one ex-prisoner on his own initiative may perform the operation of finding suitable employment much more efficiently than an employment agency for discharged prisoners while another ex-prisoner simply may not be able to find any suitable work by his own efforts.

If one accepts a range of variation of the extent to which a person has acquired a deviant status, role and identity, it would seem quite reasonable to suggest that ex-prisoners will perform somewhat differently from one another in finding employment after release. The aim should be directed towards discovering which men are likely to be helped and which men may well be harmed by a particular service.

The fact that men may be set further back by the good intentions of an agency is clearly recognized nowadays by academic sociologists, particularly with regard to the part 'defining agencies' (of which Apex is of course one of many) may play in the continuation of deviant roles. The practitioner, though, may not so readily acknowledge that 'treatment' may be quite contrary to the expected result; but, as Gibbons says, 'although one official function of correctional agencies and processes is the reformation of the offender, the actual outcome is often the isolation of the person, reinforcement of the deviant role, and rejection of society by the offender, the final result being nonreformation'.[16]

Within the context of the Apex study it is worthwhile to consider whether men who rejected the offer of the Apex service may well be reacting in the most favourable manner. Certainly there are many reasons why men reject a particular service and it is naturally dangerous to generalize too freely. However, one should perhaps beware of trying to persuade some of these men to change their minds and to accept the Apex service when their initial reaction is otherwise. This is perhaps particularly the case for those men whose statistical chance of being reconvicted is small anyway, for the very fact of organizing their own resources in finding employment may be beneficial. The follow-up of some of the men in the rejection group in fact suggested that they had done very well in settling down in suitable employment without the assistance of Apex and one sometimes suspected that the intervention of an employment agency would have been detrimental in some of these cases. The surgeon may sometimes recognize that it is best to leave well alone and that the use of his knife could even have the disastrous effect of spreading a malignancy to other parts of the body. It is perhaps more difficult to recognize that the action of dispensing such a socially acceptable medicine as finding employment for ex-prisoners may not always have the intended effect.

Following the almost heretical view that one should not too readily assume that prisoners are always being unwise in rejecting potential help which is offered, one should go on to consider whether it is a useful procedure to try to help all those who accept the offer of the Apex service. One should recognize once again that there are potential dangers. If, for example, one is unable to arrange interviews for certain types of men, one could argue that this outcome may reinforce a man's view of himself as an inevitable failure rather than strengthen his resolve to find work for himself after an employment agency has failed. Similarly the present Apex procedure of finding suitable interviews is hardly likely to help the man who has a pathological fear of attending interviews.

Apart from the potentially demoralizing effects on its clients, it is clearly very uneconomic for an employment agency (particularly one which has no pretensions of extending its social work beyond its placing activities) to continue to try to assist men who will certainly fail to start any work arranged for them. The problem would seem to be one of recognizing the almost certain 'failures' before rather than after the provision of a service. The usual procedure of social agencies is to attempt to select their clients either consciously or unconsciously on an intuitive basis. Our own evidence indicated that the attempt to estimate on a subjective basis the likelihood of a man attending an interview was certainly no better than chance and there was a tendency if anything to be more often wrong than right! It would seem that a more profitable procedure is to make the judgement on objective criteria as we have outlined in Part III.

Although we have tried to indicate the possible application of statistical techniques in examining the value and effectiveness of after-care service, one must avoid suggesting that one has completed twenty years' work in one project of less than five years. The evidence of the present study is still incomplete. We have probably shown satisfactorily that this particular service of finding employment is not a universal panacea. Similarly, we have probably moved a little way towards evolving a procedure by which one may identify more closely the men who *may* be helped by such a placing service, but one must humbly recognize at this stage that a person staying, say, three months at a job arranged by Apex might have performed equally well in finding work and staying in the job if Apex had not been in existence. Clearly, therefore, we have not performed the crucial test in examining the value of finding employment in isolation, which would presumably be on the lines of selecting a group of men most likely to benefit and who are interested in accepting the Apex service, placing them in matched pairs and then tossing a coin to decide which member of the pair will in fact have the possible benefit of the placing service.

After acknowledging the limitations of a research design, one is still perhaps entitled to glance briefly at some of the possible implications of this sort of approach. Although the present study

K*

produces more evidence on those whom Apex is unlikely to help than on those who may benefit, it is still useful to perfect a procedure by which almost certain 'failures' can be identified beforehand. The ideal of after-care would be approaching if the almost certain 'failures' of one type of service could be offered alternative and more appropriate services. In this study one has perhaps been more concerned to find ways of making the labour-intensive and hence expensive approach of Apex a more viable economic proposition if carried out on a wider scale. It is perhaps relevant to point out that we have not begun to consider the possibility that it may still be useful if the community engages in this sort of operation, even if in direct economic terms it is not viable. Indeed, we should seriously consider whether the greater benefit of after-care may be to 'us' (providing the structure of after-care) rather than to 'them' (the ex-prisoners). Even if this were shown to be the case it would not necessarily mean the abandonment of after-care services, but the introduction of a more appropriate measure of effectiveness.

Returning to the more traditional theme of how to assist men and women discharged from prison, we will assume for a moment that one can pinpoint even more exactly than at present the men who may be helped by the Apex service (and for this moment one could also assume that one was able to pinpoint fairly exactly those likely to be assisted by other after-care schemes as well). A computer would be able to calculate in a matter of seconds which members of the total prison population would be most likely to benefit from a particular service. The problem would be in terms not of the time taken to calculate the various formulae by a computer but of the preparation of the punched cards containing the appropriate data for each man. It is at this point that one should avoid seeing this as a separate enterprise from other developments which may take place in the future.

The objective criteria for calculating the formulae used in this project (see Appendix A) are items of information which would be useful in other spheres. The two spheres which spring most readily to mind are sentencing procedure and the compilation of the *Criminal Statistics*. It is one possibility that the sentencer will have to become accustomed in the future to receiving a print-out from a computer which will itemize a man's previous criminal record together with various prediction scores with the aim of guiding him in making an appropriate sentence. Similarly, it is not too far-fetched to recognize that the prison welfare officer could receive guidance from a computer print-out in planning the most appropriate way of assisting a man. It would help the welfare officer to identify a suitable after-care plan, and would indicate the possible dangers in following a particular procedure.

Inevitably, a hint of trying to transform the work of the prison welfare officer from an art to a science will provoke feelings of pleasure as well as horror. In conclusion, therefore, it may be of interest to outline briefly the form that this could take. He could perhaps be presented with a print-out from a computer which would indicate what may be the most appropriate procedure for each person on his caseload. This print-out, however, should be regarded as his servant, not his master, and, without pressing the analogy too far, comparable with the help that an epidemiological study should give a doctor.

As an example, we can consider the indications which a combination of various formulae could give a welfare officer. We will assume that subsequent work has proved these measures both valid and reliable. The print-out could be as shown in Table 42.

These are only three cases in the project who fully accepted the Apex service, but they are useful for the purpose of illustration. Table 42 suggests that of the three men, only case 0001 has a 'high' chance of staying at the job arranged for three months or more. If, on the other hand, the welfare officer decided to use the placing service for cases 0009 and 0012, the print-out would suggest to him that one of the danger points may be in whether case 0009 will manage to start that job even though he may well attend the interview arranged. In contrast, for case 0012 if one could overcome the problem of attending the interview arranged, he would seem to have a good chance of being accepted by the employer and starting the job. If a welfare officer was provided with a profile of this kind for each man and for each service he could offer, it could have the dual purpose of identifying the most appropriate service for a particular man (one message may of course be, for men who can rely on their own resources – 'beware of doing anything'!) and the points where a breakdown may occur.

Inevitably, in a study devoted to an examination of the effectiveness of offering an employment service to discharged prisoners, one has concentrated on one particular aspect. Many of the principles suggested in this study, though, are equally applicable to other aspects of after-care. For example, we should wish to know the value of providing after-care hostels or clubs specifically for ex-prisoners. Similarly, a prison welfare officer may well find it helpful to know the chances of a person taking up a hostel place he is trying to arrange, the chances of a person being accepted

TABLE 42 *Example of computer print-out for three cases*

| Case number | Chances of interview being arranged | Chances of attending interview | Chances of being accepted by employer | Chances of starting job as agreed | Chances of staying three months |
|---|---|---|---|---|---|
| 0001 | 0·01579 High | 0·00839 High | 0·01077 High | −0·02564 High | 0·06719 High |
| 0009 | 0·01196 High | 0·00678 High | 0·00545 High | −0·04973 Low | −0·00880 Low |
| 0012 | 0·00628 High | 0·00301 Low | 0·01447 High | −0·02474 High | −0·01121 Low |

by a hostel warden and the chances of a person staying for a time at the hostel.

Rather than continue with speculation on the possible future of after-care which may excite some and disturb others, Alfred Lord Tennyson's words probably enable one to recognize the likely time-scale of such developments: 'Science moves, but slowly slowly, creeping on from point to point'.[17]

It would be welcome if this tentative attempt to put after-care on a much sounder basis produced some further interest, for, as Martin has pointed out,

> one has only to compare our ignorance about after-care needs with the quality and extent of research into, for example, the demand for higher education, for hospital beds, for residential accommodation for the aged, for hearing aids, to appreciate how backward is penological research in this respect.[18]

# REFERENCES

1 Martin, J. P., 'After-Care in Transition' in Grygier, T., Jones, H., and Spencer, J. C. (eds.), *Criminology in Transition*, London, Tavistock (1965), p. 107.

2 The Salmon Committee, p. 93.

3 The ACTO Report 1963, p. ii.

4 Cressey, D. R., 'Crime', in Merton, N. K., and Nisbet, R. A. (eds.), *Contemporary Social Problems*, London, Hart-Davis (1969), p. 71.

5 Ibid., p. 72.

6 Loc. cit.

7 Ibid., p. 73.

8 Volkman, R., and Cressey, D. H., 'Differential Association and the Rehabilitation of Drug Addicts', in Rubington, E., and Weinberg, N. S. (eds.), *Deviance: The Interactionist Perspective*, New York, Macmillan (1968), pp. 407–22.

9 Cressey, op. cit., pp. 73–4.

10 Ibid., p. 72.

11 Ibid., p. 73.

12 Becker, H. S., *Outsiders: Studies in the Sociology of Deviance*, New York, Free Press of Glencoe (1963), p. 31.

13 Schwartz, R. D., and Skolnick, J. H., 'Two studies of legal stigma', in Becker, H. S. (ed.), *The Other Side*, New York, Free Press of Glencoe (1964), p. 107.

14 Ibid., pp. 107–8.

15 Martin, op. cit. (1962), p. 33.

16 Gibbons, D. C., *Society, Crime, and Criminal Careers*, Englewood Cliffs, Prentice-Hall (1968), p. 226.

17 Tennyson, Alfred Lord, *The Complete Works of Alfred, Lord Tennyson*, London, Macmillan (1898), p. 101.

18 Martin, op. cit. (1965), p. 106.

# APPENDIX A

# Variables Used in Discriminatory Analysis and Correlational Analysis

*A. Age at time of sentence*

| | |
|---|---|
| 0 | 20–24 |
| 1 | 25–29 |
| 2 | 30–34 |
| 3 | 35–39 |
| 4 | 40–44 |
| 5 | 45–49 |
| 6 | 50–54 |
| 7 | 55–59 |

N.B. There were no men under 20 years of age or over 59 years of age in the sample.

*B. Age at first conviction or finding of guilt*

| | |
|---|---|
| 0 | 10–14 |
| 1 | 15–19 |
| 2 | 20–24 |
| 3 | 25–29 |
| 4 | 30–34 |
| 5 | 35–39 |
| 6 | 40–44 |
| 7 | 45–49 |
| 8 | 50–54 |
| 9 | 55–59 |

N.B. Any man for whom the age at first conviction or finding of guilt is below the age of 10 is included in category '0'.

*C. Previous convictions as an adult*

| | |
|---|---|
| 0 | 0–2 |
| 1 | 3–5 |
| 2 | 6–8 |
| 3 | 9–11 |
| 4 | 12–14 |
| 5 | 15–17 |

|   |       |
|---|-------|
| 6 | 18–20 |
| 7 | 21–23 |
| 8 | 24–26 |

N.B. Any man who has more than 26 adult convictions is included in category '8'.

*D. Period in freedom since last custody*

|   |                    |
|---|--------------------|
| 0 | Less than 1 year   |
| 1 | Less than 2 years  |
| 2 | Less than 3 years  |
| 3 | Less than 4 years  |
| 4 | Less than 5 years  |
| 5 | Less than 6 years  |
| 6 | Less than 7 years  |
| 7 | Less than 8 years  |
| 8 | No previous custody |

N.B. Any man who has had previous custody but has been in freedom for 8 years or more is included in category '7'.

*E. Probation experience*

|   |       |
|---|-------|
| 0 | Nil   |
| 1 | Once  |
| 2 | Twice |

N.B. Any man who has had more than two experiences of probation is included in category '2'.

*F. Proportion of working life spent in custody*

|   |             |
|---|-------------|
| 0 | Nil         |
| 1 | 25% or less |
| 2 | 50% or less |
| 3 | 75% or less |
| 4 | 100%        |

*G. Longest period in any job*

|   |                |
|---|----------------|
| 0 | Up to 1 year   |
| 1 | Up to 2 years  |
| 2 | Up to 3 years  |
| 3 | Up to 4 years  |
| 4 | Up to 5 years  |

N.B. Any man who maintains that he has stayed 5 years or more in his longest job is included in category '4'. This limitation helps to minimize the effect of possible exaggeration by the men on this item.

*H. Time since longest job*

| | |
|---|---|
| 0 | Present job |
| 1 | less than 2 years |
| 2 | less than 4 years |
| 3 | less than 6 years |
| 4 | less than 8 years |
| 5 | less than 10 years |
| 6 | less than 12 years |

N.B. Any man who maintains that he left his 'longest job' twelve years or more ago is included in category '6'.

*I. Time in job when committing present offence (present job time)*

| | |
|---|---|
| 0 | Unemployed |
| 1 | Up to 6 months |
| 2 | Up to 12 months |
| 3 | Up to 18 months |
| 4 | Up to 24 months |
| 5 | Up to 30 months |
| 6 | Up to 36 months |
| 7 | Up to 42 months |
| 8 | Up to 48 months |

N.B. Any man who maintains that he has been more than 4 years at his present job is included in category '8'. This limitation helps to minimize the effect of possible exaggeration by the men on this item.

CORRELATION ANALYSIS

*Intercorrelational matrix of variables used in discriminatory analysis*

(Figures in each cell are product moment correlations)

| | | A | B | C | D | E | F | G | H | I |
|---|---|---|---|---|---|---|---|---|---|---|
| Age at time of sentence | A | | 0·5465 | 0·4104 | 0·0565 | −0·2226 | −0·0525 | 0·5069 | 0·3044 | 0·1126 |
| Age at first conviction | B | | | −0·2305 | 0·3860 | −0·4792 | −0·4693 | 0·4614 | −0·1091 | 0·2992 |
| Previous adult convictions | C | | | | −0·5297 | 0·2990 | 0·4490 | −0·0493 | 0·4424 | −0·2566 |
| Period in freedom | D | | | | | −0·3795 | −0·7430 | 0·2991 | −0·2749 | 0·3786 |
| Probation experience | E | | | | | | 0·3825 | −0·2279 | 0·2190 | −0·1831 |
| Proportion of working life spent in custody | F | | | | | | | −0·3540 | 0·2370 | −0·2825 |
| Longest period in any job | G | | | | | | | | 0·0751 | 0·3287 |
| Time since longest job | H | | | | | | | | | −0·3063 |
| Present job time | I | | | | | | | | | |

# Brief Discussion of Men Who Made Partial Acceptance of the Apex Service

This brief discussion is included because men will not conform to the unreasonable demands of a research design! We have already described why it was necessary to introduce the concept of partial acceptance, for it seemed unreasonable to place men who were making strictly limited demands in the same category as men who definitely maintained that they wished Apex to find them a job interview on release.

There seemed to be two types of response to the Apex offer within the partial acceptance group of 56 men. Forty men seemed to show a somewhat vague and limited interest in the Apex service, but maintained that they were not interested in Apex finding them suitable work immediately on release, although many had no specific employment plans of their own. They simply seemed to want an assurance that they were able to contact Apex after release if they subsequently felt it necessary. Although this was an assurance that the research officer gave to everyone interviewed, these men tended to need to know that they were 'on the books', as it were, awaiting their instructions. For this reason many were sent individual letters after the prison interview or were interviewed by the director of Apex to assure them that he was interested in them after release if necessary. Before release many of them resembled drowning men who were unable to grasp in any definite manner the straw of Apex help. If one pressed for an answer as to what they intended to do on release, one quickly seemed to enter the realms of either phantasy, utter helplessness or dubious faith that everything would work out satisfactorily this time.

Ten (6 Wormwood Scrubs, 4 Pentonville) of this group of forty men contacted Apex after release, but only three were subsequently placed by Apex. The jobs of two of these men lasted only a few days and for one of them this was a pattern repeated several times. These men tended to re-establish contact with Apex almost invariably as the result of an extraordinary number of coincidences which suggested that several at least of this group were probably drifting around from social agency to social agency. Only four of the men made their first contact with Apex after being more than one month in freedom but the impression was that these were the more purposeful contacts in the sense that there seemed to be a more genuine desire for work rather than the magical solution which the others seemed to demand – and require.

An impression was that a higher proportion of the older men who expressed limited interest in the Apex service were only marginally employable. Although this impression could not be tested by Apex, as so few contacted Apex after release, there is some support for this view if one examines the previous work records of the partial acceptance group. Every police record available was inspected and all the reasons for leaving jobs mentioned in the employment histories of the police reports were documented. The various reasons for leaving previous jobs showed a similar distribution for both the full acceptance and rejection groups. However, the partial acceptance group had a significantly higher proportion of men who had left previous jobs for medical reasons, but a lower proportion with specifically unfavourable comments from former employers. This begins to suggest that the partial acceptance group consisted of more disturbed and unsettled (rather than troublesome) individuals than the other two groups.

While tending to emphasize how some men in the partial acceptance group display an almost pathological inability to make a decision about whether to accept the Apex service, there was in contrast a group of sixteen men who asked Apex to take specific action on their behalf. These men often seemed to reject the Apex service and then, almost as an afterthought, make a specific request regarding employment. Sometimes this involved making an enquiry about a particular field of employment, such as being a fireman or deep-sea diver, while at other times it involved the simple action of discovering whether they could return to their last employment. The link which brought all requests under one category was that, when an enquiry had been made, the men did not want any further action to take place on their behalf. For example, the young man who wished to return to his last job as a cinema attendant simply wanted Apex to discover whether this was possible, but whatever the outcome (which in this case happened to be successful) he did not want Apex to make any further efforts on his behalf.

The variation within the 'specific request' group was largely in terms of the appropriateness of their plans. The requests for work as a deep-sea diver and fireman illustrate this point, for in the former case the request was appropriate while the latter could reasonably be considered inappropriate. Deep-sea diving for the ex-marine with considerable experience of the techniques but who had drifted into trouble for the first time a few weeks after ending his service career was appropriate enough. In contrast, the young man who had a remarkable number of previous convictions and amount of institutional experience nursed a child-like ambition to join the London Fire Brigade. The recruiting centre of the Fire Brigade clearly stated their feelings on the matter:

One of the prescribed conditions is that a recruit 'shall be of good character at the time of his appointment' and it is difficult to see how any man who has recently served a prison sentence could qualify.

There were, in fact, only one or two men in the group who made specific requests which could be regarded as fairly hopeless from the outset. Generally, the requests were fairly straightforward. Some simply wanted Apex to explain their present predicament to a former employer and by this means a cinema attendant and a chauffeur were re-engaged, while others wanted specific employment information but did not want Apex to identify the individual who made the request. Examples of the latter type of request were information about work on trawlers, whether film studios knowingly employ ex-prisoners, the effect of a prison sentence on an army career. Despite the range of requests and the likelihood of fulfilling their various aims, this group seemed at one end of a scale in being able to specify their interest on release while in general those who expressed limited interest in the Apex service seemed particularly vague as to what they intended to do after release. In the final analysis, most of the men in the latter group remain the same enigma as they were during and immediately after the prison interview. The problem stems from whether 'limited interest' is a term which even begins to summarize their often perplexing reaction to the Apex offer. If one can appreciate that some of these men seemed to be accepting and rejecting the Apex offer at the same time, but failing to communicate either reaction very effectively, one can begin to grasp the problem of categorization and the inadequacy of the term 'limited interest in the Apex service'.

# Possible Effect of the Order of Interviewing and of any Change in the Pre-Release Procedure

We have emphasized how we attempted to give a similar employment-placing service to all those who fully accepted the offer of Apex, trying to find them a suitable interview to attend immediately on release. Clearly, though, however conscientiously one attempts to maintain a certain standard of service over a period of time, there are factors which inevitably tend to lower performance after a while and must be taken into account in assessing the effectiveness of a service. The most pertinent factor in the present case could be postulated as some sort of 'battle fatigue' when the director sees many of his tremendous placing efforts being dissipated by men who simply fail to attend the arranged interview. One could speculate that he will start his activities for the first few men with enthusiasm, drive and energy in the belief that his work will have a positive effect on the well-being of the prisoners, but his performance may demonstrably fall off when it is apparent that his placing efforts seem rarely to have a favourable outcome. Furthermore, placing activity which consists of scores and scores of fruitless telephone calls to employers is the type of work that for some could rapidly pall, and a 'fatigue effect' could become manifest. On the other hand, one could maintain that there are other factors which are likely to improve performance over time. It is perhaps a daunting thought to telephone an employer for the first time to try to interest him in interviewing the first ex-prisoner one has agreed to help, but over a period of time one suspects that a certain expertise will be built up in presenting a case to an employer. Further, as knowledge of general market conditions and knowledge of the requirements of particular industries increases, it is reasonable to suggest that placing activity may improve as a result of making more appropriate submissions to employers. In other words, when placing activity is investigated over a period of time, these two types of factor have opposite effects, for in one case there is the possibility of a deterioration in performance while in the other case there is the possibility of an improvement in performance. The purpose of the present section is to investigate whether either of these effects seems to have any important bearing on the placing activities of Apex over the period of two and a half years, which was the duration of the project.

These possible effects could begin to be measured in a straightforward manner if the interviewing procedure and the personnel had remained constant throughout the experiment. Unfortunately neither of these conditions was exactly fulfilled, for during the Wormwood Scrubs study there were two changes of director and these in turn brought the modification to the general procedure which has been briefly indicated in the text. However, during the entire Pentonville study there was the same Apex staff and there was no known modification in procedure.

With these various points in mind, it may perhaps be instructive to consider whether there are any differences in terms of the proportions starting work at the different periods during the life of the project. Comparing the first and last hundred interviewed in each prison, this shows for the Wormwood Scrubs sample that 17 (or 33·3 per cent) started in the Apex job out of 51 men who fully accepted from the first 100 interview, while 16 (or 36·4 per cent) out of 44 men were the comparable figures for the last 100. This is studied in more detail in the Ph.D. thesis, but generally the figures are remarkably similar considering the changes in personnel during the year. The Pentonville figures are proportionately lower than the Wormwood Scrubs figures. There is a slight indication that a smaller proportion of the last 100 (10 out of 55) started the Apex job compared with the first 100 (13 out of 54), but this is not statistically significant.

While starting in the job arranged by Apex is one measure of successful placing work, a more interesting and sophisticated one is how long the men stayed in the job, for *ceteris paribus* one may reasonably assume that to stay longer in a particular job is a function of suitable placing action. In other words, if two placing officers have the same percentage of men starting the work arranged, but the men placed by one placing officer stay at their jobs for significantly longer periods, then one may suggest that this placing officer is perhaps placing men in more suitable employment. Quite often, though, other things are not equal, for if one placing officer deals with skilled men while the other deals with unskilled men, this could easily explain the apparent success of one placing officer compared with the other.

Of the last seven men in the Wormwood Scrubs sample who started work arranged by Apex, six men stayed at the job for three months or more (five actually stayed for over a year at the final check). This compares favourably with the remaining thirty-two men in the Wormwood Scrubs sample who started work at the Apex job, for only seven of these stayed three months or more (three actually stayed for over a year at the final check). The former group were placed by the present director of Apex after he had been at Apex for a couple of months. There are two ready explanations for this apparently higher success rate – a chance factor or simply that he was dealing with potentially more promising material than had emerged during the earlier interviews. The other explanation is, of course, that this may be an example of particularly able placing work, but before this is fully credited one must judge whether these men were of higher than normal calibre and so liable to bias the outcome somewhat.

This is extremely difficult to assess, for while in terms of previous criminality and recent employment record they seemed fairly average candidates, the level of employment at which an interview was arranged for these men was a little higher than the average and could be used as evidence that these were in fact higher calibre men. However, what seemed to happen in at least some of these cases was that the director of Apex arranged interviews on a level commensurate with their ability before their recent deterioration.

There were two particularly outstanding cases to demonstrate this – one was a ship's engineer and the other was a high-grade architect. Both of these men had suffered mental breakdowns three or four years earlier and by a rather haphazard process had arrived in Wormwood Scrubs. The research officer felt that the gap in their employment record suggested that they were unlikely at this juncture to hold down a job which was appropriate to their undoubted ability, but the director of Apex felt otherwise and also maintained that the risk was worthwhile. Both were found jobs appropriate to their skills as an engineer and an architect respectively, and both (at the time of writing) have stayed over a year at the first job arranged. They have gained in confidence to such an extent that a *post hoc* examination would indicate that they were obviously higher calibre employment prospects, but this is not a valid procedure, for at the time of the initial interview by the research officer they were both highly anxious and in some ways rather pathetic characters who seemed somewhat lost and exhausted by their recent experiences. While these two cases suggest that it may sometimes be worthwhile to attempt to place men at a level of employment nearer their actual ability than their present plight indicates, it is perhaps essential to record that coincidentally with the intervention of Apex both these men had positive help from another organization to overcome the problem of accommodation.

The numbers are too small to say authoritatively whether the type of approach of the director was of significant value in terms of placing technique; it is also impossible to estimate from the case histories of the other members of the Wormwood Scrubs full acceptance group whether this policy could have been profitably tried with any others. What is clear, however, is that it rarely succeeded with the Pentonville sample for the simple reason that there were only a few men who seemed to have genuine skills or abilities to 'recover' in this way.

Even if more of the men in the Wormwood Scrubs sample stayed three months or more after being placed by one particular director, it is relevant to record that he did not manage to get a higher proportion of those who accepted the Apex service to start work. If he was in fact placing men more effectively, this would tend to suggest that good placing work is likely to improve the length of time the men stay at the jobs arranged by Apex rather than to get a further group of men to start work. If this is the case, this is further support for the belief that employment in isolation is going to help only a small proportion of men. The quality of placing work in this context can, therefore, reasonably be measured only in terms of the outcome for this small proportion of men rather than in terms of what proportion of the total prison population start work. In other words, the way to increase the proportion of men who can benefit from an employment service on release is likely to lie elsewhere than simply in improving the quality of that service.

# INDEX